MEASUREMENT IN PSYCHOLOGY

This book traces how such a seemingly immutable idea as measurement proved so malleable when it collided with the subject matter of psychology. It locates philosophical and social influences (such as scientism, practicalism, and Pythagoreanism) reshaping the concept and, at the core of this reshaping, identifies a fundamental problem: the issue of whether psychological attributes really are quantitative. It argues that the idea of measurement now endorsed within psychology actually subverts attempts to establish a genuinely quantitative science and it urges a new direction. It relates views on measurement by thinkers such as Hölder, Russell, Campbell and Nagel to earlier views, such as those of Euclid and Oresme. Within the history of psychology, it considers among others contributions by Fechner, Cattell, Thorndike, Stevens and Suppes. It also contains a non-technical exposition of conjoint measurement theory and recent foundational work by leading measurement theorist R. Duncan Luce.

JOEL MICHELL teaches psychometrics, measurement theory and the history and philosophy of psychology in the Department of Psychology, University of Sydney. He is the author of the textbook *An Introduction to the Logic of Psychological Measurement* (1990) and co-editor of the collection *At Once Scientific and Philosophic* (1996), and has published papers in psychological and philosophical journals.

IDEAS IN CONTEXT

Edited by QUENTIN SKINNER *(General Editor)*
LORRAINE DASTON, WOLF LEPENIES, J. B. SCHNEEWIND
and JAMES TULLY

The books in this series will discuss the emergence of intellectual traditions and of related new disciplines. The procedures, aims and vocabularies that were generated will be set in the context of the alternatives available within the contemporary frameworks of ideas and institutions. Through detailed studies of the evolution of such traditions, and their modification by different audiences, it is hoped that a new picture will form of the development of ideas in their concrete contexts. By this means, artificial distinctions between the history of philosophy, of the various sciences, of society and politics, and of literature may be seen to dissolve.

The series is published with the support of the Exxon Foundation.

A list of books in the series will be found at the end of the volume.

MEASUREMENT IN PSYCHOLOGY

Critical History of a Methodological Concept

JOEL MICHELL

CAMBRIDGE UNIVERSITY PRESS
Cambridge, New York, Melbourne, Madrid, Cape Town, Singapore, São Paulo

Cambridge University Press
The Edinburgh Building, Cambridge CB2 2RU, UK

Published in the United States of America by Cambridge University Press, New York

www.cambridge.org
Information on this title: www.cambridge.org/9780521621205

© Joel Michell 1999

This publication is in copyright. Subject to statutory exception
and to the provisions of relevant collective licensing agreements,
no reproduction of any part may take place without
the written permission of Cambridge University Press.

First published 1999
This digitally printed first paperback version 2005

A catalogue record for this publication is available from the British Library

Library of Congress Cataloguing in Publication data

Michell, Joel
Measurement in Psychology: critical history of methodological concept/Joel Michell.
p.   cm. – (Ideas in context)
Includes bibliographical references.
ISBN 0 521 62120 8
1. Psychometrics – History. 2. Psychology – Methodology – History.   I. Title.   II. Series.
BF39.M545   1999
150'.28'7–dc21   98–39566   CIP

ISBN-13 978-0-521-62120-5 hardback
ISBN-10 0-521-62120-8 hardback

ISBN-13 978-0-521-02151-7 paperback
ISBN-10 0-521-02151-0 paperback

To the memory of my father
JOEL BLAMEY MICHELL
1917–1997

'We must not ask nature to accommodate herself to what might seem to us the best disposition and order, but must adapt our intellect to what she has made, certain that such is the best and not something else.'

(Galileo to Prince Cesi)

Contents

Preface	*page*	xi
Acknowledgments		xv

1 Numerical data and the meaning of *measurement* — 1
Two examples of psychological measurement — 5
Quantitative relationships and the concept of measurement — 12

2 Quantitative psychology's intellectual inheritance — 24
The classical concept of measurement — 25
The measurability thesis — 33
The quantity objection. — 40
Aporia and nexus — 44

3 Quantity, number and measurement in science — 46
The theory of continuous quantity — 47
The theory of (measurement) numbers — 59
The theory of quantification — 67
Stevens' definition and the logic of quantification — 76

4 Early psychology and the quantity objection — 78
Fechner's model for psychological measurement — 79
Applying Fechner's *modus operandi* — 90

5 Making the representational theory of measurement — 109
Russell's transformation of the concept of measurement — 110
Campbell's theory of fundamental and derived measurement — 121
Nagel's positivistic representationalism — 131
From ratios to representations — 137

6 The status of psychophysical measurement — 140
The Ferguson Committee — 143
The response to the Final Report — 155

x *Contents*

7 A definition made to measure   162
   Stevens' thoroughgoing representationalism   164
   Stevens' operationism   169
   Stevens' concept of number   177
   Stevens' 'revolution'   185

8 Quantitative psychology and the revolution in
   measurement theory   191
   The revolution that happened   193
   Eluding the revolution   211
   In fine   216

Glossary   220

List of references   224

Index   243

Preface

This is a book about an error, an error in scientific method fundamental to quantitative psychology. This error became locked into established ways of doing things in that science, that is, it became systemic. Then it was compounded by a higher order error, the effect of which was to disguise the first. Because science is a cognitive enterprise, because scientific methods are fallible methods, and because all scientists are fallible cognisers, the making of errors is par for the course in science and so any particular instance of error is usually only of passing interest. In so far as scientists invite criticism and put their ideas to the test, there is some chance that errors will eventually be corrected. On the other hand, errors that become systemic are of more than passing interest because they show that science's mechanisms for correcting error are themselves fallible and able to break down. Then it is of interest to inquire into the conditions of such errors because they may teach us something about the workings of science. This book is written as a contribution to that endeavour.

In the case studied here, the first of the two errors mentioned was of a familiar enough kind. It was the error of presuming an answer to a scientific question, rather than investigating it empirically. Quantitative psychologists presumed that the psychological attributes which they aspired to measure were quantitative. There is no question that presuming instead of testing was an error in scientific method. Quantitative attributes are attributes having a quite specific kind of structure. The issue of whether psychological attributes have that sort of structure is an empirical issue because there is no necessity that such attributes should be so constituted. Despite this, mainstream quantitative psychologists (that is, the dominant tradition of those attempting either to measure psychological attributes or to theorise about them quantitatively) not

xi

xii *Preface*

only neglected to investigate this issue, they presumed that psychological attributes are quantitative, as if no empirical issue were at stake. This way of doing quantitative psychology, begun by its founder, Gustav Theodor Fechner, was followed almost universally throughout the discipline and still dominates it.

The second, higher order, error involved in this case was of a kind far from familiar. It involved accepting a defective definition of a fundamental methodological concept, that of measurement. Given that measurement has been central to science since ancient times and also a more or less permanent feature of non-scientific life since then, it is surprising that quantitative psychologists were able to pull this manoeuvre off. It is even more surprising that it was done, so far as I can tell, entirely in good faith. This definition continues to dominate the discipline. Most quantitative psychologists think that measurement is simply the assignment of numerals to objects and events according to rule. This definition was proposed by the psychologist Stanley Smith Stevens in 1946. Its understanding of the concept of measurement is clearly mistaken because it ignores the fact that only quantitative attributes are measurable. Of course, that feature is no accident, as will be revealed.

Because this second error disguises the first so successfully and has persisted within psychology now for more than half a century, this tissue of errors is of special interest. Errors such as these are not likely to be accidental. They are more likely to be motivated. Locating the motivation is one of my aims. I argue that these errors are connected with ideologies underlying the development of modern psychology. These ideologies are scientism and practicalism. Scientism is a commonly invoked concept and what I mean by it is the view that methods successful in certain 'paradigmatic' sciences must also apply to others. The concept of practicalism is one that I have taken from the philosopher John Anderson. I use this term to refer to the view that success in science derives from the solving of 'practical' problems. This is to be contrasted with the classical view that success in science simply means finding out how natural systems work. Anderson thought that 'modern science does not exemplify disinterested inquiry. Its spirit has been "practical", it has been concerned with "getting things done" ... not just with finding out what is the case and with the "criticism of the categories" that that involves.' I show that modern psychol-

Preface xiii

ogists almost universally, from Fechner to Stevens, neglected 'criticism of the category' of quantity and its relation to the scientific method of measurement. Inquiry in psychology had to serve the social interests of a discipline anxious to present itself as 'scientific' and of a profession equally anxious to present itself as an 'applied science'. Because these interests were pursued within a wider milieu dominated by views such as Pythagoreanism, presuming that psychological attributes are quantitative would have seemed a much smaller step than, in reality, it was.

It is a curious feature of the recent expansion of interest in 'science studies' that few works on the history of errors in science have so far been produced. Perhaps this is because, when it comes to errors, it seems that scientists themselves 'are far better placed to do that critical job than historians, sociologists, or philosophers', as Steven Shapin puts it. While scientists, like everyone, need all the help they can get in identifying errors, the history related here confirms Shapin's observation by showing how internal criticism, when valid, can eventually lead to a revolution in ideas. The fact that, in this case, revolutionary developments have had minimal impact upon established practice, shows how much an understanding of science requires an understanding of the mechanisms of the cognitive affliction I call *systemic error*.

For most of my adult career I have been involved with attempts at psychological measurement in some form or another. I served an 'apprenticeship' in applied psychometrics and worked for several years as a students' counsellor and guidance officer before completing a Ph.D. in the area of attitude measurement. Since then I have taught psychometrics and measurement theory at the University of Sydney, supervised theses on psychological measurement and published in the area. Being an insider has both advantages and disadvantages when it comes to writing history. The advantages are obvious and the disadvantages considerable. There are the problems of being too close to a subject. There is also the problem that by training the insider is usually neither an historian nor a philosopher. I make no claim to be either. Hence, in this book I lean heavily, but selectively, upon historians and philosophers of science. Selectively, because I am reluctant to conform to what I adjudge, albeit as an 'outsider', to be the false gods currently worshipped within those disciplines. The result may not please some. This is a risk I am prepared to take because I think xiv *Preface*

that with a topic such as this we enter disciplinary borderlands, wherein scientists may also have their say and no one claim the last word.

There certainly is more work to be done on the questions investigated in this book. First, I have confined my attention to published material because it is at this level that the errors and their history impinged upon me. In this case, the public surface of science reveals patterns worth reporting. However, I am sure that there are deeper currents than those identified here. Second, with a couple of notable exceptions, I have confined attention to material available in English. This leaves gaps because the initial error identified occurred first in German psychology and I am sure that the study of the 'quantity objection' within the nineteenth-century German psychological literature would reveal subtleties glossed over in my work. Third, the philosophy of scientific quantification remains a patchy area of study and it still awaits more comprehensive and systematic treatment than I have been able to give it here. Finally, the errors investigated here are not free-standing errors: they form part of a ubiquitous syndrome. There is a particularly pernicious form of Pythagoreanism, according to which the ostensively qualitative features of human life are squeezed, insensitively and without second thought, into a quantitative mould. This has happened especially in a range of areas where human performance is considered and evaluated. It deserves closer philosophical scrutiny. There are many things in human life which may not be quantitative. They are no worse for that. If nonquantitative, they can be investigated in terms of their own 'categories' and such investigation is no less scientific than measurement. Quantitative structure is but one (important) kind amongst many and it holds no franchise over scientific method in its entirety.

Acknowledgments

A first draft of most of this book was written between January and June 1995, while I was a visiting professor at the Catholic University of Leuven, Belgium. I was accorded the privilege of using Professor Luc Delbeke's personal library of books on measurement for that period and I thank him for his generosity. Professor Paul De Boeck oversaw my visit and gave me all the support I needed for my research. I thank him heartily, as well. The University of Sydney provided the financial resources necessary for that visit through its programme of special study leave and I am indebted to it, as I am to Professors Robert Boakes and Helen Beh, who as head of the Department of Psychology and acting dean of the Faculty of Science respectively, lent their support to my application. Prior to my time in Belgium, a considerable amount of the preparatory research for this book was funded by the Australian Government via ARC Grants awarded through the University of Sydney. That support was crucial. Subsequently, the Department of Psychology at the University of Sydney supported my research through departmental research grants.

The manuscript was completely rewritten between July 1997 and February 1998, during most of which time I was a Fellow with the Research Institute of Humanities and Social Sciences of the University of Sydney. I am grateful to the Director, Professor Paul Patton, and the Selection Committee for finding merit in my application, and to Professors Stephen Touyz and Ian Curthoys, head and deputy head, respectively, of the Department of Psychology, for supporting my application and for smoothing the way for my acceptance of that honour.

During the period of my research on this project, my research assistants, Fiona Hibberd and Kate Toms, were indispensable. As well, Fiona, with characteristic dedication and enthusiasm, dis-

xvi *Acknowledgments*

charged my normal teaching duties while I enjoyed my fellowship. In recent times, despite the vicissitudes of academic life, Kate has been unstinting in her generous support and personal loyalty. I will always be grateful to them both.

Friends, students and colleagues have commented critically upon earlier drafts, to a greater or lesser extent. I will not list them all, but thank them just the same, especially David Grayson, George Oliphant and Agnes Petocz. At various times I have taken encouragement while engaged in this research from remarks by David Armstrong, John Bigelow, Duncan Luce, Louis Narens and Phil Sutcliffe. Catherine Max of Cambridge University Press has, from the start of negotiations, lent her support and provided useful guidance, especially with respect to the choice of a title. She organised reviews of my first draft and the consequent revisions significantly improved the presentation of my argument. I thank them all.

Finally, over the summer of 1997/98, I took the opportunity to complete this book. I thank Anne for her indulgence and more especially for the understanding and support she has given me throughout this entire project.

JOEL MICHELL

CHAPTER 1

Numerical data and the meaning of measurement

There is no safety in numbers, or in anything else.
(James Thurber)

He that forsakes measure, measure forsakes him.
(Fergusson's Scottish proverbs)

There is a myth about the way in which science works. Scientists attempt to find out how natural systems work. From what little they can glean initially by unaided observation and by analogy with what they think are similar systems, they form hypotheses about the workings of the systems they are studying and put these hypotheses to the test. They do this by making predictions from their hypotheses and then checking these predictions via observations aided by scientific methods, which may include experiments, measurements, and so on. These methods often involve elaborate equipment, stringent controls and highly standardised procedures. Because of their sophistication they are thought to provide a transparent window on reality. They show us how things really are. Observations made, the predictions can be checked against the data and science moves a step forward: the hypothesis is confirmed or falsified and this general procedure repeated. In this way, it is thought, science moves ever closer, by successive approximations, to an understanding of how natural systems work.

Like many myths, this one contains some truth. But if research in the history and philosophy of science over the past half-century has shown anything of value, it has shown that the methods that scientists use to test their hypotheses are not transparent windows on the world. Philosophers and historians divide over what kind of 'windows' these methods might be. Some think they are like the windows of Chartres cathedral, where what is seen is located within the window itself and not in the world beyond. Others think that while there are distortions and discolouration, something of the world behind the window can, at least sometimes, be glimpsed. Obviously, the latter view is the most that any kind of research could ever force us to, for while methods may contaminate observations, possibly in ways we do not suspect or cannot easily see, blanket scepticism about methods of knowing is self-refuting and, incidentally, likewise defeating for the historian or philosopher of science as well.

The lesson to be learned is that scientific methods are imperfect tools and all observations are, in principle, fallible. Because scientific methods are imperfect, the only safe way to use them is critically. By this I mean that caution in science requires investigating one's methods as well as using them. I have heard scientists disclaim the need for this, arguing that one does not need to know how a car works in order to drive it. That might be true around the city, but try driving across Australia's Simpson Desert, without roads, on unchartered territory, without knowing how your car works! The scientist in the classroom giving demonstrations to students is like the driver in the city; the scientist in the laboratory, investigating as yet untested hypotheses, is like the driver in the desert.

The critical investigation of methods has two parts: empirical and conceptual. Any observational method, even 'naked' observation, because it involves a causal process between the observer and the observed, presumes a theory about how that method discloses some of nature's secrets to us. A good example is the way theories of optics underwrite the use of the telescope. These theories need to be empirically investigated, just like any others in science. But deeper than the empirical lies the conceptual underpinnings of methods. The critical investigation of methods, and their proper use, requires conceptualising the method correctly. If we consider an entire class of methods, such as methods of measurement, the conceptual problem resides in defining the method. This is neither a trivial nor an arbitrary exercise. Methods are interwoven inextricably into the fabric of science and the definition given of a concept such as measurement must be consistent with its place in that fabric. It is possible that uncritical scientists in a particular area could, for socio-historical reasons, come to misunderstand a concept such as measurement and use it in ways inconsistent with its wider theoretical commitments.

Then the methods called 'measurement' within that science would not disclose the sort of facts about the world that they might be thought to and those scientists would misunderstand what they were doing.

Modern psychology, quantitative and experimental, began with the publication in 1860 of *Elemente der Psychophysik* by the German scientist, G. T. Fechner. A physicist preoccupied with psychological questions, Fechner was guided by the uncompromisingly imperialistic metaphysical vision of natural science. In proposing a feasible scientific theory about how any natural system works, a metaphysical promissory note is thereby contracted, the scope of which encompasses all natural systems connected spatio-temporally, however distantly, with the system theorised about. This promissory note entails that the categorial features presumed in that theory infuse the spatio-temporal realm entirely. Categorial features are the warp and weft of being, so general that they permeate every situation, no matter where, no matter when. Two such, of fundamental importance to theories in physics, are causality and quantity. The category of causality underwrites the experimental method, that of quantity, measurement. These methods, experiment and measurement, are often seen as marks ratifying true science, and so are automatically imposed upon newer areas of scientific investigation. This was the case with Fechner's psychophysics, delivered already swaddled in measurement and experiment.

If quantity is present in every situation, it may seem that measurement is required of all sciences. Not so. This issue is more complex than at first appears, particularly in the case of psychology. The relationship between quantity, as a category of being, and measurement, as a method of science has never been rigorously examined. The founding fathers of modern psychology, almost to a man, simply presumed that measurement was a scientific imperative and, accordingly, thought to contrive quantification. Whether they were correct or not is a matter requiring careful analysis.

Can the existence of psychological measurement be seriously questioned, now, at the close of the twentieth century, with psychology so long and (seemingly) securely established as a quantitative science? Is it not a fact that psychologists measure an array of psychological attributes? Certainly, psychologists claim to be

4 *The meaning of measurement*

able to measure such an array: psychological attributes like general intellectual ability ('intelligence'); various specific intellectual abilities (verbal ability, spatial ability and so on); the intensities of different kinds of sensations (loudness, brightness, etc.); the subjective probability of occurrence of various possible events (such as winning some gamble); the strength of attitudes towards social policies (e.g., euthanasia or abortion); the subjective value of various commodities (such as laptops or wilderness areas); degrees of personality traits (introversion, neuroticism, etc.); strength of association between a stimulus and the overt response elicited (such as Hull's 'habit strength'); levels of skill (e.g., social skill or typing skill); and levels of achievement in various areas (such as spelling or arithmetic). Not only psychologists, but the wider community accept that psychologists measure at least some of these. But science as knowledge, as distinct from science as a social movement, is often indifferent to the confidence of scientists and the vicissitudes of popular opinion.

In fact, there are signs that this presumption of successful psychological quantification is premature. One very disturbing sign is that many psychologists misunderstand what measurement is. In taking over the concept of measurement from the established sciences and fashioning their own quantitative theories and practices, psychologists are, like all scientists, logically committed to the traditional view of measurement; but in endorsing and promoting their claim to measure, psychologists typically invoke a definition of 'measurement' at odds with the traditional view.

The claim that psychologists measure psychological attributes is embedded in a complex matrix of concepts and practices. This matrix has three dimensions. First, there is an observational dimension: the sets of observational and analytical procedures applying, according to the relevant theories, to each such attribute. Second, there is a theoretical dimension: the character that each supposedly measurable attribute is taken to have, both its intrinsic character (i.e., how different levels of this attribute interrelate) and its extrinsic character (i.e., how the attribute relates to others). Third, there is a philosophical dimension: the understanding of measurement professed, in virtue of which psychologists think of their practices as measurement. There is a dissonance between these dimensions, a dissonance largely unacknowledged. It can be revealed via a brief examination of some examples of psychological 'measurement'.

For half a century or so after the publication of Fechner's *Elemente der Psychophysik*, psychophysics remained the principal area within which psychological quantification was attempted. During the twentieth century interest in psychophysics waned and attempts to measure intellectual abilities became the central focus of quantitative psychology. The technology of ability measurement, so-called, is perhaps the most significant contribution, for better or worse, that modern psychology has made to our society. The examples considered in this chapter, accordingly, are taken from these two areas.

First the observational dimension will be examined, then the theoretical. What kind of thing is it that psychologists suppose they are able to measure? In discussing this question, interest will not be in how sensation intensity and intellectual ability should, separately, be defined. Instead, it will be in the general character they are thought to share in virtue of being hypothesised as measurable. Within psychology, it is supposed that sensation intensity and intellectual ability are both quantitatively related to other attributes. Theorising of this sort carries implications about the internal character of the attributes involved, and these, in turn, entail a view of measurement.

The definitions of measurement which psychologists typically present in their publications will then be considered. It transpires that the definition of measurement entailed by the theory and practice of psychology is quite different from the definitions which psychologists explicitly profess. It will be argued that in formulating their own, special definition of measurement, psychologists undermine the understanding of measurement implicit in the theories they propose and on which their quantitative practices depend.

TWO EXAMPLES OF PSYCHOLOGICAL MEASUREMENT

Much of what passes for psychological measurement is based upon the counting of frequencies. A sequence of situations is constructed, each of which delivers just one of two possible outcomes via the behaviour of participants, some of whose attributes it is

6 *The meaning of measurement*

intended to measure. Responses to mental test items, classified either as correct or incorrect, is a typical example. The number of outcomes of one kind or the other is counted, and a mathematical theory linking these frequencies (or, perhaps, associated probabilities) to the attributes to be measured is accepted as true and, via that theory, measures of those attributes obtained. This pattern is easily replicated for many different psychological attributes because dichotomous situations are easily contrived. The following examples display this pattern.

Psychophysics

The aim of psychophysical measurement, as conceived by its founder, Fechner, is to quantify the intensity of sensations. Consider a set of stimuli, all of which vary only with respect to a single, directly discernible, quantitative, physical attribute (e.g., a set of spherical marbles, all of the same colour and volume, but varying in weight). The idea behind Fechner's psychophysics was that the presentation of each stimulus gives rise to a mental state, a sensation (e.g., the sensation of heaviness produced by a marble held in the palm of the hand) and it was thought by Fechner, and many after him, that the physical magnitude of the stimulus and the intensity of the corresponding sensation are related by some mathematical formula (or function), one specific to that attribute (e.g., weight)[1]. There are a variety of procedures by which it is thought that the intensity of sensations can be measured. The instance considered here is the method of pair comparisons.

This method involves presenting elements from the stimulus set, two at a time, to the person whose sensations are being measured, with instructions to report for each pair which of the two is the 'greater' in some prescribed sense (e.g., which of two marbles is the heavier). This procedure is repeated many times under standard conditions, including repetitions of the same pair. Ideally the procedure is continued until a relatively stable estimate is

---

[1] Of course, Fechner recognised that the same stimulus presented to the same person on different occasions but under otherwise identical external conditions could give rise to sensations of different intensity, in which case what may be said to correspond psychologically to the physical magnitude of the stimulus is a probability distribution over a range of possible sensation intensities. The mathematical psychophysical functions which Fechner and others proposed were intended to relate to something akin to the average of these distributions.

Two examples of psychological measurement

obtained of the person's probability of judging, under these conditions[2], each particular stimulus, say x, greater than each other stimulus, y. Alternatively, if it is thought that individual differences in the sensations produced are not too great, then repeated observations on the same stimulus pairs may be obtained from different people[3]. Over many repetitions of each stimulus pair, the number of times x is judged greater than y in the required sense may be counted for all pairs, x and y, and these frequencies converted to proportions. These proportions or, more correctly, the probabilities that they are thought to reflect, are taken to vary systematically with the magnitude of the difference between the sensations produced by the stimuli involved. If the precise relationship between such probabilities and differences were known as a general law, then the sensation differences could be measured via the proportions. Such a law cannot be known *a priori*, but a number of mathematical relationships have been hypothesised. Perhaps the best known is L. L. Thurstone's Law of Comparative Judgment (Thurstone, 1927a, b).

In the 1920s and later, Thurstone's theoretical work in psychological measurement synthesised and organised many of the previously disparate ideas in the area. One important idea which had not been explicitly developed theoretically until then was the idea that magnitudes of the relevant stimulus attribute do not unvaryingly cause fixed intensities of sensation.[4] A stimulus of a given magnitude (e.g., a marble of a particular weight), says Thurstone, may give rise to any of a range of sensations, some being more likely than others. Here Thurstone employs the so-called Normal (or Gaussian) probability distribution form:[5] the probability

---

[2] It is now recognised that the relevant conditions are not only physical but psychological. In particular, motivational and cognitive factors are known to be important.

[3] Repetitions of pair comparisons involving the same stimulus pairs can be very boring for subjects, and so can have a dramatic effect upon motivational states. This is just one of the difficulties in making such measurements which I shall ignore in developing this example.

[4] This will be because of small fluctuations in the state of the causally relevant parts of the nervous system which cannot be experimentally controlled with existing technology and not, of course, because of any intrinsic indeterminism in the sensory system.

[5] This distribution form is named after the German mathematician, Karl Friedrich Gauss (1777–1855). Its form is that of the now familiar bell-shaped frequency distribution, widely referred to in many sciences where statistics are analysed, especially the biological, behavioural and social sciences. It was already very well known in psychology when Thurstone proposed his theory and in that context, some adjudge it a not implausible hypothesis (see Luce, 1977, 1994).

8 *The meaning of measurement*

distribution of sensation intensities associated with stimulus x is Normal with mean, μ_x, and variance, σ_x^2. Thus, the expectation is that x will produce a sensation in the vicinity of μ_x, the likelihood of something too much greater or less than μ_x diminishing with distance from that mean value, the extent of diminution being dependent upon the magnitude of σ_x^2. Similar expectations hold for each other stimulus, say y, where the relevant parameters are μ_y and σ_y^2 respectively. Simplifying by assuming no response biases (i.e., that the person making the judgment uses a simple response rule[6]), that for all stimulus pairs, x and y, $\sigma_x^2 = \sigma_y^2$ and that the sensation intensities elicited by x and y on any occasion are independent of one another, Thurstone's 'law' becomes

$$z_{xy} = \frac{\delta_{xy}}{\sigma} \qquad (1)$$

(where z_{xy} is the Normal deviate[7] corresponding to $P_{x>y}$ (the probability of judging x greater than y), $\delta_{xy} = \mu_x - \mu_y$, and σ is the standard deviation (i.e., the square root of the variance) of the distribution of differences in intensity between sensations elicited by any one stimulus in the set and those by any other, a constant for all stimulus pairs under the simplifications assumed here. For convenience, the unit of measurement can be set at σ, in which case σ equals 1). This mathematical relationship can be described approximately in less mathematical terms as follows: when $\delta_{xy} = 0$ (i.e., when $\mu_x = \mu_y$),$P_{x>y} = .5$; as δ_{xy} increases from 0, $P_{x>y}$ increases from .5, at first rapidly approaching 1, but never reaching it because the rate of approach gradually and continually slows down; and as δ_{xy} decreases from 0, a mirror-image process happens, with the probability now approaching, but never reaching, 0.

Taking the proportion of times that x is judged greater than y as an estimate of $P_{x>y}$, this probability can be transformed to z_{xy} and the difference between μ_x and μ_y, δ_{xy}, can, accordingly, be estimated. When repeated for all pairs in the stimulus set, measures

---

[6] Thurstone assumed this simple response rule: if on any occasion the intensity of the sensation produced by x exceeds that produced by y then the person involved will always judge x greater than y. Subsequently, it has been thought that people may not always behave in this straightforward way.

[7] The Normal deviate corresponding to a probability is the point under the standard Normal curve (i.e., the Normal curve with a mean of 0 and a variance of 1) below which the proportion of the total area under the curve equals that probability.

of the μ values for all stimuli can be estimated on a scale with arbitrary zero point (see Bock & Jones (1968) for an account of the estimation procedures). If Thurstone's conjecture and the simplifying assumptions are true, then the estimated μ values can be interpreted as the expected value of the sensation intensity produced by the stimulus involved under the kind of observational conditions employed. Here, then, is one case of putative psychological measurement.

Intellectual abilities

It is a commonplace observation that people differ in their performances on intellectual tasks. Two people invited to solve an arithmetic reasoning problem, for example, will often give different solutions. This fact has been used, at least since the work of Binet (1903) and Spearman (1904) to attempt to measure intellectual abilities. Intellectual abilities are hypothesised properties of persons which are supposed to be responsible for differences in performance on intellectual tasks. Of course, such differences in performance will have a variety of causes within the persons involved, not all of them intellectual. For example, it is widely believed that motivational factors play a part. Intellectual abilities are usually thought of as distinct from such factors, having to do exclusively with what the person involved knows (the person's cognitive state) or with the neural mechanisms sustaining such knowledge. Since the time of Spearman a variety of theories has been proposed for the measurement of intellectual abilities.

These theories typically apply to scores on psychological tests. Such tests are fixed sets of intellectual problems administered under relatively standardised conditions. The individual problems involved are called test items. When administered to a person, the person's solutions to the items (that person's responses) are recorded. These responses are then classified as *correct* or *incorrect* and, typically, the number of correct responses (the person's total score) is the datum from which a subsequent measure of ability is inferred. That is, it is generally thought that intellectual abilities relate in a systematic way to total scores. It is pertinent that the relationship between the sets of item responses and total scores is not one to one. Obviously, with the exception of the two possible extreme scores on any test, two people could get the same total

10 *The meaning of measurement*

score by getting different items correct. Thus, if total scores relate systematically to intellectual abilities, the relationship between abilities and item responses must be less systematic, because it must be possible for two people, having exactly the same level of ability and getting the same total score,[8] to get different items correct. Most theories in the area cope with this requirement by postulating a probabilistic relationship between abilities and item responses.[9] Current theories of this sort are called *item response theories*.

Item response theories connect the probability of a person getting a test item correct to some combination of the person's ability and attributes of the item. The relevant item attributes are usually taken to be the difficulty of the item, the discriminating power of the item and the probability of getting the item correct by random guessing. To illustrate the measurement of intellectual abilities using this approach, imagine a test in which differences in total scores between people depend only upon differences between them in one ability. Of course, this is an idealisation, but it may be approximated in the case of certain simple tests.

An item's difficulty level is located on the same scale as the person's ability: the difficulty for any item is the level of ability required to have a 50:50 chance of getting the item correct. If a person has less ability than this, the chances of failing the item should exceed those of passing it, and if they have more ability they are more likely than not to pass it. This last feature relates to the item's discriminating power. The more rapidly the probability of getting an item correct increases as ability increases above the item's difficulty (or the more rapidly this probability falls away with decreases in ability below the item's difficulty) the better the item discriminates between different levels of the relevant ability.

Suppose now that the probability of getting an item correct on this imaginary test varies with just two attributes: the person's level of the relevant ability, and the item's difficulty (all items having the same discriminating power). Each item classifies

---

[8] Of course, two people with the same level of ability need not get the same total score either.

[9] Again, the probabilistic relationship need not be taken as implying indeterminism. It no doubt simply reflects the failure of the psychometrician to control all relevant causal factors.

people into two groups, *correct* and *incorrect*, and the probability of those in the correct group having more ability than those in the incorrect group for any item is, it is supposed, relatively high (but never 1). If it is assumed, as is usual in this area, that responses to items are independent of each other,[10] it follows that a greater total score on the test is indicative of a greater level of ability (Grayson, 1988). Depending on the number of items in the test, and on the discriminating power of the items, an ordering of people according to total score may be expected to be a more or less accurate ordering of them according to ability level.

Of course, few psychologists are content with just (approximately) ordering people according to ability, but one can proceed beyond this, to measure ability, only if it is known exactly how the probability of getting an item correct relates to the person's ability and the item's difficulty. As with psychophysical measurement, there are a number of theories about this relationship. The simplest such theory for the idealised example considered here is that proposed by Rasch (1960). Recall that the difficulty of an item is the level of ability required in order to have a 0.5 probability of success. If person i's level of ability is denoted A_i and item x's level of difficulty is denoted A_x then this is achieved if

$$Pr\{correct \mid i \ \& \ x\} = \frac{A_i}{A_i + A_x} \qquad (2)$$

(where $Pr\{correct \mid i \ \& \ x\}$ is the probability of person i getting item x correct). Despite appearances, this theory is similar to (1): when the difference between A_i and A_x is zero, the $Pr\{correct \mid i \ \& \ x\} = 0.5$; as this difference increases from 0, so the probability increases from 0.5, at first rapidly, then slowing down so that a probability of 1 is never attained; and as the difference decreases from 0, a mirror image relation obtains. There are, of course, versions of item response theory utilising the Gaussian distribution form instead of (2) and versions of psychophysical theory employing the kind of distribution form entailed by (2) (the logistic form), rather than the Gaussian.

Using (2), levels of A can be estimated from test scores (e.g.,

---

[10] Independent in the sense that for a fixed level of ability, the response to any item in no way influences the response to any other item.

12 *The meaning of measurement*

see Hambleton & Swaminathan, 1985, for some technical details). If Rasch's hypothesis is correct, the estimates can be regarded as measures of the ability involved. Some psychologists claim to be able in this way to measure intellectual abilities.

QUANTITATIVE RELATIONSHIPS AND THE CONCEPT OF MEASUREMENT

In the above examples, a mathematical relation is conjectured to hold between a hypothetical attribute it is hoped to measure and another quantity, in each example the probability of some event. Each of these mathematical relations possesses a special feature: it remains true under changes in the unit of measurement of the hypothetical attribute, but not under other mathematical transformations. Changing the unit of measurement (in the case of length measurement, changing from yards, say, to metres) is equivalent to multiplication by a positive real number.[11] For example, in the case of equation (2), if the measures of ability undergo a change of unit, that is equivalent to obtaining measures, kA_i and kA_x, on a new scale of ability, where before one had A_i and A_x. Then equation (2) would become

$$Pr\{correct \mid i \; \& \; x\} = \frac{kA_i}{kA_i + kA_x} = \frac{kA_i}{k(A_i + A_x)} = \frac{A_i}{A_i + A_x}$$

To repeat, changing the unit of measurement makes no difference to the hypothesised mathematical relationship. The same is true of equation (1): a change in the unit for measuring differences of sensation intensity leaves (1) unchanged. By contrast, a different kind of mathematical transformation (e.g., adding the same constant, k, to each measure, or raising each measure to the same constant power, k) would in general change the mathematical relationship, though it might preserve the order of the magnitudes involved.

This fact, that the (conjectured) mathematical relationship is insensitive to (or invariant with respect to) changes of unit but not to other transformations, is not peculiar to these examples. All attempts at psychological measurement, if they involve the

---

[11] For example, if length in metres is multiplied by .914 then a close approximation to length in yards is obtained.

Quantitative relationships and the concept of measurement 13

postulation of quantitative relationships between the attributes to be measured and some other quantities, have this property. Nor is it peculiar to psychology; it is a general feature of quantitative science. For example, in physics, the relationship known to hold between mass, volume and density (density = mass/volume) is similarly invariant under changes of the units involved (e.g., changing from imperial to metric units).

This very general feature of quantitative science is intimately connected to measurement. In any instance where a supposedly measurable attribute is hypothesised to, or known to, stand in a quantitative relationship to other quantities, and this relationship is invariant with respect to changes in the unit of measurement, the measurable attribute must possess a certain kind of internal structure which is capable of sustaining this invariance. Now, by definition, the unit of measurement on any scale for any quantitative attribute (e.g., the metric scale of length) is that magnitude of the attribute whose measure is 1. In the case of the metric length scale, this magnitude is that length given the name, *the metre*.[12] The measure of any other magnitude of the same quantitative attribute is just its ratio to the unit of measurement.[13] For instance, the measure of any length, x, in metres is the positive real number, r, when x is r metres long (i.e., $x/metre = r$). Similarly, in the case of abilities, if on a scale for measuring some ability, the measure of ability level A_1 is 1, then the measure of person i's ability, A_i, on this scale is the ratio of A_i to A_1. If the unit of measurement is changed from, say, A_1 to A_2, the measure of A_i goes from $A_i/A_1 = r$ to $A_i/A_2 = s$, and the constant, k, by which r must be multiplied to produce s (i.e., $r \times k = s$) is just A_1/A_2 because $(A_i/A_1) . (A_1/A_2) = A_i/A_2$. In other words, the mathematical relationship between ability and other attributes is insensitive to change of units only so long as there are ratios between different levels of ability (i.e., the magnitude of one level relative to another must be a positive real number).

Now, for there to be ratios between different levels of an

---

[12] The metre is this specific length: 'the length of the path travelled by light in a vacuum during a time interval of 1/(299 792 458) second' (Jerrard & McNeill, 1992, p. 98).

[13] Discussion of precisely what is meant by *ratio* here is deferred to Chapters 2 and 3. For the moment it will simply be said that the ratio of one magnitude, m, of a quantitative attribute, to another, n, of the same attribute, is the positive real number, r, such that $m = r.n$.

14 *The meaning of measurement*

attribute, these levels must be additively related to one another. That is, considering A_i and A_j (any two levels of ability), if $A_i > A_j$ then there is a level of ability which is the difference between them (call it A_k). That is, $A_i = A_j + A_k$. If ability has such a structure (and meets some further conditions mentioned in Chapter 3), there are ratios between any two levels of ability. Without this kind of structure there are no such ratios, and the ability cannot possibly be measured.

If the structure of ability does sustain ratios, then it is easy to see how any level, A_i, may be measured relative to a unit, A_1. The measure of A_i relative to A_1 is r if and only if $A_i/A_1 = r$. That is, quite generally, measurement is just the process of discovering or estimating the measure of some magnitude of a quantitative attribute relative to a given unit. That is, measurement is the discovery or estimation of the ratio of some magnitude of a quantitative attribute to a unit (a unit being, in principle, any magnitude of the same quantitative attribute).

This understanding of measurement, that it is the process of discovering ratios, is not novel. It is, in fact, standard within quantitative science. For example, consider this discussion by Terrien (1980):

Quantities are abstract concepts possessing two main properties: they can be measured, that means that the ratio of two quantities of the same kind, a pure number, can be established by experiment; and they can enter into a mathematical scheme expressing their definitions or the laws of physics. A unit for a kind of quantity is a sample of that quantity chosen by convention to have the value 1. So that, as already stated by Clerk Maxwell,

$$\text{physical quantity} = \text{pure number} \times \text{unit}.$$

This equation means that the ratio of the quantitative abstract concept to the unit is a pure number. (pp. 765–6)

Passages showing a similar understanding of measurement abound in discussions of the concept in the physical sciences (e.g., Beckwith and Buck, 1961; Clifford, 1882; Massey, 1986; Maxwell, 1891). As I have said, and as Terrien and many others confirm, and as will be shown in detail in Chapter 3, this understanding of measurement follows from the structure of quantitative attributes: they are so structured that different magnitudes of them are related by ratios; these ratios are expressed as real numbers;

Quantitative relationships and the concept of measurement   15

and measurement is the attempt to discover what, in particular cases, these real numbers are.

The definition of measurement in psychology

Despite the ubiquity of this understanding of measurement in the natural sciences, and despite the fact that it is entailed by the quantitative theories proposed in psychology, psychologists are strangely ignorant of it. To be sure, psychology texts are more apt than those in other sciences to attempt to define measurement, but the resulting definitions given rarely resemble anything in the last section. Consider the definition of Corsini and Auerbach in the *Concise Encyclopedia of Psychology*: 'Measurement is the process of assigning numerals to objects or events according to rules' (Brown, 1996, p. 546). Within psychology, this definition is typical. Most psychologists would instantly recognise it as a variant of a definition made famous by S. S. Stevens. In his publications on measurement theory over a period of almost 30 years, Stevens repeated this refrain: 'Measurement is the assignment of numerals to objects or events according to rule' (see Stevens, 1946, 1951, 1958, 1959, 1967, 1968, 1975), sometimes adding 'any rule'. Stevens' opening chapter of his *Handbook of Experimental Psychology* (1951) had an influence on the thinking of psychologists which is difficult to appreciate now. For most psychologists of that time, Stevens' treatment of measurement 'stood', as Newman said, 'like the Decalogue' (1974, p. 137), a judgment confirmed by the fact that so many texts published shortly afterwards (for example, Guilford, 1954, Lindzey, 1954, and Lorge, 1951) quoted it as definitive.

Since the 1950s, Stevens' definition of measurement has been, for psychologists, the model for definitions of the term. Go to any university library, locate the psychology section and search at random anywhere in that section. You will very soon find a book that offers a definition of measurement and it will be one of this form: 'measurement is the assignment of X to Y according to Z' (see Michell, 1997b, for the results of such a survey). That Stevens' definition is still, in the late 1990s, virtually the only definition of measurement mentioned in psychology texts is testimony to its durability over the last 50 years. Sometimes it is quoted directly and with due acknowledgment (e.g., 'The classic definition

of measurement was offered by the experimental psychologist
S. S. Stevens (1951), as the "assignment of numerals to objects or
events according to rules" ' (Salkind, 1994, p. 96). Often, however, Stevens' dictum is paraphrased without any acknowledgment
(e.g., 'Measurement may be defined as the application of rules for
assigning numbers to objects' (Kaplan and Saccuzzo, 1993, p. 30)
and 'Tests are designed to measure attributes of the test taker,
and measurement implies the assignment of numerical values'
(Friedenberg, 1995, p. 6) as if propagating an oral tradition which
communicates psychology's collective wisdom.

This extraordinary discrepancy between psychology and the
natural sciences becomes all the more interesting when it is
realised that Stevens' definition and the traditional understanding
of measurement are mutually incompatible: if the traditional
understanding is correct, Stevens' is not, and vice versa. The
incompatibility resides in two main points of opposition between
them: assignments of numerals according to rule versus discovery
of numerical facts; and objects or events versus ratios.

In measurement, according to the traditional view, numbers (or
numerals)[14] are not assigned to anything. If, for example, I discover by measuring it, that my room is 4 metres long, neither the
number four nor the numeral *4* is assigned to anything, any more
than if I observe that the wall of my room is red, either the colour
red or the word *red* is thereby assigned to anything. In neither
case am I dealing with the assignment of one thing to another.
Considering the ratios of magnitudes and the numbers involved
in measurement, it is clear that one is not dealing with the
relation of assignment. One is dealing, rather, with predication.[15]
That is, it is not that my room or its length is related to the
number four, the length of my room relative to the metre simply
is the number four.

---

[14] The conventional distinction between numerals and numbers is this: numerals are the
names of (i.e., signs standing for) numbers, while numbers are whatever it is we think
are named (or signified) by numerals (views on this latter issue differing markedly,
especially amongst philosophers). Stevens' terminology in his definition of measurement
is quite confusing. He claimed that he wanted to avoid *number* because of its ambiguity
(Stevens, 1951), but his solution hardly assisted the cause of clarity. I discuss what
numbers are in Chapter 3 and Stevens' concept in Chapter 7.

[15] The difference here is not, as it might appear, that assignment and predication are
different relations. Strictly speaking, predication cannot be taken as a relation at all
without entailing a vicious, infinite regress (see, e.g., Armstrong, 1989, 1997).

Quantitative relationships and the concept of measurement 17

This might appear to be a trivial linguistic point but it is not. It is a fundamental, logical one. Stevens was correct to link assignments to rules, because the assignment of one thing to another is a conventional allocation, often based upon an explicit rule. Measurement does not involve assignments because it is not conventional in that way.[16] Measurement is the attempt to discover real numerical relations (ratios) between things (magnitudes of attributes), and not the attempt to construct conventional numerical relations where they do not otherwise exist. The difference would be most dramatically seen if the attributes involved were not actually quantitative. Then there would be no ratios to discover, and measurement would be logically impossible. Nonetheless, numerical assignments according to some rule could always be made to the objects and events involved. This highlights the logical distinction: the making of numerical assignments entails no commitment to truth; predication always does. A numerical assignment may be many things (e.g., useful, convenient, rewarding), but true (or false) is not one of them. On the other hand, to claim that my room is four metres long is to assert something which is either true or false. In measurement, a numerical relation is taken to obtain. Only because measurements involve a commitment to truth can they count as data in science.

Of course, one rule for assigning numbers to things could be: assign to x the number which expresses the ratio of x's length to the metre. Then the numerical assignment involves measurement. But just because some numerical assignments (according to rule) are assignments of measurements it by no means follows that all numerical assignments (according to rule) are measurements, any more than it follows from the fact that some newspaper reports are reports of deceptions that all newspaper reports are deceptions. Such an invalid inference involves an obviously illicit attempt to infer all from some but, interestingly, it also involves a sleight of hand with respect to the second term of the proposition, in which assignments of measurements and measurements are equated. As will become

---

[16] The conventional element in measurement is the unit adopted. No matter which magnitude is taken as the unit, the numerical relationship (ratio) in which it stands to any other magnitude exists independently of its being the unit. Selecting a unit determines which numerical facts the measurer is interested in. It never constructs 'facts' which would otherwise not exist.

18   *The meaning of measurement*

evident in Chapter 7, this error was no accident on Stevens' part.

The second point of opposition between Stevens' definition and the traditional notion has to do with the location of numbers in measurement: are they assigned to objects or events (as on Stevens' view) or are they predicated of ratios of magnitudes (as on the traditional view)? This is a fundamental difference, and one which by itself disqualifies Stevens' definition.[17] The relevant distinctions are as follows: there are objects (e.g., my room) and events (e.g., my room's changing colour); there are attributes of objects (e.g., the length of my room) and attributes of events (e.g., the time it takes to paint my room); and there are relations into which those attributes enter (e.g., ratios to other attributes of the same kind, for instance, to the metre or to the second). As far as measurement is concerned, numbers are only identified when relations of ratio are considered. In measuring the length of my room, for example, that length's ratio to some unit (another length) is estimated. This relation is intrinsically numerical, and cannot therefore be described in other than numerical terms. Stevens' definition shifts the focus of attention, suggesting, falsely, that objects or events are measured, rather than attributes. In so doing it ignores the conceptual dependence of measurement upon ratios, and it ignores the logical link between ratios and numbers.

Because it shifts the locus of measurement from numerical facts to rules for making numerical assignments, and from quantitative attributes to objects or events, satisfaction of Stevens' definition is trivial. Procedures for assigning numbers or numerals to objects or events according to some rule can be devised on request, and without limit. This obvious fact has not escaped the attention of some psychologists. For example, Suen (1990) remarks that, 'The hazard of educational and psychological measurement is that almost anyone can devise his or her own set of rules to assign some numbers to some subjects' (p. 5). Stevens' definition is extremely wide, and excludes only random assignment.[18] To

---

[17] Stevens also proposed a much more general definition of measurement, one not often recognised, that does not fall victim to this objection. This is the following: 'whenever a feature of one domain is mapped isomorphically in some relation with a feature of another domain, measurement is achieved' (Stevens, 1968, p. 855). This is not to say that it is not wrong for other reasons.

[18] 'The only rule not allowed would be random assignment, for randomness amounts in effect to a nonrule' (Stevens, 1975, p. 47).

Quantitative relationships and the concept of measurement   19

labour the point, in relation to any psychological attribute one can easily contrive ways to count frequencies or obtain numerical ratings, and via that process make numerical assignments to the relevant objects or events, thereby according to Stevens attaining measurement. According to Stevens' definition, every psychological attribute is measurable.

On the other hand, according to the traditional understanding of measurement, only attributes which possess quantitative structure are measurable. This is because only quantitative structure sustains ratios. Unless every attribute really is quantitative, to conclude that, because one can make numerical assignments to things, the attribute involved must be measurable, is to presume upon nature. True, some scientists have believed that all attributes are quantitative. This belief, called *Pythagoreanism*, is discussed in later chapters. Not only do I not know of any sound argument for Pythagoreanism, I know of no argument for it at all. Until Pythagoreans present arguments, it would of course be premature to assume their doctrine true. Hence, we have no good reason to believe that all attributes are quantitative. So, before we can conclude that any attribute is quantitative (and therefore measurable), we must ask how the presence of quantity can be detected. What are the marks of quantity?

This is a question which those who accept Stevens' definition will not understand. It emphasises the fundamental, practical difference between the two concepts of measurement. Those who accept Stevens' definition will believe that they can measure whenever they have a rule for assigning numerals to objects or events, regardless of whether the relevant attribute is quantitative. Thus, given equations (1) or (2), for example, they will believe that they can measure sensation intensities or intellectual abilities without further ado. That this is the thinking of many quantitative psychologists is evident from inspection of almost any text on psychological measurement. Such texts assume that the models or theories sustaining numerical assignments always enable the measurement of something.[19] Those who accept the traditional notion of measurement believe otherwise. They would want to

---

[19] I exclude from this generalisation psychological texts influenced by the writings of the mathematical psychologists R. D. Luce and P. Suppes on the theory of measurement. More is said about their contributions in Chapter 8.

20 *The meaning of measurement*

know, first, whether or not the relevant attribute is quantitative and, second, whether or not the rule for making assignments links numbers to ratios in the correct way. Before accepting equations (1) or (2), for example, they would want to investigate the hypotheses that sensation intensities or intellectual abilities really are quantitative attributes. Stevens' definition of measurement hides a scientific question (Is the attribute we hope to measure a quantitative attribute?), a question fundamental to quantitative science.

This last claim might be thought to be an overstatement. Stevens also distinguished between what he called different kinds of *scales of measurement* and, in particular, accepted the desirability of what he called *interval* and *ratio* scales.[20] These kinds of scales cover the measurement of what, according to the traditional understanding, are quantitative attributes. It might be argued then that Stevens' definition, correct or not, is fairly harmless conjoined with his theory of measurement scales. This view is seriously mistaken. Recognition of the distinctions between Stevens' kinds of measurement scales is not at all sufficient to counter the effects of accepting his definition. Most psychologists accept his theory of scales of measurement, along with some variant of his definition. Furthermore, most psychologists claim that they can measure their favoured psychological attributes on interval or ratio scales. However, hardly any psychologists recognise the need to establish that their favoured attributes are quantitative before accepting such claims. Stevens' definition rationalises this scientific negligence.

The textbook by Lord and Novick (1968), widely regarded as the definitive work on measurement via psychological test scores, exemplifies this attitude. They are fully aware of the fact that Stevens' concept of an interval scale

specifies a one-to-one correspondence between elements of the behavioral domain and the real numbers, with only the zero point and the unit of measurement being arbitrary. Such a scale assigns meaning not only to scale values and their relative order but also to relative differences of scale values. (p. 21)

---

[20] See Chapter 7 for a discussion of Stevens' theory of scales of measurement. Measurement, in the traditional sense, he called ratio scaling, and if an attribute is such that differences between its levels are quantitative, this allows for the construction of what Stevens called an interval scale.

Quantitative relationships and the concept of measurement 21

That is, they recognise that having an interval scale of measurement entails that differences between levels of the attribute are quantitative. But this in turn implies that claiming to measure on an interval scale is gratuitous unless some attempt has been made to test the hypothesis that the relevant differences are quantitative. And, like the majority of quantitative psychologists, Lord and Novick seem not to recognise this implication.

It is obvious from their discussion that Lord and Novick do not recognise that the issue of whether or not an attribute hypothesised to underlie test performance (some relevant ability) is quantitative is a fundamental scientific issue, one upon which the entire edifice they construct is based. Their response to this problem is simply to stipulate that total test scores are interval scale measures of theoretical attributes and to state that to the extent that a set of test scores produce 'a good empirical predictor the stipulated interval scaling is justified' (p. 22). They then see it as being a 'major problem of theoretical psychology ... to "explain" the reason for the efficacy of any particular scaling that emerges from [such] empirical work' (p. 22). The fact that a set of test scores is found to be a good predictor of some criterion (e.g., success in some course of study) is, of course, a fact which invites scientific explanation, but any proposed theory only explains it if true. A typical psychological theory here would hypothesise that the test scores relate systematically to some quantitative property of the people tested, and that property is a determinant of performance on the criterion. But proposing such a theory and testing it, in particular testing the crucial hypothesis that the supposed property is quantitative, are two quite different things. Only when such a theory has been subjected to some experimental test sensitive to the presence or absence of quantitative structure in the hypothesised attribute can any conclusions be drawn about whether or not test scores are interval scale measures of anything. Weaker tests, such as the test scores being a good predictor of related criteria, are not sensitive to the presence or absence of quantitative structure in the underlying attribute because no matter which way they turn out they cannot rule out the hypothesis that this attribute is quantitative. No discussion of scientifically crucial tests figures at all in the text by Lord and Novick.

In their quest for mental measurement, psychologists have contrived devices (tests or experimental situations) which, when appropriately applied, yield numerical data. These devices are treated as windows upon the mind, as if in the fact of yielding numerical data they revealed quantitative attributes of the mind. However, the windows upon the mind presumption dissolves the distinction between cause and effect, in this case the attributes of the mental system causing behaviour and attributes of the effects this behaviour has upon the devices contrived. That the latter possess quantitative features in no way entails that all of the former must. Hence, the windows on the mind presumption is questionable and, so, in the absence of additional, relevant evidence, not a sound basis for accepting the conclusion that the numerical data procured via the contrived devices is a measure of anything. Stevens' definition of measurement obscures these facts.

The fact that the majority of psychologists accept Stevens' definition of measurement rather than the traditional one, and have done so for almost half a century, should be a warning sign regarding the presumption that psychology is a quantitative science. The fact that acceptance of this definition hides from view questions fundamental to the development of quantitative *science* means that this warning sign must be taken seriously. Acceptance of Stevens' definition carries, of course, secondary gains. Not only is the fundamental scientific question obscured, but the definition is used to license the conviction that psychologists practise quantitative science. As a bonus, they feel safe to continue to market their practices as applications of scientific measurement and to reap the ensuing rewards.

There are, then, solid *prima facie* grounds for wanting to look further at the history of this definition. Where did it come from, and why was it so readily and so widely accepted? In accepting Stevens' definition, psychologists have lost touch with the implications of their own theory and practice of measurement. Hence, when they claim to be able to measure psychological attributes, they do not mean *measurement* in the standard scientific sense (to which they are bound to by their own quantitative theories and practices), they mean *measurement* in Stevens' contrived sense. The question, 'Is there any such enterprise as psychological measurement?' is one which psychologists, in so far as they endorse Stevens' definition, are not presently competent to answer.

The following chapters explain how this anomalous situation has come about. The causes lie in a number of directions. First, they are to be found in the peculiar combination of ideological forces which existed at the birth of quantitative psychology in the nineteenth century (see Chapter 2). Second, they lie in the social pressures which shaped the young science (see Chapter 4). Third, they reside in the changes in the understanding of measurement which took place in the philosophy of science during the twentieth century (see Chapter 5). Fourth, an important catalyst was an inquiry in the 1930s into the status of psychophysical measurement (see Chapter 6). All of these forces shaped Stevens' definition and prepared the ground for its long term acceptance within psychology (see Chapter 7).

However, this book is not just a history of the concept of measurement in modern psychology. It is a critical history of quantitative psychology. All criticism presumes an underlying logic, in this case a logic of quantification. Hence, what is also shown in the following chapters is what measurement really is (Chapter 3) and how the hypothesis that psychological attributes are quantitative can be tested (Chapter 8). Unbeknown to most psychologists, the mathematical and logical work necessary for quantitative psychology's rehabilitation has already been done.

CHAPTER 2

Quantitative psychology's intellectual inheritance

> Whatever exists at all exists in some amount. To know it thoroughly involves knowing its quantity.
>
> (Edward L. Thorndike)
>
> This is only to ring changes on words, and to make a show of mathematical reasoning, without advancing one step in real knowledge.
>
> (Thomas Reid)

If we view the present through lenses partly constructed by the past, then clearer vision comes through locating the historical conditions shaping them. I have talked with psychologists so convinced of their own clearsightedness that they claimed not to comprehend even the possibility that psychological attributes might not be quantitative. Yet the merest acquaintance with the history of science shows that quantitative thinking has not always held sway. Kuhn's (1970) picture of the history of science as a succession of conceptual convulsions may hold a germ of truth but it is one distorted by his conviction of radical discontinuity in the flow of ideas. Superficially, conceptual discontinuities appear in the history of science, but these disguise deeper continuities. The thesis that nature sustains quantity and measure, which has flowed through Western thought since at least Pythagoras, has a trajectory surfacing here, submerged there, here combining with other ideas, there in opposition to dominant trends. Intellectual currents, being propositional, interact in logical ways. Some of the tensions in the history of ideas happen because of the tensions created when there is a confluence of contradictory intellectual currents.

As scientists, psychologists inherited the world view that had developed out of the scientific revolution two centuries earlier.

Consequently, they aspired to make psychology quantitative. This aspiration, in its turn, conflicted with another element of that same world view, the presumption that the mental is non-quantitative. The character of this conflict may be displayed as follows. Those seeking a place for measurement within psychology were required to resolve the following inconsistent triad of intellectual currents:

1 *The Classical Concept of Measurement*: All measurable attributes are quantitative.

2 *The Measurability Thesis*: Some psychological attributes are measurable.

3 *The Quantity Objection*: No psychological attributes are quantitative.

Each of these propositions is contradicted by the other two conjoined. Progress requires rejecting at least one.

Where had these intellectual currents come from? Why did they exert such strong pressure upon the new science of psychology? This chapter provides some answers to these questions. Then it will be clearer what the conceptual problems were facing those who wished to promote the cause of psychological measurement.

The classical concept of measurement originated in ancient Greece and the measurability thesis in the Middle Ages. Both derived fresh impetus from the scientific revolution of the seventeenth century and the subsequent progress of quantitative science. The roots of the quantity objection also lay in the scientific revolution, especially in the metaphysical vision then replacing the Aristotelean system that had influenced European thought since the thirteenth century. In the following sections, an impressionistic sketch of each is provided.

THE CLASSICAL CONCEPT OF MEASUREMENT

The classical concept of measurement is that all measurable attributes are quantitative. This concept of measurement derives from Book V of Euclid's *Elements* (see Heath, 1908). Euclid presents a theory about ratios of magnitudes of a quantity and about relations of proportion between such ratios. As the understanding of measurement unfolded, especially during and after the scientific revolution, a close conceptual link between the concepts of quantity and measurement was forged via the concept of ratio.

26 *Quantatitive psychology's intellectual inheritance*

This was that only quantitative attributes are measurable because these are the only attributes that sustain ratios and measurement depends upon ratios. Until the twentieth century, the classical concept was taken to be almost definitional: because of their character, magnitudes of quantities were thought to entail ratios which, in turn, made the application of arithmetic possible. It seemed that measurement could only be of quantities.

What was the Euclidean view? A context for understanding Euclid's theory of ratios of magnitudes[1] is provided by Aristotle's definition of quantity:

> We call a quantity that which is divisible into constituent parts of which each is by nature a one and a 'this'. A quantity is a *multitude* if it is numerable, a *magnitude* if it is measurable. (*Metaphysics*, v, 13, 1020ᵃ 7-10, as quoted in Stein, 1990)

A multitude is an aggregate of individual things, all of the same kind (e.g., an aggregate of sheep). Obviously, Aristotle was not contemplating infinite multitudes here. Hence, the fact that a multitude is numerable is just the fact that it is finite and entirely constituted of discrete units. As a result, any two aggregates of things of the same kind (say, two aggregates of sheep) will always be commensurable[2] because they are aggregates of the same kind of unit. In Aristotle's terminology, the size of a multitude is not measured, it is numbered (i.e., counted). For Euclid, 'a number is a multitude composed of units', where 'a unit is that by which each existing thing is called one' (*Elements*, Bk. VII), that is, a unit is just a definite kind of thing, such as a sheep. The ancient Greek view was that number was always only whole number.

Magnitude is different from multitude, according to the early Greek view: two magnitudes of the same quantity (two different lengths, say) need not be commensurable. Euclid held that 'a magnitude is a part of a magnitude, the lesser of the greater, when it measures the greater' and 'the greater is a multiple of the less when it is measured by the less' (*Elements*, Bk. V, Dfns. 1 & 2; in

---

[1] The 'beautiful theory of proportion' (Kneale & Kneale, 1962, p. 379) given in Book V of Euclid's *Elements* is widely attributed to Eudoxos, a contemporary of Plato (see, e.g., Heath (1908, p. 112)). Simply for convenience, I call it Euclid's theory.

[2] Two aggregates or multitudes are commensurable if and only if they are each entirely composed of whole numbers of units of the same kind, i.e., aggregates b and c are commensurable if and only if $b = na$ and $c = ma$, where a is the unit and m and n are whole numbers.

The classical concept of measurement

Heath, 1908, p. 113).[3] Euclid's parsimonious style of expression can cause intellectual indigestion in the modern reader. His view is that for each magnitude of a quantity (each specific length, say) there is a series of multiples of that magnitude (where *multiple*, of course, is always taken relative to a whole number). That is, a magnitude is always an aliquot[4] part of other magnitudes, which in turn must be aliquot parts of further magnitudes and so on indefinitely. A consequence of these propositions is that, unlike the concept of multitude, the concept of magnitude does not rule out the possibility of incommensurability. It is not required by Euclid's definition that any two magnitudes of the same quantity (e.g., any two specific lengths) must have any aliquot parts in common or that the series of multiples of them must ever coincide.

While the specification of the unit enables the numerical characterisation of any multitude (via reference to the relevant whole number), specification of a magnitude as the unit does not always enable the numerical characterisation of any other, arbitrary magnitude of the same quantity in this way. For example, as was known to Aristotle and Euclid, the lengths of the side and the diagonal of a square are not commensurable with each other. However, the great strength of Euclid's theory is that a general, numerical characterisation of magnitudes can be achieved via the concept of *identity of ratio*. Euclid (Bk. V, Dfn. 3) defined a ratio of magnitudes as a 'type of relationship' between magnitudes of the same kind in respect of size and then proceeded to give the following condition for the identity of two ratios (Bk. V, Dfn. 5).[5] Two ratios of magnitudes, a to b (sometimes written as $a{:}b$) and c to d ($c{:}d$) are the same when and only when, for all pairs of whole numbers m and n,

1. $ma < nb$ if and only if $mc < nd$ (i.e., $a{:}b < n/m$ if and only if $c{:}d < n/m$),
2. $ma = nb$ if and only if $mc = nd$ (i.e., $a{:}b = n/m$ if and only if $c{:}d = n/m$),

---

[3] This is a special sense of measure, viz., measures by a whole number of units.

[4] An aliquot part is one into which the whole divides exactly (i.e., without remainder), some whole number of times, i.e., a is an aliquot part of b if and only if there is a whole number, n, such that $na = b$.

[5] It should not be presumed that Euclid's concept of ratio of magnitudes was exactly the same as ours. See Fowler (1987), Grattan-Guinness (1997) and Rusnock & Thagard (1995) for discussions of what Euclid may have understood by ratio.

28   *Quantatitive psychology's intellectual inheritance*

3. $ma > mb$ if and only if $mc > nd$ (i.e., $a{:}b > n/m$ if and only if $c{:}d > n/m$).

This says that two ratios of magnitudes are identical when and only when they are each less than, equal to, and greater than exactly the same numerical ratios. Any particular ratio of magnitudes is completely characterised by three classes of numerical ratios (or, as it would now be put, by three classes of rational numbers): for any pair of magnitudes, a and b, of the same quantity, $a{:}b$ is characterised by the three classes, $\{n/m \mid ma < nb\}$, $\{n/m \mid ma = nb\}$, and $\{n/m \mid ma > nb\}$. If a and b are commensurable, then the second of these classes is non-empty and this class completely determines the other two (any element of the second class is sufficient to precisely specify that class and, thus, the other two classes). If a and b are incommensurable, then the second class is empty and either the first or third class uniquely specifies the other because they are mutually disjoint and together exhaust all numerical ratios. Therefore, ratios between incommensurable magnitudes are precisely specified by either the first or the third of these classes.[6] Hence, taking any particular magnitude, a, as a unit and attempting to characterise any other magnitude of the same kind, b, relative to it, while a might not measure b in the narrow sense of being an aliquot part of it, there is always the ratio of b to a. This ratio gives the measure of b in units of a in the more general sense of completely specifying b numerically via a. In modern terms, it locates $b{:}a$ relative to the series of rational numbers. From a practical viewpoint, this ratio can only ever be estimated. Theoretically, however, it is important to understand what this estimate is an estimate of.

This theory is one of the great intellectual triumphs in the history of science. It provides a conceptual basis for the understanding of measurement. However, as a theory of measurement it is incomplete. It needs to be supplemented in three ways. First, the concept of magnitude must be defined. No doubt Euclid had in mind magnitudes of geometric quantities, such as length, plane angle, area, and volume (and, possibly, other sorts of quantities as well) and there was small chance of his contemporaries misunder-

---

[6] Euclid's thinking here is very close to the idea that Dedekind was to use when he developed his theory of real numbers (Dedikind, 1872); (see Bostock (1979) and Stein (1990)).

standing the range of applications of his theory.[7] However, by the Middle Ages, when the concept of intensive quantity was introduced,[8] the range of possible applications was no longer obvious. Attributes, such as charity, were said to vary in intensity without it being clear whether or not they were capable of quantitative variation (as opposed to merely qualitative variation). However, such attributes were sometimes taken to be quantitative (Sylla, 1972). This idea was also applied to physical attributes like velocity. From then on, there was a need within the philosophy of science for a precise definition of magnitude, for only via such could this issue be satisfactorily settled. Hölder's (1901) axioms for magnitudes of a continuous quantity provided one of the earliest and best known, precise specifications of this concept.

Second, a theory of the classical concept of measurement must not only explain what magnitudes are and how they sustain ratios of the kind defined by Euclid, it must also explain the relationship between these ratios and numbers. For Euclid, as for ancient Greek mathematicians generally, number meant *whole number*. Hence, ratios of magnitudes were not thought of as being of a kind with numbers. However, over the following two millennia the concept of number was broadened. From the seventeenth century onwards, number was defined as the ratio between magnitudes of the same quantity (e.g., see Klein, 1968, especially his section on Wallis' *Mathesis Universalis*), thus strengthening the conceptual connection between measurement and quantity. In particular, the real numbers proved to be especially important in quantitative science and, employing Dedekind's (1872) concept of continuity, Hölder (1901) rigorously explicated the relationship between real numbers and continuous quantity.

Third, as a practice, measurement bridges mathematical and empirical science and, so, the theory of measurement is only complete when an account is given of the contexts in which the real

---

[7] This matter was not entirely without ambiguity in ancient times, however. In the *Categories*, Aristotle says that 'Qualities admit of variation of degree' (10^b26; see McKeon, 1941, p. 27), thereby admitting the possibility that some qualities may be quantitative, a possibility explored in the fourteenth century by, amongst others, scholars at Merton College, Oxford, and Nicole Oresme in Paris via the concept of intensive quantity (see Grant, 1996; Sylla, 1972).

[8] The occasion for the introduction of this concept seems to have been the theological debate over the intension and remission of forms (see, e.g., Crombie, 1952b; Grant, 1971, 1996; Sylla, 1972).

30   *Quantatitive psychology's intellectual inheritance*

numbers find their proper empirical applications. Of course, in the most general sense, real numbers find application in quantitative contexts. The problem, however, is to understand the ways in which quantitative contexts can be identified observationally. While Euclid's geometric examples were unambiguously quantitative, the justification of other applications is not always so obvious. This is no less difficult a supplement to Euclid's theory than the other two and it is one that is especially pertinent to the subject matter of this book (viz., measurement in psychology). Important breakthroughs in this area were also not made until the twentieth century with the work of Hölder (1901), Campbell (1920), Luce and Tukey (1964) and Luce *et al.* (1990).

In mentioning these three supplements to Euclid's theory here, I mean only to give a foretaste of matters dealt with in more detail in later chapters. My main concern in this chapter is with the force that this classical conception exerted upon the minds of the founders of quantitative psychology. Because it was one of the permanent features of scientific and philosophical thinking, from ancient times to the birth of modern psychology, it exerted enormous force. Even during the later Middle Ages, when Aristotelianism dominated the intellectual world, and mathematics and physics were generally thought to have quite separate subject matters, the classical understanding of measurement held its ground.

One of the most important factors determining the historical strength of the intellectual tradition embodying the classical concept of measurement was the fact that until the middle decades of the nineteenth century, Euclid's *Elements* was regarded as the undisputed classic of geometry, and until the early decades of the twentieth century it (or texts based directly upon it) was a universal feature of mathematics education. De Morgan's (1836) assessment, that Book V of Euclid was one of the 'two most unobjectionable and unassailable treatises which ever were written' (p. 1), was an entirely typical pre-twentieth century view and even as late as the First World War, Hill (1914) was written as a teachers' college textbook devoted exclusively to this book of Euclid. Book V of Euclid provided a common conceptual framework for understanding measurement. As a result, when philosophers, mathematicians, and scientists considered measurement, they did so in terms of ratios of magnitudes (sometimes using the terms *pro-*

The classical concept of measurement

portion[9] and *quantity*[10] instead). Only during the early Middle Ages, when Euclid's *Elements* was almost totally unknown, did its influence seriously wane. However, with the revival of learning in the later Middle Ages, the *Elements* became a core part of the quadrivium, the main source of scientific knowledge for medieval university students (Grant, 1996). Its influence upon the thinking of the Mertonians, Oresme and other scientists of the Middle Ages (see Sylla, 1972; Lindberg, 1982; Grant, 1996) is evident. For example, in his *Tractatus de Proportionibus*, Thomas Bradwardine expressed laws of nature as ratios of magnitudes (Grant, 1974) and when Nicole Oresme, in his *Tractatus de Configurationibus Qualitatum et Motuum* (Clagget, 1968), wanted to discuss the measurement of what he thought of as intensive quantities (like velocity), he did so by analogy with ratios of line lengths.

What can be seen in the history of quantitative thinking from the later Middle Ages to the Renaissance is a gradual extension in influence of the central Euclidean concepts of ratio and proportion. Before these concepts came to play a decisive role in the scientific revolution, they had already left an indelible mark upon the Renaissance. Artists such as Piero della Francesca, Leonardo da Vinci and Albrecht Dürer, fascinated by mathematical issues relating to light, perspective and proportion, produced works that carried forward the influence of Euclid's concept of ratio (Bairati, 1991; Crosby, 1997; Field, 1997; Grattan-Guinness, 1997; and Strieder, 1982). These artists were expert mathematicians and some made important contributions there, as well. For example, Dürer wrote and published in 1525 a *Manual of Measurement*, based in part upon a Latin translation of Euclid's *Elements* he had obtained in Venice.

Most importantly for the subsequent history of science, Euclid's theory of ratio influenced the central works of the scientific revolution itself, in particular the work of Galileo. Mertz (1980, p. 236) notes that

---

[9] Strictly speaking, calling ratios proportions is confusing because, for Euclid, proportions were relations between pairs of ratios and, thus, quite different to ratios themselves. Grattan-Guinness (1997, p. 161) notes that this usage was present in the fourteenth century in Nicole Oresme's *De proportionibus proportionum*. This confusion is still commonplace, if not quite standard.

[10] The distinction between magnitude and quantity favoured here (see glossary) has never been standard and quotations from other authors do not always accord with it.

32   *Quantatitive psychology's intellectual inheritance*

... within the area of inquiry which Galileo deals with mathematically, only a single theory is rigorously applied. This is the theory of proportionality of general magnitudes developed by Eudoxos and found in the Fifth Book of Euclid's *Elements*.

Galileo's devotion to Euclid's Fifth Book was intense, from the time when, as a young man, he preferred it to his medical studies, through his years of teaching mathematics at the universities of Pisa and Padua, and even to his deathbed, where in September 1641 he began a final commentary on it (Drake, 1978). Its centrality to Galileo's work is summed up by Mertz in these terms:

> The Eudoxean theory is significant in that it establishes proportionality between continuous magnitudes and so makes for a rigorous application of mathematics to the continuous distances and change (e.g., acceleration) observed in nature. (1980, p. 236)

This feature cannot be stressed too strongly: Euclid's concept of ratio provided a principled rationale for the application of arithmetic to continuous magnitudes and, hence, of measurement itself.

If the Euclidean conceptual framework was crucial to Galileo's thinking in re-establishing quantitative physics, the same conceptual framework is evident, also, in Descartes' attempts to work out a world-view suited to the new scientific era. At the beginning of his philosophical career, his imagination fired by his mathematical research, Descartes' vision was of a *mathesis universalis*, a unified mathematics of measurement applicable to any scientific subject. This vision was realised most famously in *The Geometry* (1637/1954), wherein his recognition of the identity of structure between ratios of (geometric) magnitudes and (real) numbers sustained his revolutionary methods for solving geometrical problems by algebraic means (Gaukroger, 1995, Mancosu, 1992). Indeed, Grosholz (1991) notes that the mathematical theory of proportion served as a model for Descartes' more general philosophical method as well.

The influence of Euclid's theory of ratios of magnitudes is also clear in Newton's quantitative physics. He explicitly defined number as the abstracted ratio of a magnitude of a quantity to a unit (Newton, 1728) and his *Principia* is notable for the manner in which physical laws are expressed as equations of proportionality. Conjoined, this definition of number and this form of expression made explicit the way in which measurement (as the assessment

The measurability thesis

of ratios) applies to such laws and, also, how it was that geometrical analogies could be fruitfully employed (Grosholz, 1987).

The success of the scientific revolution, in which quantitative triumphed over qualitative physics, ensured that the classical concept of measurement persisted well into the nineteenth century in the thinking of most scientists and philosophers. Thus, De Morgan's (1836) treatise, *The Connexion of Number and Magnitude*, which explains how numbers apply to ratios of magnitudes, was really an extended commentary upon the fifth book of Euclid. The paradigmatic understanding of measurement was as explained by Maxwell in his *Treatise on Electricity and Magnetism*:

> Every expression of a Quantity consists of two factors or components. One of these is the name of a certain known quantity of the same kind as the quantity expressed, which is taken as a standard of reference. The other component is the number of times the standard is to be taken in order to make up the required quantity. (1891, p. 1)

Without using the term ratio, Maxwell here explains what a ratio of magnitudes is in measurement: the number of units required to constitute a given magnitude of a quantity. This kind of understanding was often summed-up in a single sentence, like

> Every quantity is measured by the ratio which it bears to some fixed quantity, called the unit. (Clifford, 1882, p525)

Because measurement was understood as necessarily numerical and because the only avenue through which numbers could enter scientific discourse was presumed to be via ratios of magnitudes, it followed that measurement could only be of quantities. To the minds of pre-twentieth-century scientists and philosophers, the proposition that measurement could be of non-quantitative attributes would have seemed impossible because there was no rational basis for applying numbers to such attributes. To the founding fathers of modern psychology, the classical concept of measurement was a necessary and non-negotiable feature of the scientific framework within which they attempted to found the science of psychology.

THE MEASURABILITY THESIS

The measurability thesis is the view that at least some psychological attributes are measurable. While Oresme had included psychological attributes like pleasure and pain amongst the class of

34   *Quantatitive psychology's intellectual inheritance*

intensive quantities (Clagget, 1968), after the scientific revolution it was not until the eighteenth century that psychological attributes were again considered measurable (Brooks and Aalto, 1981; Leary, 1980; Ramul, 1960; Zupan, 1976) and it was not until the nineteenth century that the measurability thesis gained serious scientific attention. Following the scientific revolution, the exemplar of scientific success was quantitative physics. Emerging sciences were naturally modelled upon physics, as novices in any field model their efforts upon the obviously successful. This tendency was noted by the German psychologist, Ebbinghaus, who wrote that 'The brilliant results produced in the natural sciences by measurement and calculation suggested the idea that something similar might be done for psychology' (1908, p. 13). This tendency to take quantitative physics as their model was strengthened by the fact that the founders of the discipline (e.g., Fechner and Wundt) had often been trained in natural sciences and, so, for them the paradigm was quantitative science.

There are reasons, additional to this one, explaining why psychologists came to accept the measurability thesis. A second seems an obvious one, although it may well have been the least influential. Measurement has one apparent advantage over non-quantitative methods, viz., exactness or precision. Some psychologists aspired to the level of accuracy and precision attained in the physical sciences through measurement. This practical advantage was seen by some as a reason for adopting the measurability thesis. For example, James McKeen Cattell wrote that 'Psychology cannot attain the certainty and exactness of the physical sciences, unless it rests on a foundation of experiment and measurement' (1890, p. 373).

Cattell's claim is mistaken and the error involved, as far as measurement is concerned, had been identified some sixteen years earlier by another early psychologist, Franz Brentano, when he wrote that

Mathematics appears to me necessary for the exact treatment of all sciences only because we now in fact find magnitudes in every scientific field. If there were a field in which we encountered nothing of the sort, exact description would be possible even without mathematics. (Brentano, [1874] 1973, p. 65)

If it is allowed that some attributes of interest to science are non-quantitative, then it follows that a description may be exact even

The measurability thesis

though not quantitative. That is, if some object, X, is Y (where Y is a non-quantitative predicate) then the proposition that X *is* Y is an exact description of that situation. Furthermore, to attempt to describe the fact that X is Y quantitatively would be to attempt an inexact (i.e., false) description. Of course, if it is assumed that all attributes studied in science are really quantitative, then it follows that non-quantitative descriptions are inexact, but this assumption is not necessarily true and, so, needs its own justification.

There is more to this issue of exactness and precision than just description, however. Equally important in science is the formulation of theories, hypotheses and laws in quantitative form. While a non-quantitative law, *All X are Y*, may be both exact and precise (given that neither X nor Y is quantitative), if an hypothesis or law relates two scientific attributes, rather than just two properties, then it may seem that a quantitative, functional relationship is more exact and precise than any non-quantitative proposition could ever be. Again, this is an illusion and for the same reason. There can be precise and exact non-quantitative relationships between attributes and, of course, such relationships can be expressed in a mathematical form, for mathematics, as is now recognised, treats more than quantity. However, at a time when mathematics was taken to be the science of quantity, such an illusion was prevalent.

A third reason for adopting the measurability thesis was the metaphysical view, Pythagoreanism. If the view attributed to Pythagoras, that all things are made of numbers,[11] is interpreted to mean that all attributes are fundamentally quantitative (despite the often 'superficially' non-quantitative guise presented to us via sense perception), then it follows that the attributes studied by psychologists must be quantitative and, so, in principle at least, measurable.

The Pythagorean view persisted over many centuries as a significant feature of European thought (Crombie, 1994).[12] Plato adopted and developed it in his *Timaeus* and from there it found

---

[11] Aristotle wrote that 'For they [the Pythagoreans] construct the whole universe out of numbers – only not numbers consisting of abstract units; they suppose the units to have spatial magnitude' (*Metaphysics*, 1080^b16–20; (see McKeon, 1941, p. 898)). Burnet tells us that 'Briefly stated, the doctrine of Pythagoras was that all things are numbers' (1914, p. 52).

[12] Pythagoreanism was not always associated with views that today would be thought of as scientific. See Fehér (1995) for an indication of some of these alternative manifestations.

36 *Quantatitive psychology's intellectual inheritance*

its way, via the Augustinean monasteries, into the intellectual culture that helped shape the scientific revolution of the seventeenth century (Crombie, 1952a, b, 1994). For example, consider the parallels between Grosseteste's thirteenth-century claim that 'All causes of natural effects can be discovered by lines, angles and figures, and in no other way can the reason for this action possibly be known' (*De Lineis, Angulis et Figuris*, see McEvoy (1982, p. 168)) and the well-used quotation from Galileo that 'The book of nature is written in mathematical language, and the letters are triangles, circles and other geometrical figures, without which means it is humanly impossible to comprehend a single word' (*Il Saggiatore*, see Drake (1957, pp. 237-8)). Koyré (1968) has shown just how radical Galileo's Pythagoreanism was in the context of the Aristotelian view of the cosmos which prevailed prior to the scientific revolution. It was not just that Aristotle's physics was non-quantitative. His position was that the essential properties of physical objects could not be mathematical. The triumph of Galileo's quantitative over Aristotle's qualitative physics resulted in Pythagoreanism being incorporated into the new scientific-philosophical orthodoxy.

The Pythagorean vision of the physical world found its most complete and influential expression in the work of Descartes, who equated physical existence with quantitative extension in space and saw science as coextensive with the study of quantity: 'I recognise no matter in corporeal things apart from that which the geometers call *quantity*' ([1644] 1985, Vol. 1, p. 247). The influence of Descartes and the development of quantitative physics at the hands of Newton meant that the Pythagorean view dominated scientific thinking during the eighteenth and nineteenth centuries.

Mundy (1994) has coined the term *eighteenth-century methodological consensus* to describe the special Pythagorean vision that physicists then came to share: all physical laws were to be expressed using the quantitative conceptual apparatus of ordinary or partial differential equations. As Mundy notes, 'This conceptual apparatus has dominated subsequent physical science' (1994, p. 60). Pythagoreanism was such a significant feature of nineteenth-century scientific ideology (*scientism*)[13] that one of its best known

---

[13] See also Hacking (1983), Kuhn (1961) and Wise (1995) for discussions of the extent to which measurement and quantification were taken to be necessary features of science in the nineteenth century.

The measurability thesis

expressions by W. Thomson (Lord Kelvin) is still in circulation in modern psychology:

> I often say that when you can measure what you are speaking about and express it in numbers you know something about it; but when you cannot measure it, when you cannot express it in numbers, your knowledge is of a meagre and unsatisfactory kind; it may be the beginning of knowledge, but you have scarcely, in your thoughts advanced to the stage of science, whatever the matter may be. (Thomson, 1891, pp. 80–81)

Some idea of the ubiquitous influence of this ideology is gained from the fact that a segment of Lord Kelvin's saying came to adorn the facade of the Social Science Building at the University of Chicago (Merton, Sills and Stigler, 1984).

To the modern mind Pythagoreanism seems to be an out-dated view, but it must be remembered that until the end of the nineteenth century the quantity view dominated mathematics. This was the view that 'mathematics is the science of quantities' (Kant, [1764] 1970, p. 280). Kant equated empirical science with applied mathematics: 'a doctrine of nature will contain only so much science proper as there is applied mathematics in it' (Kant, 1786, p. 7). This view endured through the nineteenth century, at the end of which it was a commonplace observation that 'science recognizes only *quantities*' (Freud, 1895, p. 309).[14] Of course, a much wider view of the subject matter of mathematics is taken now and many kinds of structure other than quantitative ones are included. These other kinds of structure have found ample empirical application (e.g., the application of the theory of formal languages to empirical linguistics, machine theory and cognitive psychology). These applications constitute a decisive refutation of Pythagoreanism. However, it would be anachronistic to require such modern conclusions of nineteenth-century thinkers. Pythagoreanism, if not the dominant scientific philosophy of that century, was a very powerful intellectual force.

While Pythagoreanism may have been one of the metaphysical doctrines driving the scientific revolution, the success of that revolution in eventually establishing science as the most dynamic social movement of the nineteenth-century was, itself, the major factor in

---

[14] Freud, it should be said, changed his mind about this, his more mature view locating the causes of behaviour in both quantitative (motivational) and qualitative (cognitive) structures (e.g. Freud, 1915).

giving Pythagoreanism the hold it had over the nineteenth-century mind. The spectacular development of quantitative science from the seventeenth to the nineteenth centuries and the successful extension of quantification from dynamics into not only the study of thermal and electrical phenomena but also chemistry and biology, made it appear that the progress of science and the development of measurement went hand in hand. Furthermore, there seemed to be 'no apparent limit to the ultimate extension of quantitative science' (Jevons, [1873] 1958, p. 274). This view, which is not just that science and measurement are inextricably linked but that measurement is necessary if a discipline is to be scientific, I have called the quantitative imperative (Michell, 1990).

The quantitative imperative is not synonymous with Pythagoreanism. Certainly, Pythagoreanism seems to entail the quantitative imperative. However, the quantitative imperative was also, sometimes, justified inductively from observation of the history of science and success of quantification. Venn, like Jevons, argued that because the advance of science into new areas had resulted in those areas becoming quantitative, it followed that quantification was a necessary part of science:

... we might almost say that the extension of science from time to time is correspondent to the discovery of fresh measurable elements in nature; and that, within the limits of such extent at any given time, our progress is correspondent to the improvements made in the accuracy of measuring those elements. (1889, p. 433)

To many psychologists the kind of justification provided by Venn carried weight equal to that of Pythagoreanism. Whatever the justification assumed, the quantitative imperative resonated through the early history of modern psychology, the following sentiments being typical:

... until the phenomena of any branch of knowledge have been submitted to measurement and number, it cannot assume the status and dignity of a science. (Galton, 1879, p. 147)

The history of science is the history of measurement. Those departments of knowledge in which measurement could be used most readily were the first to become sciences, and those sciences are at the present time the furthest advanced in which measurement is the most extended and exact. (Cattell, 1893a, p. 316)

... there is yet another [method] so vital that, if lacking it, any study is thought by many authorities not to be scientific in the full sense of the word. This further and crucial method is that of measurement. (Spearman, 1937, p. 89)

The justification of the quantitative imperative takes the form of a practical syllogism: all science is quantitative; psychology aspires to be a science; therefore, psychology must be quantitative. The first premise could be either a deductive inference from Pythagoreanism or an inductive generalisation from the history of science. However it is obtained, the logic of this argument entails that if psychology is not quantitative, then psychology is not scientific. As is now obvious, the first premise of the above practical syllogism is merely a species of scientism. It is the mistaken view that a method which applies to only some scientific disciplines (albeit those once thought of as paradigms of science), should characterise all scientific disciplines.

Had neither Pythagoreanism nor the quantitative imperative been accepted by psychologists and even had they not hankered after the exactitude characteristic of the physical sciences, simply because some of them wished to establish psychology as an academic, scientific discipline and as an allied profession, they would still have had another reason to accept the measurability thesis. The fact that Pythagoreanism and the quantitative imperative were widely accepted within the nineteenth-century scientific community meant that if psychology was to be 'sold' within that milieu as a science and as a science-based profession, it had to be 'packaged' as quantitative. In this way, both scientism and practicalism motivated psychologists to adopt the measurability thesis opportunistically, as an ideological means to a social end.

There are then, these five reasons why psychologists adopted the measurability thesis: (i) the tendency to model psychology upon quantitative natural science, (ii) the belief that pursuit of the goals of precision and exactness required measurement, (iii) Pythagoreanism, (iv) the quantitative imperative, and (v) the perceived need to 'sell' psychology as quantitative. No doubt different combinations of these reasons operated upon each of the founders of quantitative psychology, but whatever the combination, they constitute a potent mix and explain why rejection of this thesis seemed to most psychologists to be completely out of the question.

THE QUANTITY OBJECTION

The quantity objection, the claim that psychological attributes are not quantitative, has its philosophical roots in the scientific revolution. This revolution in human thought was accompanied by a radical change in world view. Following the successes of Galileo's physics, the older, Aristotelian view, according to which the natural world was thought to contain both qualitative and quantitative features, was rejected. It was replaced with a comprehensively quantitative view of the physical world. Within this new view, the apparently qualitative features of things (such as colours, odours, flavours, etc.) were extracted from the common-sense picture of the natural world and relocated within human 'consciousness'. This banishment of qualitative features to 'consciousness' was closely linked with the distinction between primary and secondary qualities articulated in various versions by thinkers such as Galileo, Hobbes, Boyle, and Locke. The primary qualities were understood to be the quantitative attributes of things and they were taken to be their only real physical properties. The secondary qualities were defined either as combinations of primary qualities apt to cause qualitative experiences in consciousness, as in Locke (i.e., as physical dispositions)[15] or as the qualitative, conscious experiences themselves, as in Galileo.[16] The content of these qualitative experiences was thought of as having no existence independent of the mind involved. One version of this new philosophical picture was given by the English philosopher, Thomas Hobbes. Hobbes held that the secondary qualities were 'in the object ... but so many motions of matter; ... neither in us are they anything else, but divers motions; for motion produceth nothing but motion. But their appearance to us is fancy, the same waking, that dreaming' (Woodbridge, 1930, pp. 139-40). As *fancy*, the secondary qualities were held to exist when and only when experienced and, so, to have no independent, physical existence at all. In this way the

---

[15] '*Secondly*, such qualities which in truth are nothing in the objects themselves but power to produce various sensations in us by their primary qualities, i.e., by the bulk, figure, texture and motion of their insensible parts, as colours sounds, tastes, etc. These I call *secondary qualities*' (Locke, [1690] 1894, Bk. 2, Ch. 8, Sect. 10).

[16] 'I think that these tastes, odours, colours, etc., on the side of the object in which they seem to exist, are nothing else than mere names, but hold their residence solely in the sensitive body; so that if the animal were removed, every such quality would be abolished and annihilated' (Galileo, [1623] 1932).

The quantity objection

world was seen as containing only matter, which in turn possessed only quantitative attributes.

The most thoroughgoing version of this metaphysical picture was constructed by Descartes. As already mentioned, early in his intellectual career he was attracted to the possibility of a *mathesis universalis*, a set of principles underlying all science. He was convinced that these principles would be quantitative. The apparently non-quantitative features of things (the 'sensible qualities', as he called them) were present only in the mind. For example, sensory qualities such as colours, do not really exist in physical objects, but only in our minds when the brain is stimulated in certain ways. Descartes is famous in philosophy for his sharp, metaphysical distinction between the mental and the physical orders of reality. He summed it up neatly in his replies to some objections:

> ...there are *certain* activities, which we call *corporeal*, e.g. magnitude, figure, motion, and all those that cannot be thought of apart from extension in space; and the substance in which they exist is called *body* ... Further, there are other activities, which we call *thinking* activities, e.g. understanding, willing, imagining, feeling, etc., which agree in falling under the description of thought, perception, or consciousness. The substance in which they reside we call a *thinking thing* or *the mind*, or any other name we care, provided only we do not confound it with corporeal substance, since thinking activities have no affinity with corporeal activities, and thought, which is the common nature in which the former agree, is totally different from extension, the common term for describing the latter. ([1641] 1934, p. 64)

The basis for his distinction was explained in his *Rules for the Regulation of the Mind*. The attributes of physical things (e.g., extension, motion, etc.) he took to be quantitative and, so, measurable. The sensible qualities (e.g., colour, warmth, etc.) he took to be non-quantitative and, so, not measurable. Our ideas of physical things, he thought, are *clear and distinct*; those of sensible qualities, *obscure and confused*. At best, sensible qualities can be ordered but, Descartes correctly saw, order by itself is not sufficient to sustain ratios and, hence, insufficient for measurement. He recognised that sensible qualities are correlated with the physical properties stimulating our brains, but concluded that this correlation could never be expressed mathematically because the sensible qualities, by their nature, cannot be measured (Buroker, 1991). The conclusion of this argument is that because the sensible qualities do

42   *Quantatitive psychology's intellectual inheritance*

not exist in the physical world and are not amenable to mathematical treatment and because science is based upon mathematical treatment (i.e., measurement), consciousness is not a proper subject for scientific investigation and, so, not a proper subject for measurement.

In one form or another, this kind of philosophical picture has informed all modern Western philosophy. It has brought in its wake a host of philosophical problems to do with epistemology, the relationship between mind and matter and, of course, the subject matter of psychology. From the start of modern science, psychology was excluded from the realm of the quantitative. When philosophers, such as David Hume, began in the eighteenth century to formulate psychological laws (in Hume's case, laws of the association of ideas) and, so, to found a 'moral science' of psychology, no attempt was made to express these in quantitative form, so entrenched had the non-quantitative view of mental phenomena become. This was despite the fact that Hume was modelling his psychology upon Newton's physics and attempted to understand the association of ideas by analogy with gravitation.[17]

The divorce between quantification and psychology was deeply entrenched. For example, the German philosopher, Immanuel Kant, agreed with Hume's position in this respect and thought that because mental phenomena exist only in time, and not space, they could not be measured:

> ... mathematics is inapplicable to the phenomena of the internal sense and their laws, unless one might want to take into consideration merely the law of continuity in the flow of this sense's internal changes ... The reason ... lies in the fact that the pure internal intuition in which the soul's phenomena are to be constructed is time, which has only one dimension. ... It can, therefore, never become anything more than a historical (and as such, as much as possible) systematic doctrine of the internal sense, i.e., a natural description of the soul, but not a science of the soul. ([1786] 1970, p. 8)

This attitude persisted well into the nineteenth century and ves-

---

[17] 'Thus Hume's second task as a methodologist was to show that the Newtonian "methods of philosophizing" are as applicable in the moral as they are in the physical sciences ... General laws must be propounded, on the model of the Newtonian laws of gravitation; Hume thought he could point to such laws in the form of associative principles, which "are really to *us* the cement of the universe"' (Passmore, 1952, p. 8).

The quantity objection

43

tiges of it remain today in the phenomenological movement in European philosophy and its derivatives within psychology.[18]

The quantity objection, however, produced a philosophical tension of its own as, increasingly, attempts were made in the eighteenth and nineteenth centuries to establish a science of psychology. As explained, the quantity objection derived from the dominant scientific world view. On the other hand, the view that there is really only one order of reality, which must include the mental along with the physical, is also implicit in the scientific view of things. The mental and the physical interact causally, and they can only do this if they both belong to the same realm of being, the world that science purports to study. Ingenious philosophies can be devised partitioning mind and matter into distinct realms, but such philosophies cannot be sustained very easily in the face even of ordinary experience, let alone of scientific thinking. So, the impulse to include psychology within the natural sciences is a natural one. Given the quantitative imperative, it was also only natural that this impulse should be accompanied by another, viz., to measure mental phenomena. However, whenever attempts were made to do this, the quantity objection was put.

A good example is Thomas Reid's objections to Francis Hutcheson's proposed quantitative moral psychology. Hutcheson (1725) proposed a moral algebra, a set of mathematical hypotheses relating moral and psychological attributes (see Brooks and Aalto (1981) for a discussion of his theory). His proposal provided the occasion for *An Essay on Quantity* (Reid, [1748] 1849). In this paper, Reid begins by advancing a version of the classical concept of measurement, one that clearly shows the influence of Euclid. Quantities are said to be additively composed of parts and these stand in relations of proportion or ratio to one another. It is this that makes measurement possible and only quantities can be measured. Later, he turns his attention to the issue of 'applying measures to things that properly have not quantity', things that are only capable of 'more and less', that is, of nothing more than

---

[18] The intellectual trajectory of the quantity objection, interpreted radically as a non-negotiable metaphysical principle, moving from the phenomenological movement, through the so-called 'third force' in American psychology (Pandora, 1997) to 'postmodern' qualitative methodology (e.g., Denzin & Lincoln, 1994), although always a minor tradition in modern psychology, deserves its own history and will not be considered further here.

44 *Quantatitive psychology's intellectual inheritance*

order. He presents the usual list of secondary qualities, 'Tastes, smells, the sensations of heat and cold, beauty, pleasure, all the affections and appetites of the mind, wisdom, folly, and most kinds of probability' (p. 717), and adds *virtue* and *merit* to this list. According to Reid there are only two legitimate routes to quantification. One is by showing directly that different levels of the attribute involved stand in ratios to one another. The other is by showing that the levels of the attribute vary at least monotonically (this is not his term, of course) with something that is known to be quantitative. Since, this has not been done for these secondary and moral qualities, attempts to describe them quantitatively 'is only to ring changes on words, and to make a show of mathematical reasoning, without advancing one step in real knowledge (p. 717).

The quantity objection has two sides. The first is conceptual: mental phenomena cannot meaningfully be said to be quantitative. The other is more empirical: the hypothesis that mental phenomena are quantitative is meaningful, it is just that, as a matter of fact, mental phenomena do not possess quantitative structure. While Descartes' was of the first, Reid's objection is of the second kind. In the thinking of those who opposed Fechner's psychophysics and later developments in quantitative psychology, these two sides remained fairly distinct. Some, such as von Kries (1882) and Bergson ([1889] 1913), were to emphasise the conceptual side. Others, such as Campbell (1940), emphasised the empirical. The respective merits of these will be considered in later chapters. The important thing to note here is that the quantity objection did not suddenly appear at the end of the nineteenth century. It was an important feature of the post-seventeenth-century world view.

APORIA AND NEXUS

These, then, were the inconsistent triad of presumptions confronting those nineteenth-century scientists who aspired to make psychology a quantitative science: the classical concept of measurement, the measurability thesis, and the quantity objection. Interestingly, the force that each had attained derived from the scientific revolution and the subsequent success of science. This revolution and the success of quantitative science reinforced

Aporia and nexus

the position of the classical concept of measurement by installing quantity as a fundamental scientific category and measurement as a fundamental scientific practice. The success of quantitative science in turn encouraged a thoroughgoing quantitative vision of reality and the apparent success of that vision made it seem necessary that any aspiring scientific discipline should also aspire to be quantitative. Finally, the apparent success of the quantitative vision of reality helped to banish psychological states from the domain of quantitative science and, when psychologists attempted to introduce such states into that domain, this quantitative vision itself became an obstacle.

It was the singular misfortune of quantitative psychology to inherit this aporia at its birth. Logically, what is required in order to resolve it is recognition of the contingent character of both the measurability thesis and the quantity objection. The quantity objection is an empirical hypothesis. Its truth or falsity can only be sensibly ascertained by scientific research. If it is true, then the measurability thesis is false; if it is false, then the measurability thesis is true, at least in principle. They are linked by the classical concept of measurement, which sustains these implications. The only way of severing this nexus is the rejection of this concept of measurement.

Acceptance of Stevens' definition of measurement is a rejection of the classical concept. Therefore, the widespread acceptance of Stevens' definition within psychology after 1950 broke the nexus between the measurability thesis and the quantity objection. Indeed, it made the quantity objection seem quite irrelevant. To those interested in establishing a quantitative psychology, the central problem lay in the force of the quantity objection. As long as the charge could be made that there was no scientific evidence to support the hypothesis that psychological attributes are quantitative, psychological measurement would have its detractors. Widespread acceptance of Stevens' definition of measurement marginalised the detractors and sustained the conviction that psychology, like physics, was a quantitative science. But was acceptance of Stevens' definition a genuine resolution?

CHAPTER 3

Quantity, number and measurement in science

Every measurable thing . . . is imagined in the manner of continuous quantity.

(Nicole Oresme)

Quantity communicates with number.

(Samuel Alexander)

What must the world be like, in its most general features, given that at least some attributes can be measured and given that it is possible that some quantitative theories are true? Answering this question requires unfolding the metaphysics or logic of quantification. That logic unfolded, one has a framework within which attempts at quantification can be critically assessed. In particular, this enterprise provides a basis for a critical history of quantification in psychology and a critical analysis of Stevens' definition of measurement.

If measurement of an attribute such as, say, length (or distance), is sometimes successful and some quantitative theories such as, say, the theory that the area of a rectangle is its length times its breadth, are true, then attributes such as length and area must be quantities. Thus, a part of understanding the logic of quantification is defining the concept of quantity. This much tells us the kind of attributes that are measurable. Another part is showing how magnitudes of a quantity relate to numbers. This tells us what measurement is. A third part is showing how the hypothesis that an attribute is quantitative can be tested by observational methods and how procedures for discovering quantitative relations can be established. This tells us how to quantify.

In investigating these issues and proposing a logic of quantification I will be largely synthesising answers given by others. I propose little that is original regarding this logic. In the first

The theory of continuous quantity

instance, I lean very heavily upon a paper by the German mathematician, Otto Hölder, on the axioms of quantity and theory of measurement.[1] No matter how much the logic of quantification must utilise mathematical results, it is not a part of mathematics. It is a branch of philosophy. I have drawn upon relevant philosophical works of a number of modern metaphysicians (Anderson, 1962; Armstrong, 1997; Bigelow, 1988), philosophers of measurement (Helmholtz, 1887; Mundy, 1987, 1994; Nierderée, 1992; Swoyer, 1987, 1991) and philosophers of mathematics (Frege, 1903; Whitehead and Russell, 1913; Bostock, 1979; Stein, 1990).

THE THEORY OF CONTINUOUS QUANTITY

If any attribute is measurable, length is. That is, a claim that an object, say, *this pen, X, is 12 centimetres long* may be true.[2] If this particular claim is true, then the world must contain the following situation, that of X's length being 12cm. So, in its being possible, we are committed to the possibility of these sorts of situations (Anderson, 1962) or states of affairs (Armstrong, 1997) obtaining. In their most general form, situations are always a matter of a thing or things of some kind having a property, or a thing or things of some kind standing in relation to something else. In this case, the pen, X, would be of a specific length and that length would stand in a specific numerical relation to another length (the unit of measurement).[3] The rest of this section is an attempt to spell out just what these presuppositions entail.

Of course, X's being 12cm long is just an example. We could be

---

[1] Hölder (1901). For an English translation see Michell & Ernst (1996, 1997).

[2] I accept the relatively simple view of truth that scientists, in attempting to understand the way natural systems work, implicitly espouse: 'a claim is true when things are as it states them to be' (Mackie, 1973).

[3] Situations or states of affairs are all we need the world to be composed of in order to make sense of the thesis that scientific observations or theories may be true. We do not need to decompose situations into particulars (say, the pen, X) and universals (such as, *the length of 12 cm*), as if these were capable of some independent existence. It makes more sense to say that particularity and universality are features of every situation. Neither do we need to suppose that the form of reality is other than situational. That is, things may not always be as we take them to be (I may take X to be Y when it is not), but the logical form of things must be situational (i.e., a matter of things having properties or standing in relations to other things). To think otherwise is not only to make all discourse impossible, it is to invite the logically intractable tangles of those who think that the situational form is something we impose on things, that it is merely a feature of our representations of reality.

48 *Quantity, number and measurement in science*

considering objects of any conceivable length. That is, there is not just one length possible, the length of X. Length's being measurable allows an indefinitely large range. Where we deal with a range of properties, all of the same general kind, such as the class of all lengths, the class constitutes what is here meant by an *attribute*.[4] What makes the properties in some range an attribute is the fact that they are mutually exclusive in relation to one another. That is, if the pen, X, is of one length, then it cannot at the same time be of another: if, for example, X's length is 12cm, then it cannot at the same time be a different length, say 30cm. Indeed, as is evident, different lengths stand in numerical relations to one another (e.g., the length of X is 12 times the length known as a centimetre). It is the possibility of this sort of relation between different levels of an attribute, one level being r times another (where r is a positive real number), that distinguishes quantitative from non-quantitative attributes. Non-quantitative attributes do not stand in numerical relations of this sort to one another. Before we can understand what it means for one length to be, for example, 12 times another, we need to understand what makes such numerical relations possible. That is, the range of lengths must have a special kind of character sustaining such numerical relations, one which non-quantitative attributes lack.

Numerical relations require *additive* structure. We know that lengths are additive because of facts of the following sort. Suppose we have a set of rigid, straight rods of various lengths. We might have a rod, X, of length a and another rod, Y, of length b. If X and Y are combined end to end, so that Y becomes a linear extension of X, then the length of this concatenation of rods will be $a + b$. If we call the concatenation of these two rods Z, and call Z's length c, then $c = a + b$. That is, the lengths, a, b and c stand in an additive relation to one another. Of course, the lengths stand in this relation whether or not the operation of concatenating rods X and Y into Z is carried out. In this sense, the additive relation between these lengths is a permanent feature of the length attribute, one independent of anything we might do with objects.

The fact that the range of all lengths possesses additive structure can be expressed as follows. Let a, b, c, . . ., *etc.* be any lengths

---

[4] Some attributes, such as the lengths of objects, are ranges of properties; others, such as the distance between two points in space, are ranges of relations.

The theory of continuous quantity

in the range of all lengths. Then the fact that length is additive is just the fact that the following four conditions obtain.

1. For any lengths, a and b, one and only one of the following is true:
   (i) $a = b$;
   (ii) there exists c such that $a = b + c$;[5]
   (iii) there exists c such that $b = a + c$.
2. For any lengths a and b, $a + b > a$.
3. For any lengths a and b, $a + b = b + a$.
4. For any lengths a, b and c, $a + (b + c) = (a + b) + c$.

The first of these conditions is that any two lengths, a and b, are either identical or different and if the latter, then there is another length, c, making up the difference between them. The second says that a sum of lengths always exceeds each length summed. The third says that the additive relation between lengths is indifferent to the order of the addition. The fourth says that the additive relation is indifferent to the order of compound additions: the addition of three lengths, a, b and c is identical whether it is the addition of a to the sum of b and c or c to the sum of a and b. Note also that the first and second conditions entail that lengths are ordered according to magnitude: for any pair of lengths, a and b, a is greater than b if and only if (ii) is true. Hence, for each pair of different lengths, one is always greater than the other.

If the range of all lengths has the structure imposed by these four conditions then it is quantitative. That means that the content of claims like $a = 12b$ can be unfolded. What such a claim means is that

$$a = 11b + b$$

(where $11b = 10b + b$, $10b = 9b + b$, ..., $2b = b + b$). Moreover, numerical relations involving numbers that are not whole numbers can also be understood. Claims like $a = 9.45b$ are equivalent to $100a = 945b$ and both $100a$ and $945b$ can be interpreted by analogy with $12b$ above. In general, claims of the sort $na = mb$ (where n and m are natural[6] numbers) have a definite meaning.

What is missing from the above characterisation of length as a

---

[5] For example, if the length of my pen is b and the length of my page is a, then there will be a part of my page, the length of which is c, such that $a = b + c$.

[6] By a natural number I mean just a whole number, i.e., one of the series, $1, 2, 3, \ldots, etc.$

50 *Quantity, number and measurement in science*

quantity is the understanding that every length in the complete range of lengths is measurable relative to any other length taken as the unit. In claiming that length is measurable, we do not mean that just some lengths stand in numerical relations to the unit. They all do. Furthermore, we recognise that the unit employed is always arbitrary, in the sense that while the metre or yard (or some part thereof) is conventionally selected, any other length might have been taken had it been convenient to do so. That is, before we understand what it is for length to be a measurable quantity we need to characterise the range of lengths so that every conceivable length is measurable relative to any length as unit. This may involve talking about lengths that are not instantiated in objects.[7] In the attempt to understand what it means for length to be measurable, restricting ourselves simply to those lengths present in our local region of space-time is far too egocentric.

That is, within the range of lengths we need to consider every conceivable measurable length, so a set of conditions is required to describe the complete range of measurable lengths possible. This is done as follows.

5. For any length a, there is another b, such that $b < a$.
6. For any pair of lengths, a and b, there is another c, such that $c = a + b$.
7. For every non-empty class of lengths having an upper bound, there is a least upper bound.

These three conditions ensure that all possible, measurable lengths are included in the range of lengths considered. Condition 5 simply says that there is no smallest length: diminishing, lengths just keep getting smaller. However, lengths are bounded below: condition 2 entails that there is no length zero or less.[8] Condition 6 implies that there is no greatest length. This condition also means that the class of all lengths is unbounded above. However, this does not ensure that there are no gaps in the sequence of lengths ordered according to magnitude. This is why condition 7 is necessary. In order to understand 7, the concepts of *upper bound* and *least upper bound* must be explained. Consider a non-empty class, L, of lengths. A length, b, is an upper bound of L if and only

---

[7] If it is allowed that distances between points in space have length and that space is continuous and unbounded, then every conceivable length will be instantiated.

[8] In this respect, the concept of distance is wider than that of length. Distances may be zero or negative. Differences between lengths are distances.

The theory of continuous quantity 51

if every length, a, in L is such that $a \leq b$. A least upper bound of L is an upper bound, c, of L such that $c \leq b$ (where b is any upper bound of L).

Condition 7 ensures that the class of all possible lengths is continuous. What continuity means is that if any arbitrary length, a, is selected as unit, then for every positive real number, r, there is a length b such that $b = ra$. How 7 completes the class of lengths may be illustrated as follows. Consider the side and diagonal of any arbitrary square. Take the length of the side, s, as the unit of measurement. Suppose that the class L contains only every length strictly less than the length, d, of the diagonal. Note that L does not contain an upper bound within itself: for any length, a, less than d there is always one greater than a but still less than d (e.g., the length mid-way between a and d). Now consider the class of all lengths strictly greater than that of the diagonal. Let us call this class L^*. Each of these lengths is, by definition, an upper bound of L. But analogously, there is no least upper bound of L amongst them: for any length, b, greater than d there is always one less than b but still greater than d (e.g., the length mid-way between d and b). Thus, if the class of all lengths consisted only of the lengths in the two classes, L and L^*, then there would be a length missing, one measurable by a real number relative to s as unit, viz., the length d, which of course, by Pythagoras' theorem, must be $s\sqrt{2}$. However, condition 7 ensures that d is not missing because it requires that the *least* upper bound of class L be included in the range of lengths. In this way, condition 7 ensures no gaps anywhere in the sequence of lengths ordered according to magnitude.

With these seven conditions, the complete class of lengths and the structure that they must have if they are measurable has been specified. Of course, length has simply been employed here as an example. If it is the case that any attribute, Q, is measurable, then analogously with the example of length, what is entailed is the analogue of the above seven conditions for Q. That is, if an attribute is measurable, then this is what the world must be like.[9]

As Hölder (1901) set these conditions out, they are slightly, but

---

[9] Of course, it is recognised that for some quantities (e.g., velocity in relativity theory) there are strong theoretical reasons to restrict its range in some way. Then the above conditions must be modified slightly for that special case.

52 *Quantity, number and measurement in science*

not greatly different from the above. Since it is to Hölder's proofs that reference will be made, his conditions are displayed below. Let Q be an attribute and let a, b, c, ... be different levels (or *magnitudes*, as they will be called henceforth) of it. Then Hölder's conditions, with his wording slightly modified, are as follows. (In each case the conditions are also described approximately, using minimal mathematical symbolism.)

1. Given any two magnitudes, a and b, of Q, one and only one of the following is true:
    (i) a is identical to b $(a = b, b = a)$;
    (ii) a is greater than b and b is less than a $(a > b, b < a)$; or
    (iii) b is greater than a and a is less than b $(b > a, a < b)$

(any two magnitudes of the same quantity are either identical or different and if the latter, one is always greater than the other).

2. For every magnitude, a, of Q, there exists[10] a b in Q such that
    $b < a$

(for every magnitude of a quantity there is another that is less).

3. For every ordered pair of magnitudes, a and b, from Q, there exists c in Q such that $a + b = c$

(for every pair of magnitudes there exists another, their sum).[11]

4. For all a and b in Q, $a + b > a$ and $a + b > b$

(every sum of two magnitudes is greater than each of those summed).

5. For any a and b in Q, if $a < b$ then there exists x and y in Q such that $a + x = b$ and $y + a = b$

(if one magnitude is less than another then there exists a third that makes up the difference between them).[12]

6. For all a, b, and c in Q, $(a + b) + c = a + (b + c)$

(the sum of three magnitudes is the same whether it is the addition of the third to the sum of the first two or the addition of the first to the sum of the last two).

7. For every pair of classes of magnitudes in Q, ϕ and ψ, such that

---

[10] Hölder is using the term *exists* here in a sense familiar to mathematicians but, perhaps, not to non-mathematicians. He does not necessarily mean to imply that magnitude b is spatio-temporally located. He can be interpreted as specifying what magnitudes he takes to be possible.

[11] This explanation of Hölder's third axiom is slightly stronger than the axiom itself because it ignores the order in which the parts are taken. Hölder (1901) proves that + is commutative (i.e., for any two magnitudes, a and b, of a quantity, $a + b = b + a$) and, so, the stronger proposition does follow from the set of axioms as a whole.

[12] Again, this explanation is slightly stronger than the axiom stated in that commutativity is assumed.

The theory of continuous quantity

(i) each magnitude belongs to one and only one of φ and ψ,

(ii) neither φ nor ψ is empty, and

(iii) every magnitude in φ is less than each magnitude in ψ, there exists a magnitude x in Q such that for every x' in Q if $x' <$ x then x' is in φ and if $x' > x$ then x' belongs to ψ. (Depending on the particular case, x may belong to either class.)

(*Given any two sets of magnitudes, an 'upper' and a 'lower' set, such that each magnitude of a quantity belongs to either set but none to both and each magnitude of the upper set is greater than any of the lower, there must exist a magnitude no greater than any in the upper set and no less than any in the lower.*)

In considering these conditions, it is very easy to misunderstand what they claim.[13] Hölder's conditions describe the structure of quantity. They say nothing directly about how we might relate to any given quantity. Thus, the relations (+, =, <, and >) involved are not to be thought of as always directly observable by us in the behaviour of objects instantiating the relevant magnitudes. For example, one may be able to think of operations for establishing that two objects are of equal length. However, any such operation will never apply across the class of all objects, let alone the class of all lengths. One way is to compare side by side the span of two transportable objects, but the success of this operation depends upon other properties possessed by the objects and not just upon length. Its employment also depends upon our sensory-motor capacities. Hence, there will be conditions under which such an observable relation between objects will not hold while the relation of identity between magnitudes obtains.

In characterising a quantity, such as length, the relations mentioned are between specific lengths. So, =, +, >, and < are to be understood, not as relations between objects, but as relations between the magnitudes. For example, considering length again, a + b = c, by itself, does not say anything about the outcome when two objects are concatenated lengthwise and compared with a third. Neither should it be understood as saying anything about what results when two lengths are put together or combined, if such an operation is possible. It simply asserts the existence of a ternary relation of a specific form between lengths. Whether or not that ternary relation is directly evident when either objects or

---

[13] For the sort of misunderstanding I refer to see Nagel (1931).

54   *Quantity, number and measurement in science*

lengths are operated upon by us is a further matter and one not dependent upon the existence of that relation alone. That is, while all quantities must be additive (in the sense of satisfying Hölder's conditions 3–6), it does not necessarily follow that there will exist a (humanly) performable operation upon either objects or lengths that directly reflects this additivity. That is, all quantities must be additive, but they need not all be *extensive* (as this term is now understood).

Extensive quantities are those in which the additivity of the quantity (i.e., the truth of Hölder's conditions 3–6, especially) is evident to us more or less directly from the behaviour of some objects manifesting magnitudes of the quantity. For example, using a set of rigid, straight rods of humanly manageable dimensions, the additivity of length can be illustrated more or less directly. I say more or less because testing a condition like Hölder's sixth, for example, involves matching the lengths of different rods and this can only ever be done by us, with our limited perceptual capacities, approximately. Furthermore, if additivity is assessed via the concatenation or division of rods, as seems natural, this can only ever be done over a very restricted range of lengths. In this very limited sense then, some quantities are extensive. (It should be stressed that no quantity is extensive across the entire range of its magnitudes.) Being quantitative (i.e., additive) is only necessary and not sufficient for being extensive. What is also required for a quantity to be extensive is a certain kind of complex relation between objects instantiating magnitudes of the quantity and us (i.e., human observers). The fact that certain attributes are quantitative first came to attention because certain quantities (such as length, area, volume, etc.) are extensive, but the existence of non-extensive quantities is a possibility.

In the Middle Ages, when the application of quantitative concepts to (then apparently non-extensive) physical attributes, like velocity, was being considered, the concept of *intensive quantity* was proposed.[14] Intensities were understood as quantities (i.e., as able to sustain ratios in Euclid's sense), but they were not considered

---

[14] As mentioned earlier, this conceptual advance arose out of the controversy over the intension and remission of qualities when 'Peter Lombard had put the question whether the theological virtue of charity could increase and decrease in an individual and be more or less intense at different times' (Crombie, 1994, p. 410).

The theory of continuous quantity

55

extensive. That is, they were not understood as quantities within which additivity was directly demonstrable, even for a restricted range of magnitudes. This is apparent in the following comment by Oresme about intensive quantity:

Every measurable thing except number is imagined in the manner of continuous quantity. Therefore, for the mensuration of such a thing, it is necessary that points, lines and surfaces, or their properties be imagined. For in them (i.e., the geometrical entities), as the Philosopher has it, measure or ratio is initially found, while in other things it is recognized by similarity as they are being referred by the intellect to them (i.e., to geometrical entities) ... Therefore, every intensity which can be acquired successively ought to be imagined by a straight line ... For whatever ratio is found to exist between intensity and intensity, in relating intensities of the same kind, a similar ratio is found to exist between line and line and vice versa ... Therefore, the measure of intensities can be fittingly imagined as the measure of lines. (*De Configurationibus* I, i; see Clagget, 1968, pp. 165–7).

For Oresme, hypothesising that an attribute is quantitative is an act of constructive imagination. We take it that certain non-extensive attributes have a structure capable of sustaining ratios. Such a structure we find exemplified first and foremost in the lengths of lines. Here we have extensive quantity. By analogy with length, quantitative structure can be imagined as present in other attributes (i.e., those which can be acquired successively, by which I take it he means those capable of increase or decrease.)[15] It seems clear that what Oresme believes is being hypothesised by analogy here, is the general structure of quantities and not other, contingent, features present in lines (i.e., that they can be divided or concatenated). Oresme finds it meaningful to suppose that intensities of the same kind stand in ratios, as lengths do. This analogy presumes an identity of structure (e.g., velocities relate ordinally and additively to one another, as lengths do), but it clearly does not presume an analogous capacity on our part to be able to divide or concatenate the objects or magnitudes involved. Oresme's comments indicate a significant conceptual breakthrough, one in which the concepts of quantity and extensity are

---

[15] If this is what Oresme meant, then his claim that such attributes ought to be imagined by analogy with a straight line is far too strong. Order alone does not entail quantity. The correct view is that the hypothesis that they are quantitative may be considered.

56 *Quantity, number and measurement in science*

understood as logically distinct.[16] Such a breakthrough was a necessary step leading to the scientific revolution.

One way of making this point in a more contemporary context is to consider uncontroversial cases of continuous quantity where the additivity relation upon the quantity is not directly observable. Density is one such. Density is taken to be a continuous quantity, just as mass and volume are, and it is taken to be quantitatively related to them by a continuous function (i.e., density = mass/ volume). Volume, on the other hand, is an extensive quantity: there is a concatenation operation upon certain regular solids under certain conditions, which directly reflects the additivity relations between their volumes. The same cannot be said for density. Hence, in taking density to be quantitative, its internal additive structure is taken to be of a kind with that of extensive quantities (such as volume), while its external relations with human observers are known to be quite different from that of extensive quantities.

The point is also clear in the contrast between Newtonian and relativistic velocity. According to Newtonian physics, if a is the velocity of A relative to B and b is the velocity of B relative to C (where A and B are travelling in exactly the same direction) then the velocity of A relative to C is $a + b$. Thus, according to Newtonian physics, this procedure for concatenating the velocities of objects revealed their additive structure. In relativistic physics, however, the velocity of A relative to C is taken to be $(a + b)/(1 + abc^{-2})$, where c is the velocity of light. The same concatenation procedure no longer directly reveals the additive structure of the quantity. Therefore, concatenation operations upon objects and relations of additivity between magnitudes are logically distinct concepts. While the former may sometimes allow us to see the latter, they are able to be distinguished from one another along the following lines.

Mill (1843) made a distinction between *uniformities of succession* and *uniformities of coexistence*. The former are causal regularities, stating what is dependent upon what else. The latter are not. They do not express causal dependence, rather they express non-causal, structural relationships. For example, consider Hölder's condition

---

[16] The point is that quantity is an absolute notion, while extensity is a relative one. It is relative, amongst other things, to human sensory-motor capacities.

The theory of continuous quantity 57

7 (continuity or, as it is sometimes called, *Dedekind completeness*). As originally stated by Hölder it was:

Whenever all magnitudes are divided into two classes such that each magnitude belongs to one and only one class, neither class is empty, and any magnitude in the first class is less than each magnitude in the second class, then there exists a magnitude ξ such that every $\xi' < \xi$ is in the first class and every $\xi'' > \xi$ belongs to the second class. (Depending on the particular case, ξ may belong to either class.) (Michell & Ernst, 1996, p. 38)

Now, while this wording may reflect nothing more than a fairly standard mathematical locution, the 'Whenever . . ., then . . .' form is open to a causal interpretation (i.e., such a statement tells us what happens when all magnitudes are so divided). Such an interpretation is unlikely, given the impossibility of performing the operation involved, but this misinterpretation is completely avoided if the axiom is restated as a uniformity of coexistence: a proposition about the structure of such classes (as in my condition 7), rather than about the succession of events.

The conditions of measurable quantity are all of this form. They are to be interpreted as saying nothing, by themselves, about causal relationships, i.e., about what happens when specific operations are performed upon the magnitudes involved or upon the objects manifesting those magnitudes. They do no more than specify structural relations between such magnitudes. They specify what it is for a range of properties or a range of relations to be measurable, and nothing more. Interpreting the conditions in this way means that two important questions are put to one side. These are: (i) how do we get to know that a range of attributes is quantitative? and (ii) how do we measure the attributes within such a range? These, of course, are the questions to which the scientist requires answers. However, we must be patient, for other matters provide a necessary basis for answering them and it is always important to deal with questions in their logical order. Here the logically prior question is, what must an attribute be like if it is measurable?

Hölder's conditions of quantity make it possible to prove that every magnitude of a quantity is measurable relative to any magnitude as the unit. Hölder does this as follows. He defines, for any magnitude a in Q, $2a = a + a$, $3a = (a + a) + a$, $4a = ((a + a) + a) + a$,

58 *Quantity, number and measurement in science*

etc., so that generally, $na = (n-1)a + a$. Then given any pair of magnitudes, a and b, and natural numbers, m and n,

(i) m/n is a *lower fraction* in relation to $a : b$ if and only if $na > mb$; and

(ii) m/n is an *upper fraction* in relation to $a : b \leqslant$ if and only if $na \leqslant mb$.

That is, the ratio (or measure) of magnitude a relative to unit b is located via the ordered sequence of (positive) rational numbers (i.e., numerical ratios). This, of course, is the same method Euclid used in Book V of his *Elements* for specifying when two ratios of magnitudes are equal. (In Hölder's terms, they are identical when their respective sets of upper and lower fractions are the same.) This way of locating ratios of magnitudes matches ratios uniquely with positive real numbers. Dedekind, who was also inspired by Book V of Euclid's *Elements*, noted that each positive real number is a least upper bound of a non-empty class of rational numbers (1872). He called such least upper bounds, *cuts*, and they have since become known as *Dedekind cuts*. Thus, ratios of magnitudes correspond to sets of lower fractions and each set of lower fractions corresponds to its own Dedekind cut (least upper bound), and so each ratio of magnitudes is associated with a real number. That is, Hölder proved that

For each ratio of magnitudes $a : b$, i.e., for each two magnitudes taken in a specific order, there exists a well-defined cut, i.e., a definite number in the general sense of the word. This number shall be denoted *[a : b]*. (Michell & Ernst, 1996, p. 242)

And later he also proves that

There exists exactly one magnitude, ξ, whose ratio to an arbitrarily given magnitude, b, is specified by some arbitrarily chosen cut, κ. (Michell & Ernst, 1996, p. 245)

That is, Hölder's conditions entail that for every magnitude there is a measure relative to any magnitude taken as unit and for each positive real number and unit there is a magnitude measured by that real number relative to that unit. Hölder refers to the real number, *[a : b]*, as 'the measure-number obtained when magnitude a is measured by magnitude b, in which case b is called the unit' (Michell & Ernst, 1996, p. 242). Hölder proved that the system of ratios of magnitudes of an unbounded continuous quantity is isomorphic to the system of positive real numbers. This makes explicit what is meant by the *measure* of one magnitude relative to another.

Hölder's achievement here cannot be underestimated. Measurement had existed for millennia prior to the publication of his paper. At least since the time of Euclid, it was common knowledge that measurement involved the estimation of ratios of magnitudes of a quantity (one magnitude generally unknown, the other specified as a unit). However, what had never been made explicit during the history of quantitative science was the structure which magnitudes must possess if any two of them are to stand in ratios which can be expressed numerically. Of course, in order for this structure to be specified exactly, it was necessary to define continuity. This was done by Dedekind using his concept of a cut (1872). Once that was achieved, progress with the concept of quantity was possible. Successfully using Dedekind's definition was Hölder's achievement. It filled a significant gap in the understanding of measurement: we now know precisely why some attributes are measurable and some not. What makes the difference is possession of quantitative structure. Hölder did not solve all problems by any means, but his contribution made it possible to progress to other problems in the theory of measurement.[17]

THE THEORY OF (MEASUREMENT) NUMBERS

If attributes are measurable, then the world contains continuous quantities, that is, attributes which, by virtue of their additive structure, sustain numerical relations of the appropriate kind between magnitudes. The appropriate kind of numerical relation is this: if a and b are any magnitudes of the same quantity, then $a{:}b = r$ (where r is a real number). That is, the existence of measurement not only presumes the existence of quantities, it presumes the existence of real numbers, as well. Real numbers seem to be mysterious entities. This is because they are thought

---

[17] Hölder's paper was effectively ignored in the philosophy of measurement for half a century. While his results received immediate attention from mathematicians (Huntington, 1902), in measurement theory its significance was not really appreciated until Suppes (1951). Nagel (1931) gave a critique, but one compromised by philosophical preconceptions.

60   *Quantity, number and measurement in science*

to be abstract entities,[18] detached from space and time (Quine, 1953).

Fortunately, the existence of measurement does not leave real numbers as mysterious entities because in presuming that there are continuous quantities, real numbers are implicitly entailed. Early in his paper, Hölder stated that

To unambiguously specify the formation of multiples of a magnitude I will set $2a = a + a$, $3a = (a + a) + a$, $4a = ((a + a) + a) + a$, etc. so that in general, $na = (n-1)a + a$. (Michell & Ernst, 1996, p. 238)

If Hölder is taken literally, then, $2 = (a + a)/a$, $3 = ((a + a) + a)/a$, $4 = (((a + a) + a) + a)/a$, etc., and in general $n = ((n-1)a + a)/a$. That is, the natural number, n, is the *ratio* of the magnitude, na, to the magnitude, a.[19] However, at this point care must be taken. If b is any other magnitude of the same quantity, then $2 = (b + b)/b$, or if c is a magnitude of a completely different quantity, then $2 = (c + c)/c$. Since $(a + a)/a = (b + b)/b = (c + c)/c$, 2 is what is common to all of these structures. That is, it is a kind of structure. It is one magnitude's being double or being twice another, and so on, for other natural numbers. Hence, wherever there is $2a$ and a (as magnitudes instantiated in some objects), there is 2 as well, as the relation between these two magnitudes. Just as magnitudes are located in situations, so are numbers.

One reason why numbers appear to be mysterious is because they are relations, and relations are notoriously difficult to understand.[20] Properties seem more definitely located in space and time than relations do. The redness of the car, it seems, is there, right where the car is. However, Smith's ownership of this car (a relation between Smith and his car) does not seem to be quite so palpably present. But this way of thinking is a trap for the unwary: what is spatio-temporally located is not simply properties or relations, but complex situations. That is, in this example, what

[18] For modern philosophers, the term *abstract* has a very special meaning, one that neatly demonstrates the fallacy of reification. Strictly speaking, abstracting is a special psychological relation: that of attending to one feature while ignoring others. To believe that what we attend to in abstracting is abstract is to mistake the relation between two terms for a quality of one of them.

[19] Hölder might not have agreed with this view of numbers. It is possible that he had a view something like this (Michell, 1993). Nonetheless, this view is implicit in his theory of quantity.

[20] Aristotle said that relations are 'least of all things a kind of entity or substance' (*Metaphysics* 1088a 22).

The theory of (measurement) numbers

exist (i.e., what is spatio-temporally located) are the two complex situations, the car's being red and Smith's owning the car. Similarly with respect to numbers: what exist are situations involving numerical relations.

In considering specific relations, the error to which we are prone if we are not careful is that of mistaking a relation between things for a quality of one of those things.[21] The view that numbers are properties of agglomerations of things illustrates this.[22] Frege (1884/1950) saw clearly the flaw in this: 'I am able to think of the *Iliad* either as one poem, or as 24 Books, or as some large Number of verses' (p. 28e). That is, the number of things in an agglomeration is always relative to a unit (e.g., in Frege's example, a poem, book, or verse). That is, numbers are not features of agglomerations *per se*, but are relations. The relation involved holds between the size of the agglomeration and the unit. For example, an agglomeration may be that of four books, in which case being of four books is a property it has, but it does not have the property of being four. What is four, however, is its size (being of four books) in relation to the unit (being a book), that is, its relative magnitude or ratio to a unit.

Taking the natural numbers in this way opens the prospect of generalising to the integers, rational numbers and real numbers, as noted by Forrest and Armstrong (1987). The integers, which differ from the natural numbers ($1, 2, 3, \ldots,$ etc.) in being either positive or negative and including 0 (i.e., $\ldots, -3, -2, -1, 0, +1, +2, +3, \ldots$) are, each, the ratio of a difference between two multiples of a magnitude relative to that magnitude, itself. The concept of a difference between two magnitudes is implicit in the concept of a sum: if, for any three magnitudes of the same quantity, a, b, and c, $c = a + b$, then $c - a = b$ and $a - c = -b$. Then, for example, $-2 = [(a) - ((a+a)+a)]/a$, while $+2 = (((a+a)+a)-(a))/a$. Of course, again it is not the specific magnitudes involved that are important but the kind of structure instantiated: the fact that the difference (whether positive or negative) is twice the unit. In

---

[21] Anderson (1962) was especially attuned to this form of logical confusion in the thinking of others (see also Baker, 1986, and Mackie, 1962).

[22] 'What, then, is that which is connoted by a name of number? Of course some property belonging to the agglomeration of things which we call by the name; and that property is, the characteristic manner in which the agglomeration is made up of, and may be separated into parts' (Mill, 1843, Bk. III, Ch. XXIV, § 5).

62   *Quantity, number and measurement in science*

general, for any magnitude, a, and natural number, n, $-2 = ((n - 2)a - na)/a$ and $+2 = (na - (n - 2)a)/a$.

In the case of both the natural numbers and the integers, the ratio is always that of a multiple of a to a or a difference between multiples of a relative to a. But if a wider class of relationships is considered, then rational numbers are encountered. In general terms, for example, for any natural numbers, n and m, $n/m = na/ma$. That is, the rational numbers are ratios of multiples of the same magnitude.

The real numbers are more complex structural relations than the rational numbers, but like them are already implicit in the concept of a continuous quantity. As already displayed, for any magnitudes of a quantity, a and b, and any natural numbers, n and m, $a/b > n/m$ if and only if $ma > nb$ and $a/b \leq n/m$ if and only if $ma \leq nb$. That is, a/b cuts the rational numbers into two classes: first, all n/m such that $n/m \leq a/b$; and second, all n/m such that $n/m > a/b$ (for all natural numbers, n and m). As Dedekind showed, real numbers are least upper bounds of classes of rational numbers (1872). Since a/b cuts the rational numbers into two classes, each number in the second class being greater than any in the first, the real number which is the least upper bound of the first class is then just a/b. That is, real numbers are ratios of magnitudes of a quantity.

This way of understanding the real numbers involves taking the numbers not as abstract entities, but as relations between magnitudes of the same quantity, relations that are already implicit in the concept of multiples of a magnitude and relations that exist wherever magnitudes exist. This is no new heterodoxy. It is the traditional understanding of them, one revived in recent decades. Both Bostock (1979) and Stein (1990) show how this view of the real numbers is implicit in Euclid's theory of ratios of magnitudes in Book V of the *Elements*. Of course, it would be anachronistic to attribute such a view to him. Euclid had only one concept of number (whole number) and he distinguished numbers from ratios (Fowler, 1987). Nevertheless, his definition of number as 'a multitude composed of units' (*Elements*, Bk. VII, Defn. 2; Heath, 1908, p. 277) is relational: a multitude of units is the multitude relative to the unit. While Euclid's definition was standard in ancient times and during the Middle Ages, once measurement became pivotal to science, as it did from the scientific revolution,

The theory of (measurement) numbers

his definition was obsolete because measurement as a practice typically produces rational numbers and, theoretically, it requires irrational numbers as well. Euclid's definition was too narrow. Scientists, from Oresme to Galileo, had intuitively grasped the connection between numbers and ratios and it was just a matter of time before Euclid's definition gave way to a definition in terms of ratio. The beginnings of such an understanding are clearly present in the works of the seventeenth-century English mathematician, John Wallis, who wrote that

> When a comparison in terms of ratio is made, the resultant ratio often [namely with the exception of the 'numerical genus' itself] leaves the genus of quantities compared, and passes into the numerical genus, whatever the genus of quantities compared may have been. (Wallis, *Mathesis Universalis*, in Klein, 1968, p. 222)

Wallis recognised that ratios of magnitudes are numbers. This new understanding of number became quite explicit in Newton, who defined it this way:

> By *number* we understand not so much a multitude of Unities, as the abstracted Ratio of any Quantity to another Quantity of the same kind, which we take for Unity. (Newton, [1728] 1967)

Newton, here, explicitly rejected Euclid's definition and replaced it with the much more general definition, one adequate to an understanding of the requirements of scientific measurement. By an abstracted ratio Newton did not mean an abstract entity in the modern sense, of course, he only meant that it is the bare ratio, considered independently of the specific magnitudes or kind of quantity involved. Just as a colour can be considered in the abstract, that is, without attending to whether it is the colour of a specific shirt or particular flower, so a ratio of magnitudes can be considered, ignoring the fact that the quantity involved is length or time. Then the thing considered is just the ratio on its own.

As far as just the real numbers are concerned, this understanding was Frege's. In the philosophy of mathematics, Frege is best known for his definition of the natural numbers as classes of similar classes (Frege, 1884). What is often not appreciated is that Frege (1903) defined real numbers as ratios of magnitudes.[23] In

---

[23] I am indebted to John Bigelow for giving me access to an English translation made for him by Douglas Jesseph in 1982 of the relevant sections of Frege's *Grundgesetze*. There

64 *Quantity, number and measurement in science*

doing this he saw his definition as continuous with that of Newton. What is also not widely appreciated is that Whitehead and Russell (1913) followed Frege in this respect.[24] The definition of real numbers in this way seems straightforward. However, there is one important subtlety that needs attention.

In order to show this, I will follow a line of exposition used by De Morgan (1836) in his definition of ratios. This treatment understands ratios not as binary relations between magnitudes, but as binary relations between classes of ordered multiples of magnitudes. For each magnitude, a, of a quantity, there is the ordered class of multiples based upon it: a, $2a$, $3a$, ..., etc., in general na, for all natural numbers, n. Similarly, for another magnitude, b, of the same quantity, there is the class, b, $2b$, $3b$, ..., etc. Whitehead calls each of these classes of ordered multiples a vector (Whitehead and Russell, 1913). For convenience I will follow this usage. The ratio between a and b is really a relation between these two vectors, the a vector and the b vector. Each na (for all natural numbers, n) is less than, equal to, or greater than each mb (for all natural numbers, m). That is, each step along the a vector precedes, coincides with, or exceeds, any step along the b vector. How these two vectors relate overall (that is, the pattern of how successive steps within each vector relate between vectors) is the ratio between a and b. If at some point these vectors coincide (i.e., $na = mb$, for some natural numbers, n and m), then the ratio between a and b is rational; if they do not, it is irrational. Formally, this way of defining ratios is really equivalent to Euclid's, but it emphasises more clearly the dependence of ratios upon the relation of addition involved in the quantity. This is important because if there is one such relation of addition for any continuous quantity (and there must be because the attribute is quantitative), then there is an infinite number. That is, just given an arbitrary pair of magnitudes of a quantity in isolation, there is no unique ratio between them. Instead there is an infinite number of ratios,

---

is no published English translation of the relevant sections of this important work. However, Dummett (1991) gives an exposition of Frege's argument.

[24] As Russell acknowledged, this treatment was really Whitehead's: 'My friend and collaborator Dr A. N. Whitehead has developed a theory of fractions specially adapted for their application to measurement, which is set forth in *Principia Mathematica*' (Russell, 1919, p. 64). *Principia Mathematica* is an acquired taste, so see Quine (1941, 1963) and Bigelow (1988) for more digestible expositions of Whitehead's treatment.

The theory of (measurement) numbers 65

one for each relation of addition. Ratios between magnitudes of a quantity are always relative to additivity.

Ellis (1966) gives a neat illustration of this point for the case of length, which I will embellish slightly.[25] What seems to us the most natural way for lengths to be added is exemplified by joining two rigid, straight rods, X and Y, linearly end to end to form a new rod, Z, so that if X's length is a and Y's length is b then Z's is $a + b$. However, suppose we lived in a different kind of universe and for some reason rod X could not be extended linearly by Y and that the best that could be done is to project Y at a right angle to X, so that X and Y form two sides of a right-angled triangle. Then, of course, the length (distance) between the two non-contiguous endpoints of X and Y is just the length of the hypotenuse, $\sqrt{(a^2 + b^2)}$. Creatures living in such a universe might come to think that the sum of lengths a and b is not $a + b$ but $\sqrt{(a^2 + b^2)}$. If they did form this view (which to us seems thoroughly unnatural), then they would still take length to be additive because my conditions 1–4 for additive structure still obtain. That is,

1. For any lengths, a and b, one and only one of the following is true,
   (i) $a = b$;
   (ii) there exists c such that $a^2 = b^2 + c^2$;
   (iii) there exists c such that $b^2 = a^2 + c^2$.
2. For any lengths, a and b, $a^2 + b^2 > a^2$.
3. For any lengths, a and b, $a^2 + b^2 = b^2 + a^2$.
4. For any lengths, a, b and c, $a^2 + (b^2 + c^2) = (a^2 + b^2) + c^2$.

That is, this relation between lengths also satisfies the conditions defining additive structure. I will symbolise this relation as $\oplus$. That is, $a \oplus b = \sqrt{(a^2 + b^2)}$. Just as with +, for any length, a, the vector a, $[a \oplus a]$, $[(a \oplus a) \oplus a]$, $[((a \oplus a) \oplus a) \oplus a]$, . . ., etc., exists and, similarly, for any other length, b, the b vector based upon $\oplus$. The ratio of a to b is then the pattern of equalities and/or inequalities between these two vectors, step by step along each. Now, suppose that a is the length of the side of a square and b the length of its diagonal: $b = a \oplus a$ because $b = \sqrt{(a^2 + a^2)}$, and, so, those inhabiting this universe would take a and b to be commensurable, in fact, they would say that $b = 2a$ and if we took the care to note what they mean by the sum of two lengths we would have to agree.

---

[25] A completely different example of the same point is given in Michell (1993).

66 *Quantity, number and measurement in science*

Now, Ellis's example can be generalised even further within the single quantity of length. Let $c = a * b$ if and only if $c = [a^r + b^r]^{1/r}$ (that is, c is the positive rth root of the sum of each of a and b raised to the power of r, where r is any positive real number such that $1 \leq r < \infty$). For each different value of r there is a different value of c because the sum of a and b is defined differently, but each such definition conforms to the conditions for additivity and, so, allows different ratios to be defined for each pair of lengths, a and b. Since r may take an infinite number of values, for any pair of lengths there is no unique ratio between them. A similar conclusion applies to all continuous quantities. Ratios are relative to relations of additivity.

While from our point of view, as human observers of quantitative attributes, such as length, there is 'a simplest sort of additivity' (Armstrong, 1997, p. 180) and any other proposal seems strongly counterintuitive, showing that ratios are relative in this way is by no means a purely arid point to make. I have already mentioned the point that, with respect to velocity, what seems to us the simplest sort of additivity is not the sort that reveals the additive structure of the quantity as conceptualised within relativity theory. Intuitively, we think that if A and B are travelling in exactly the same direction away from C and if A's velocity relative to B is a metres/second and B's relative to C is b metres/second then A's velocity relative to C should be $a + b$ metres/second. This is not so within relativity theory. Nevertheless, this way of understanding the additivity of velocities is perfectly coherent. It just means that for velocity as conceptualised within relativity theory it is not compatible with the, at least equally strong, intuition that velocity is the ratio of distance to time. If we were to abandon that intuition instead and retain our intuition about what it means for velocities to add together, then we would simply be working with a different relation of additivity within the quantity, velocity.[26] The upshot of this is that in any absolute sense, independent of human minds, there is no simplest sort of additivity. The relation of additivity that we come to identify within any quantity is identified because of factors extrinsic to the quantity itself. It may be identified as a result of our sensory-motor capacities or as a result, in

---

[26] See Krantz *et al.* (1971), Lucas (1984) and Luce (1997) for discussions of this point.

part, of the wider theoretical context within which our understanding of that quantity is embedded.

While it must be admitted then that ratios are slightly more complex relations between magnitudes than they at first appear, the fact that they are relative to relations of addition within the quantity involved is no impediment to their status as real numbers. However else philosophers of mathematics may wish to construe real numbers, from the point of view of the logic of measurement we need go no further than the traditional view that real numbers are ratios of magnitudes. Hence, in treating attributes as measurable, science is not committed to numbers as mysterious entities outside space and time. Numbers come as part of the same package as continuous quantity.

THE THEORY OF QUANTIFICATION

In supposing that attributes are measurable, we take them to be continuous quantities. This much is clear from the above. What is not yet clear is how we can tell whether or not an attribute is quantitative. What should be obvious from this chapter so far is that the hypothesis that some attribute is quantitative is a quite specific hypothesis, one never logically necessary. Therefore, it is one that must be put to the test. In the case of extensive, physical quantities (such as length, time, weight, etc.), the observational tests, if carried out, would be rather trivial and for this reason may never have been done explicitly. For this reason, also, their status as quantities may have acquired a false air of necessity. However, in relation to intensive quantities (e.g., velocity, force, temperature, etc.), the required tests are far from trivial. This is an issue that has long been obscured in the history of science by the doctrine of Pythagoreanism, by which I mean the thesis that all attributes are quantitative. Whatever it is that scientists and philosophers have felt compelled to believe in this regard, Pythagoreanism is obviously a contingent, empirical hypothesis. That is, it is one which might be false.[27] It is not and never has been a genuine metaphysical presupposition of quantitative science.

[27] The view that scientists study many kinds of different structures, only some of which are quantitative, is now quite uncontroversial. As a result, it is now recognised that Pythagoreanism is contingent, that is, that it may be false.

68   *Quantity, number and measurement in science*

As noted in the last chapter, since the seventeenth century this has not been recognised clearly. Prior to the seventeenth century, it may have been glimpsed. Sylla notes that

> The Mertonians, although they did not attempt to prove that their measures were extensive and additive by concise reference to experiment as a modern philosopher of science might do, were nevertheless not unaware that the additivity of their measures was an important issue. Thus in their preliminary expositions they repeatedly emphasize the continuity, homogeneousness, and additivity of the latitude of quality, and in their further discussions they frequently consider whether forces, resistances, and velocities are additive or not. (1972, p. 38)

However, it is not clear to me to what extent the Mertonians and other medieval scientists (such as Oresme) explicitly acknowledged this as an empirical issue. As Crombie (1994, pp. 413-14) notes regarding these scientists, 'Philosophers defending Aristotle's absolute distinction between quality and quantity argued that there could be no addition or subtraction of degrees of intensity of a quality as there could be of a length or a number.' He proceeds to comment further that one of the Mertonians, John Dumbleton, 'met Aristotle's exclusion of quality from quantity by accepting it in reality and presenting the quantifying procedures as abstract representations of reality' (1994, p. 414). There was a widespread reluctance amongst medieval scientists to test their theories by experiment. I know of no evidence to suggest that they or their seventeenth-century heirs explicitly recognised the issue of whether or not attributes are quantitative as one requiring experimental investigation in its own right. It seems that the opposition between Aristotelianism and Pythagoreanism (or Platonism, as it was sometimes then called) on this point was viewed as a metaphysical rather than an empirical one. This was certainly true of later thinkers, such as Descartes, who, as we have seen, drew the line between physics, as quantitative, and psychology, as non-quantitative, as a metaphysical distinction.

Recognition of the empirical character of this issue was very slow to emerge in the history of science. To my knowledge, the first scholar to notice it as an empirical question was Reid (1748). The first to discuss it as an empirical issue in a rigorous way was Helmholtz (1887). Interestingly, both raised the issue in the context of the prospect of psychological measurement. The context of Reid's paper has already been noted. Heidelberger (1993) sug-

The theory of quantification

gests that the context of Helmholtz's was Fechner's attempts at psychophysical measurement and the controversy connected with the quantity objection. Philosophically, Helmholtz's scientific work was inspired by the views of Kant, and Kant's opposition to psychological measurement was noted in the preceding chapter. If Heidelberger's assessment is correct, then it was the prospect of psychological measurement that at last forced recognition of the empirical character of this issue. As will become evident, there is some irony in this, for most psychologists declined to face the very issue that their science had thrust into the light and came to accept a definition of measurement that obscured the issue.

Helmholtz was concerned to specify the observational conditions under which we could sensibly conclude that an attribute is quantitative and, so, measurable. As he puts it,

... one must ask: what is the objective sense of our expressing relationships between real objects as magnitudes, by using denominate numbers; and under what conditions can we do this? The question resolves itself, as we shall find, into two simpler ones, namely:

(1) What is the objective sense of our declaring two objects to be alike in a certain respect?

(2) What character must the physical connexion between two objects have, in order that we may regard likenable attributes of these objects as additively combined, and consequently regard these attributes as magnitudes which can be expressed by using denominate numbers? (Helmholtz, 1887/1977, p. 75)[28]

His second question is the more important: how can we tell that an attribute possesses an additive structure?

What leads us, he says, to conclude that we are working with a quantitative attribute is the discovery of two procedures: a method of comparison that enables equivalence with respect to that attribute to be determined, and the discovery of a method of connecting or concatenating the objects that indicates the additivity of the attribute. Taking the method of comparison first, Helmholtz notes that the observable equivalence relation must be transitive and symmetric.[29] He recognises that observable

---

[28] I have made use of two different translations of Helmholtz's 1887 paper, that of Kahl (published in 1971) and Lowe (published in 1977).

[29] A binary (i.e., two-termed) relation, R, is transitive if and only if for every x, y and z that stand in the relation, if xRy and yRz then xRz (where xRy means that x stands in the relation R to y, etc.). A binary relation, R, is symmetric if and only if for every x and y that stand in R, if xRy then yRx.

70 *Quantity, number and measurement in science*

relations having these properties are quite special. Objects have many properties and the outcome of the vast majority of possible comparative procedures would generally be determined by more than just one of these. What is required is a procedure contrived in such a way that the outcome is determined only by a single attribute. As he put it,

If the method of comparison is to yield information concerning the equality or inequality of the two objects with respect to an attribute, the result of the comparison must be dependent exclusively upon the fact that the objects possess that attribute to some specified degree (presupposing, of course, that the method of comparison is properly carried out). (Helmholtz, [1887] 1971, p. 454)

In making this point, Helmholtz displayed his sensitivity to the fact that the observable equivalence relation between objects (e.g., the fact that two marbles perfectly balance one another) and the identity relation between magnitudes (e.g., the fact that the weight of two marbles is the same) are logically distinct: the latter can occur without the former and, presumably, in non-standard circumstances, the former can occur without the latter. But at the same time, Helmholtz is keenly aware of the fact that our knowledge of the latter is, in these cases, dependent upon discovering the former.

In considering weight, Helmholtz notes that

When I place two arbitrary bodies on the pans of a true balance, the balance will generally not be in equilibrium, but one pan will sink. Exceptionally, I shall find certain pairs of bodies a and b which, when placed on the balance, will not disturb its equilibrium. (Helmholtz, [1887] 1977, p. 91)

There are some caveats, which Helmholtz neglects to mention here, that it is useful to stress. The expression, 'two arbitrary bodies', must be interpreted very narrowly: it is two arbitrary bodies of the sort that can sensibly be placed on such balance pans. Also, the notion of a 'true balance' must not be unfolded in a question-begging way: it cannot just be one that remains in equilibrium for certain pairs of objects. A true balance is one satisfying certain intrinsic, physical specifications which, it must be stressed, can only ever be approximately engineered. Finally, equilibrium will be detected, ultimately, by some fallible procedure of finite resolution (i.e., in the general case, only imperfectly). It is important

The theory of quantification

to make these points, lest it be thought that talk of 'weights' is just shorthand for our observations. The concept of weight, as a quantitative property of objects, is much broader than that. Objects have weight even when they cannot be placed on balance pans, and two objects may be of the same weight even when they disturb the equilibrium of what we think is a true balance.

That weight is a quantitative attribute and that sameness of weight is a quantitative relation are facts logically independent of human observation. To recognise this is not to abandon empiricism, it is simply to reject operationism and positivism. Unless empiricism is combined with realism it assumes grotesque forms. This danger is exemplified in radical forms of empiricism where ontological and epistemological issues are consistently confused: positivists and operationists proceed to define what is or how things are in terms of how they are known or what is immediately experienced. To assert that reality is just as we experience it, is implausible, if for no other reason than that it gives an unnatural priority to the human observer. We do not need the science of psychology to tell us that human observation is both selective and fallible. Furthermore, considering our small place in the universe and our limited sensory capacities, only a foolhardy egoist could believe that there is no more to the world than what we experience directly. Weight and sameness of weight are theoretical concepts which, in most instances, are beyond the reach of immediate experience but, none the less, in these cases, open to experiential test.

A procedure for discovering whether or not two objects are the same with respect to some attribute is not sufficient warrant to form the view that the attribute is quantitative. What is also required for this step, thinks Helmholtz, is a 'physical method of connecting magnitudes' such that (i) the resulting magnitude is not affected by interchanging the magnitudes connected (i.e., the method is commutative); (ii) it is associative; and (iii) the resulting magnitude is not affected by substituting equivalent objects (i.e., objects of the same magnitude as those connected). Then the method of connecting magnitudes 'can be regarded as addition' (Helmholtz, [1887] 1977, p. 96). For example, combining two objects in a single balance pan would be such a method in the case of weight. Implicit in Helmholtz's discussion is the requirement that the method also conform to something like

72   *Quantity, number and measurement in science*

Hölder's fourth axiom, that is, that the result of combining two objects exceeds in the relevant respect each of the objects combined. Of course, similar caveats as before must apply here, as well: observationally, there will only ever be an approximation to (i), (ii), and (iii) and this will only ever be the case with a highly restricted range of objects. It should be stressed that devising appropriate empirical methods here, even for a highly restricted range of objects, is often not a simple project.

Helmholtz's failure to deal with these caveats was, in hindsight, a significant omission. Later measurement theorists, under the influence of operationism and positivism, attempted to base their accounts of measurement completely upon axiomatisations of these directly observable relations and operations. The conceptual difficulties in adopting such a basis, therefore, need to be emphasised. Take the simplest case of all, that of length. That length is quantitative is confirmed by satisfying Helmholtz's above-mentioned conditions (i), (ii) and (iii), with rigid, straight rods of humanly manageable sizes, the relevant 'physical method of connection' being that of joining rods end to end, linearly. However, the satisfaction of these conditions will generally only ever be approximate and, considering the range of all possible lengths, restricted to an extremely small band. To base the concept of length measurement upon the numerical representation of such approximations to quantitative addition within such a restricted range of lengths and objects is to adopt a conceptually limited approach. A more adequate approach is to conceptualise the length attribute as a theoretical structure (along the lines of, say, Hölder's conditions) and to see the operations upon objects (such as rigid, straight rods) as providing tests of that theory. In the case of length, the tests are relatively simple, but even there they will break down to some extent when the limits of human perceptual capacities are reached. In all such tests, one is looking for evidence of quantitative structure. The process of interpreting the results of such tests is more like that of using clues to solve a crossword puzzle (Haack, 1993) than that pictured within a rigid falsificationist framework.

Helmholtz also briefly addresses the issue of why certain procedures measure.

Magnitudes which can be added are in general also divisible. If every occurring magnitude can be regarded as additively composed, by the

The theory of quantification 73

addition procedure valid for magnitudes of this kind, out of a cardinal number of like parts, then by the associative law of addition each of these magnitudes can be replaced, wherever only its value is of account, with the sum of its parts. It is in this way then replaced with a denominate number, and other magnitudes of like kind with other cardinal numbers of the same parts. The description of the individual magnitudes of like kind can then be conveyed, to a listener acquainted with the like parts chosen as units, by simply enunciating the numbers. (Helmholtz, [1887] 1977, p. 97)

Helmholtz recognises that this account generalises to measures involving non-integer values.

Helmholtz is only too well aware of the fact that this account of quantification is incomplete. Physics treats quantities which do not conform to this picture. As examples, Helmholtz lists specific gravity, thermal conductivity, electrical conductivity, thermal capacity. He could have chosen *any* from the majority of quantities appearing in physical theories. Our knowledge of these quantities comes about, he notes, 'each time a regularity between additive quantities concerns a process which is affected by the peculiarities of a specific substance or body or by the way the process is initiated' (Helmholtz, [1887] 1971, p. 461). However, he does not treat the issues arising here in a systematic or a consistent fashion. He recognises that the distinction between these two ways of discovering quantities does not entail a distinction between two different kinds of quantities because occasionally hitherto 'non-additive' quantities, as he puts it, are found to be additive. However, he insists, as many others have done, that the discovery of quantities via the construction of observable operations of addition must always come first. This certainly does not follow from the logic of quantification. There may be indirect ways whereby the additive structure of a quantity can be detected.

Helmholtz provided an account of just one way of testing the hypothesis that an attribute is quantitative and, having confirmed that hypothesis, one way in which measurement can be achieved. If the fact that an attribute is quantitative is not logically tied to the existence of a suitable, observable additive relation of concatenation, then neither can our means of testing that hypothesis be logically tied in the same way. Helmholtz's recognition that there is no logical connection here is a sound insight (albeit, one that Oresme had attained 500 years earlier). What we regard as a

74 *Quantity, number and measurement in science*

suitable, observable additive relation is always a function, in part, of the relationship between us as human observers (with our very specific sensory-motor capacities) and the attribute in question. It would be absurd to suppose that every quantitative attribute must relate to us in such a way that a humanly observable, additive relation, always exists. It would be equally absurd to suppose that indirect evidence (i.e., evidence that does not depend upon the discovery of an additive relation) of quantitative structure cannot be attained. The causal interconnectedness of all natural processes makes it inevitable that the observation of such indirect evidence will always be a possibility. The conceptual problem is to think through what might count as indirect evidence for quantity. The mathematical task is to define structures containing no explicitly additive relations within which quantity (and, so, additivity) is definable. These are difficult issues. The hypothesis that an attribute is quantitative is an empirical one and a theoretical one. Because it is empirical it requires testing observationally. Because it is theoretical, such tests need not necessarily be direct. That indirect tests are possible was demonstrated decisively by Hölder.

In the second part of his paper, Hölder (1901) presented a set of ten conditions for directed segments of a straight line (what might be called 'intervals') that make no explicit mention of additivity and yet from which he deduces that the distances involved are quantitative (i.e., conform to the conditions of quantity given earlier in this chapter).[30] The sort of situation to which Hölder's conditions apply is that of a continuous series of points on a straight line. Any two distinct points, A and B, define an interval, AB, stretching from A to B. For such intervals, there is an implicit relation of addition: for any three points A, B and C, if $A < B < C$, then $AB + BC = AC$. Furthermore, if AB's distance is a, BC's is b and AC's c, then $c = a + b$, so the implicit additivity of intervals involves an implicit additivity of distances. Hölder's ten conditions for intervals on a straight line entail that distances are quantitative, but they make no explicit reference to additivity. Instead, they allow an indirect test. The key condition amongst Hölder's set is the following:

---

[30] See Michell & Ernst (1997).

The theory of quantification

7. If $A < B$, $B < C$, $A' < B'$, $B' < C'$, then it always follows jointly from $AB = A'B'$ and $BC = B'C'$ that $AC = A'C'$.

Since $AC = AB + BC$ and $A'C' = A'B' + B'C'$, it is obvious that Hölder's condition 7 must be true. As Oresme noted, lines constitute a model for thinking about other quantities. However, what is obviously true for intervals on a line may prove false when tested in relation to other attributes thought to be quantitative. If some way could be found of applying Hölder's theory, especially his condition 7, in other contexts, then a way of indirectly testing for additivity would exist. Hölder's work here provided an opening which others were able to exploit. Condition 7 is a very special case of the Thomsen condition, which in its more general form (and stated as the weaker 'double cancellation condition') enabled the conceptual breakthrough of conjoint measurement more than sixty years later (Luce & Tukey, 1964; Krantz *et al.*, 1971). Hölder had begun the journey down the path that would eventually allow a genuine resolution of the aporia facing those attempting psychological measurement.

Because measurement involves a commitment to the existence of quantitative attributes, quantification entails an empirical issue: is the attribute involved really quantitative or not? If it is, then quantification can sensibly proceed. If it is not, then attempts at quantification are misguided. A science that aspires to be quantitative will ignore this fact at its peril. It is pointless to invest energies and resources in the enterprise of quantification if the attribute involved is not really quantitative. The logically prior task in this enterprise is that of addressing this empirical issue. I call it the *scientific task of quantification* (Michell, 1997b).

Secondary to the scientific task is the *instrumental task of quantification* (Michell, 1997b). The scientific task having been successfully completed, it is known that the relevant attribute is quantitative and, so, it follows that it is measurable. That is, magnitudes of the quantity sustain ratios. The business of the instrumental task is to contrive procedures whereby these ratios can be discovered or reliably estimated. This is generally done by exploiting relationships between the attribute being quantified and another already quantified. Consider for example the measurement of temperature using an ordinary thermometer. Within a specific range of temperatures, it has been found that the temperature of a liquid (say, the metal, mercury) is linearly related to its volume, if pressure is held constant. Thus, in a sealed glass tube of uniform width, for a limited range, temperature varies linearly with the height of the column of liquid. By this means, it is possible to measure temperature via measurements of length.

The ease with which length can be measured makes it an ideal candidate for attempting to solve the instrumental problem of quantification. Many instruments, for measuring diverse physical quantities, employ a needle that moves along a linear scale or around a dial. Instruments of this kind provide 'pointer' measurements (Suppes & Zinnes, 1963; Luce *et al.*, 1990). In every case of the use of pointer measurement in the physical sciences, the construction of the instrument utilises established physical laws relating length to the quantity to be measured. Thus, the instrumental task of quantification is no less scientific than what I have termed the scientific task. However, the object of the instrumental task is the construction of measurement devices or instruments, while the object of the scientific task is the discovery of quantitative structure. The scientific task has logical priority in sciences aspiring to be quantitative. In relation to psychology, as far as the logic of quantification is concerned, attempting to complete the scientific task is the only scientifically defensible way in which the nexus between the measurability thesis and the quantity objection can be resolved.

STEVENS' DEFINITION AND THE LOGIC OF QUANTIFICATION

Having unfolded the logic of quantification, we are in a position to evaluate critically Stevens' definition of measurement. Because measurement is the discovery or estimation of numerical relations (ratios) between magnitudes of a quantity and a unit of that quantity, measurement could be very loosely described as 'the assignment of numerals to objects or events according to rule', but this description is so loose that taken as a definition it is conceptually pathetic. Its fundamental deficiency is its withdrawal from the metaphysical commitments of scientific measurement. As just shown, if there is measurement, then there is quantity and number as features of the world. Stevens' definition denies these commitments. Instead of numbers, Stevens only offers a human contrivance, numerals. Instead of quantitative attributes, he gives us only objects and events, neither of which allows continuous quantity.

At its most general, Stevens' definition of measurement reflects the modern nervousness about a world independent of human practices. The logic of measurement shows that quantitative science is deeply embedded in a rich metaphysics. Those who would measure the world must first possess a world complex enough to be measured. In relation to such a world, Stevens was agnostic and this is why his definition of measurement is impoverished to the point of excluding no attribute, whatever its structure, from the practice of measurement.

How does Stevens' definition relate to the two tasks of quantification? The answer to this question is both dramatic and revealing: if Stevens' definition of measurement is accepted, then the scientific task of quantification is cancelled and only the instrumental task remains. The scientific task is cancelled because Stevens' definition is indifferent to the structure of the world. His definition requires no quantitative structures. It eliminates the scientific task and leaches the instrumental task of its scientific content. This fact is so striking that it is unlikely to be an accident. Yet no one could believe, *a priori*, that a discipline seriously aspiring to become a quantitative science would come to accept a definition of a fundamental methodological concept *because* that definition removed an empirical issue from the research agenda. Only an examination of the history of psychological measurement will reveal whether or not one could be brought to believe this *a posteriori*.

CHAPTER 4

Early psychology and the quantity objection

One cannot build a house without bricks; and, when even the plan for the house has yet to be drawn, one cannot have everything right on the first try and get it all to fit together.

(Gustav Fechner)

It may be at present pseudo-science, in the sense that we have drawn conclusions without adequate knowledge, but it is none the less the best we can do.

(James McKeen Cattell)

The classical conception of measurement was accepted within modern psychology until the 1940s. From about 1950 until the present, Stevens' concept of measurement has been more or less officially endorsed. This transition required the existence of two prior conditions and a precipitating cause. First, conditions within psychology had to be favourable: by 1940 quantitative psychology had already adopted a *modus operandi* fitting Stevens' definition; the quantity objection was effectively ignored; and a wide class of number-generating operations were routinely accepted as measurement procedures. However, this was not sufficient. Psychology, as a new science, possessed neither the moral nor the intellectual resources necessary unilaterally to redefine a central scientific concept. Hence, second, relevant external conditions had to be ripe. By the 1940s, psychology was more sensitive to developments within the philosophy of science than it was to developments within quantitative science *per se*, so the external conditions required related to developments within that branch of philosophy. Supplementing these, an event was required to cause acceptance of a new definition. This catalyst was the *Final Report* of the Ferguson Committee of the British Association for the Advancement of Science.

Fechner's model for psychological measurement 79

This chapter traces the trajectory of the first of these factors, showing how quantitative psychologists at first misunderstood and then came to ignore the quantity objection. Fechner mistakenly thought he had answered it. His psychophysics was the exemplar emulated by subsequent quantitative psychologists and, so, his *modus operandi*, that of bypassing the scientific task and proceeding directly to the instrumental task, was adopted. This pattern was followed in the area of ability measurement early this century. By the 1940s, mainstream quantitative psychologists behaved as if measurement was no more than the assignment of numerals to objects or events according to rule.

FECHNER'S MODEL FOR PSYCHOLOGICAL MEASUREMENT

The foundation stone of modern quantitative psychology is Gustav Theodor Fechner's *Elemente der Psychophysik*. There had been earlier, unsuccessful, attempts to found a quantitative psychology.[1] Fechner succeeded, in that a movement, the science of psychology, grew from his achievements. Of course, external to Fechner's efforts, other factors helped, especially the research programme and influence of Wilhelm Wundt.[2] There were three reasons for Fechner's success: he not only proposed a quantitative psychology, he also linked it via his psychophysical law to quantitative physics, making psychophysics yet another extension of existing quantitative science; he supplemented his law with new research methods, initiating an experimental programme; and he persuaded enough of his contemporaries that these methods delivered measurement.[3] These were significant achievements.

It is one thing to initiate a 'science' in the sense of a social movement, and another to found a science in the sense of uncovering some of nature's ways of working, in some new area.

---

[1] In particular, the work of Johann Friedrich Herbart (1776–1841). For a description of his contribution see, for example, Leary (1980).

[2] 'The birth date of modern psychology is usually placed towards the end of 1879 when Wilhelm Wundt designated some space at the University of Leipzig to be used for the conduct of psychological experiments' (Danziger, 1990, p. 17). Neither Fechner nor Wundt have been well served by English translators. Of his psychophysical writings, only volume 1 of Fechner's *Elemente der Psychophysik* has been translated. Scheerer has added translations of two important papers (Fechner, [1851] 1987, [1887] 1987) to this list. My treatment of Fechner is, regrettably, based exclusively upon only this portion of his published work. For accounts of Wundt's contribution see Rieber (1980).

[3] The most significant disciple of Fechner in this regard was Wundt himself.

80   *Early psychology and the quantity objection*

Fechner achieved the former. As for the latter, the verdict is unclear,[4] mainly because of his inadequate response to the quantity objection. Trained as a physicist and having worked on the measurement of electric currents,[5] Fechner developed psychophysics conscious of the meaning of measurement in physics. He was aware of the quantity objection, but did not think it raised specific empirical issues. Near his death, without the slightest equivocation, he asserted that his methods provided genuine measurement and that 'all philosophical counter-demonstrations are, I think, mere writing in the sand' (Fechner, [1887] 1987, p. 215).

Like many revolutionary developments in psychology, psychophysics was philosophically motivated. It was driven by Fechner's proposed solution to the mind–body problem,[6] viz., that mind and brain are one.[7] He argued that the apparent difference between mind and body is one of perspective:

> We count as mental, psychological, or belonging to the soul, all that can be grasped by introspective observation or that can be abstracted from it; as bodily, corporeal, physical, or material, all that can be grasped by observation from the outside or abstracted from it. (Fechner, [1860] 1966, p. 7)

His idea was that there is just one basic kind of stuff, but that we can relate to it cognitively in two ways, either via introspection or via sensory observation, and this cognitive duality gives rise to the illusion of a metaphysical dualism. This sort of view was not unusual amongst the founders of modern psychology. Mill (1865/ 1965), Wundt (1896/1907) and James (1890) held similar views. Like all monistic attempts to solve the mind-body problem, it meets one of the deepest convictions of ordinary life, viz., that mind and body interact. This conviction is incompatible with a metaphysical mind-body dualism. If mind and body belong to dif-

---

[4] This judgment is confined to psychophysics. Many judge that Fechner made important contributions to other disciplines (see Brozek and Gundlach, 1988). Link (1994) assesses his contribution to psychophysics differently.

[5] For an account of Fechner's electrical research see Winter (1948).

[6] The mind-body problem is an artefact of Descartes' attempt to construct a metaphysics for modern science by stipulating that the mental is not material.

[7] While anticipating, in important respects, the modern identity theory of mind (see, for example, Armstrong, 1968), unlike most modern philosophers Fechner was motivated more by pan-psychism than by materialism or reductionism. See Heidelberger (1994) for a sympathetic summary of Fechner's position.

ferent realms of being, then there is no sphere within which they can interact. Science can only incorporate psychological phenomena stripped of any special metaphysical allegiances (such as to a distinct realm of mind or of the uncaused). Whatever the value of Fechner's solution,[8] attempting to locate the psychological within the same system of ontological categories as the physical was sound.

Fechner worked out psychophysics along the following lines. He believed that when a physical stimulus (such as, for example, a light of a certain brightness, a line of a specific length, or an object of a particular weight) acts upon the nervous system it produces a neural effect proportional in magnitude. Furthermore, he thought that the intensity of the accompanying conscious sensation was a logarithmic function of the strength of that neural effect. Hence, he concluded, there must be a logarithmic relation between stimulus magnitude and the intensity of sensation.[9] A logarithmic function, say $x = log_r y$, is one in which $y = r^x$, so that as x increases in equal steps (say, 1, 2, 3, . . ., etc.) y increases in systematically greater steps when $r > 1$ (say, 2, 4, 8, . . ., etc., if $r = 2$). As Fechner put it, 'increasing magnitudes of stimulus and sensation demand constantly greater stimulus increments in order to maintain the same increase in sensation' (Fechner, [1860] 1966, p. 52).

Fechner's hypothesis of a logarithmic function between sensation intensity and stimulus magnitude was not based upon observation. Before commencing experimental psychophysical research, he had already formed the view that a change in the intensity of a sensation was proportional to the relative change in the magnitude of the stimulus (Fechner, 1851/1987). This conviction led him to postulate a logarithmic relation between intensity of sensation and stimulus magnitude. When, later, he encountered Weber's law (which states that in order for an increment in stimulus magnitude to be just noticeable it had to be a constant proportion of that magnitude (Weber, 1834, [1846] 1978), he

---

[8] Here is not the place to attempt an evaluation of this very interesting aspect of Fechner's thought.

[9] Fechner distinguished between two areas of psychophysics: *outer* (which studies the relation between stimulus and sensation); and *inner* (which studies the relation between the stimulus' neural effect and sensation). (See, for example, Scheerer, 1987, for a more detailed discussion of Fechner's distinction.)

82   *Early psychology and the quantity objection*

concluded, mistakenly, that he could deduce his proposed logarithmic relation (see Luce and Edwards, 1958[10]). However, he also thought that this proposed logarithmic relationship could stand on its own (Fechner, [1887] 1987).

Experimentally testing Fechner's hypothesis, requires a method for determining equality of sensation differences. Fechner did not believe that subjects could directly judge the quantitative structure of their sensations.[11] He proposed three methods for doing this indirectly: the method of just noticeable differences, the method of right and wrong cases, and the method of average error. For example, the method of just noticeable differences consists in determining the minimal discernible difference between stimuli. The experimenter may begin with an easily discernible difference and reduce it to one that is just noticeable, or begin with one that is not discernible and expand it to one that is just noticeable. Fechner recommended using both procedures to obtain preliminary estimates of the value of the just noticeable difference and then calculating their mean to improve the accuracy of estimation.

Each of his methods determined, for any subject and stimulus magnitude, the value of a *just noticeable difference* (jnd). As one might expect, the value obtained is not only relative to the magnitude of the stimulus used (as Weber's law prescribes), it is also relative to the other perceptible properties of the stimulus, to properties of the subject (e.g., perceptual and motivational states), to the method used, and to the external, environmental conditions present when the methods are applied. Consideration of these additional matters will be left aside here, for the question of interest is this: assuming that for each specific stimulus, there is a jnd for each subject (conditional upon whatever boundary conditions need to be stated), is it possible thereby to determine equal sensation differences?

Of course, the answer is: not without making further assumptions. In determining jnds, it is differences between stimulus magnitudes and the judgments of subjects that are observed. The intensity of the subject's sensation is never observed by the exper-

---

[10] Luce and Edwards argue that Fechner confused a ratio of differences (the ratio between the sensation increment corresponding to a jnd and the jnd itself) with a ratio of differentials (see also Luce, 1993).

[11] Unlike Stevens who, as we shall see in Chapter 7, believed that subjects could directly estimate quantitative relations between sensations.

Fechner's model for psychological measurement 83

imenter.[12] So conclusions about sensations can only validly be drawn from observations of jnds by invoking additional premises. Fechner's additional premise was that jnds for different stimulus magnitudes correspond to equal sensation differences. If this premise is true, then a series in which consecutive stimuli are separated at each step by one jnd corresponds to a series in which the consecutive accompanying sensations are separated by equal differences in intensity. Given this, the intensity of any sensation in the series is measured by the number of jnds between the stimulus producing it and the absolute threshold (the minimal stimulus magnitude eliciting a sensation).

Fechner thought that this additional premise was a tautology. His discussion of the Plateau-Delbœuf procedure, known as the *method of bisection*, [13] makes this clear. In this method, the subject sets the magnitude of a stimulus, B, between the magnitudes of two given stimuli, A and C, so that the perceived difference between B and A equals that between C and B.

Now it might be said that if the perceived difference between A and B has been found equal to the perceived difference between B and C, then it by no means follows that the total perceived difference between A and C, if compared *directly*, will equal exactly double the two partial differences perceived separately; it might be a totally indefinite function of both. But in fact this could not be said, because to do so would mean contradicting a tautological sentence. Nor would it be possible to say in physics: If three weights A, B, C are given and if the weight difference between A and B has been found equal to the weight difference between B and C, then it by no means follows that the weight difference between A and C is twice as large as those two partial differences. We simply *call* a total difference twice as large as each of two equal partial differences of which it is composed, in the above sense, or into which it can be

---

[12] Indeed, the thesis that there are such things as sensations is not a proposition that could ever be put to any kind of scientific test (i.e., it is a purely philosophical thesis). Fechner, like many psychologists, took this assumption for granted. However, some have argued (e.g., Michell, 1988) that in perception the immediate object of awareness is always the stimulus itself and never an 'inner' mental object, such as a sensation. On this alternative, realist view, a subject's judgments inform us, not about sensations (for there are no such things) but, rather, about the subject's sensitivity to the physical stimulus, its properties and relations (see also Luce, 1972). Boring (1921) explored a similar view, as did Holt (1915). Brentano ([1874] 1973), much earlier, had written that 'a clear understanding of what is actually measured by Fechner's methods would show us that the object of measurement is not so much a mental as a physical phenomenon' (p. 69).

[13] Laming and Laming (1996) give an English translation of two of Plateau's relevant papers. See also Herrnstein and Boring (1965).

84   *Early psychology and the quantity objection*

thought to be decomposable; and I do not see any reason why in this respect there should be any difference between the mental and the physical fields. (Fechner, 1887/1987, p. 215)

It is instructive to isolate Fechner's mistake here. If a total difference is entirely constituted by two discrete and equal parts, then we do call the total twice each of the parts. However, the tautological character of the claim hinges upon the additive relationship between the parts and the whole.

Suppose it is found that weights B and X combined perfectly balance weight A and that weights C and X combined perfectly balance weight B. Expressed as $A = B + X$ and $B = C + X$, these facts seem to imply that $A - B = B - C = X$ and, therefore that, $A - C = 2(A - B) = 2(B - C)$. However, in translating the observations into quantitative propositions, weight is assumed to conform to something like Hölder's axioms. For example, the necessary algebra uses the associative law (Hölder's axiom 6): if $A = B + X$ and $B = C + X$ then $A = (C + X) + X = C + (X + X) = C + 2X$ and, so, $A - C = 2X = 2(A - B) = 2(B - C)$. If axiom 6 does not hold, then the claim that $(C + X) + X = C + (X + X)$ does not necessarily follow. It is only because weight is assumed to be a quantitative attribute that Fechner's claim appears tautological.

Similarly, the claim about perceived differences is not a tautology. Let A, B, C, and D be four stimuli in descending order of magnitude and let (A/B) be the stimulus perceived to be halfway between A and B, etc., and let $S(A)$, $S(B)$, etc., be the sensation intensities produced by A, B, etc., respectively, so that $S(A) - S(B)$ is the difference in intensity between sensations evoked by A and B. On Fechner's interpretation, $S(A) - S(A/B) = S(A/B) - S(B) = [S(A) - S(B)]/2$. If this is true, then $S((A/B)/(C/D)) = S((A/C)/(B/D))$. This last proposition is certainly not tautological, it being possible for a subject's sensations to contradict it. Thus, Fechner's claim here, that it is tautologous that a total difference is twice the parts obtained via the bisection method, is not true.[14]

The bisection method identifies a relation between stimulus magnitudes which Fechner interpreted as an additive relation between equal sensation differences. The hypothesis that this

---

[14] An experiment something like the above was carried out by Gage (1934a, b). The results did not support Fechner's contention. However, Gage's results could perhaps be reinterpreted quantitatively in the light of the more general theory of bisection operations proposed by Fagot (1961) and Adams and Fagot (1975).

relation is additive is not necessarily true. Its truth needs to be demonstrated independently. Fechner applied the same logic to interpreting the meaning of a sequence of jnds: he thought that such a sequence obviously corresponded to a sequence of equal sensation differences. Again, what is required is some way of testing this interpretation independently. In making these mistakes, Fechner was misled by an incomplete understanding of measurement. His view was not incorrect as far as it went, neither was it less than could reasonably be expected at that time. However, it was deficient exactly where it mattered.

His view was that 'the measurement of a quantity consists of ascertaining how often a unit quantity of the same kind is contained in it' (Fechner, [1860] 1966, p. 38). This definition is certainly congruent with the classical conception. He later amplified this understanding:

Given several values, in any field, which may be taken to be magnitudes inasmuch as they can be thought of as increasing or decreasing; given the possibility of judging the occurrence of equality and inequality in two or more of these values when they are observed simultaneously or successively; and given that n values have been *found* equal or, if they can be varied freely, have been *made* equal: then it is self-evident (because it is a matter of definition and therefore a tautology) that their total magnitude, which coincides with their sum, equals $n \times$ their individual magnitudes. It follows that each single value, or each definite fraction or each definite multiple of the magnitudes that have been found equal (no matter which), can be taken as the unit according to which the total magnitude, or every fraction of it, can be measured. The n equal parts that can be thought of as composing a total magnitude of course have the same magnitude as the n equal parts into which the total magnitude can be thought to be decomposable. All physical measurement is based on this principle. All mental measurement will also have to be based on it. (Fechner, [1887] 1987, p. 213)

Fechner's conviction that mental and physical measurement are based on the same principle was a sound one and his elaboration of the general character of measurement is broadly in agreement with the classical view, but it applies only to attributes already 'taken to be magnitudes'. He claims that for every magnitude, a, of a quantity, there exists a magnitude, b, such that $a = nb$ (for all natural numbers, $n > 1$), and this is a simple consequence of the classical concept (as worked out, for example, by Hölder) and related to Euclid's view that all magnitudes have aliquot parts.

Furthermore, the definition of nb as $(n - 1)b + b$, makes Fechner's judgment about a tautology in this passage appear correct, given the classical view. Even his contention that all physical measurement is based on the proposition that each magnitude is related to multiples of smaller magnitudes can be construed sympathetically. In general, the ratio of any magnitude, a, to any unit, b, is defined by the classes of upper and lower numerical ratios identified by Hölder, which in turn depend upon relations of the form $na \leq mb$ and $na > mb$ (for pairs of natural numbers, n and m) and, so, ultimately upon multiples of a and b. The fact that he couches his comments in terms relative to the human observer, does not really detract from the correctness of his claim. Fechner was only too well aware of the fragile and inexact nature of the human judgments upon which measurement of all kinds is based and he recognised that the underlying logic of measurement could be considered independently of this fact. However, his treatment fails to recognise the necessity of testing by observational methods whether or not an attribute is quantitative.

It is clear from earlier discussions of measurement (Fechner, [1860] 1966) that he recognised that the attributes we measure are only ever located in situations where they are conjoined with other attributes. In measuring something like time we are dependent upon the observation of processes (say, the movement of sand through an hour glass or a hand about the face of a clock) which possess more than temporal attributes. Time, itself, or a specific unit of time, cannot be isolated in a process independently of these other attributes. Furthermore, it may be that an attribute is measured via a unit of a different quantity. A simple example is volume. Typically, rather than attempt to measure it directly, we measure it via units of length. What is required in such a case is a relation between volume and length. Sometimes the attribute measured is hidden from direct observation and can only be assessed indirectly. Despite the perspicacity of his understanding, Fechner treats these difficulties only as obstacles encountered in developing methods of measurement (what I have called the instrumental task) and not as difficulties encountered in showing that an attribute is quantitative (what I have called the scientific task).

In this latter context, these problems are at least as serious as in the former. The fact that any object or process always possesses a multitude of attributes means that situations must be artificially contrived in which the existence of quantitative relations (such as additivity), within a single attribute, can be clearly displayed. This is the same problem that we find in all branches of science: nature's ways of working are not always openly on display and, so, the scientist must contrive situations that give some indication. Generally, in experimental science, it is causal relations that the scientist aims to detect. This is not always the case, however. In basic quantitative research, the scientist aims to discover the additive structure of attributes. In the case of attributes which are not directly observable these problems are magnified.

Fechner's neglect of the scientific task suggests that his vision was blinkered. In the preface to his *Elements of Psychophysics*, he described his project as that of providing 'an exact theory of the relation of body and mind' and proceeded to state that

As an exact science psychophysics, like physics, must rest on experience and the mathematical connection of those empirical facts that demand a measure of what is experienced or, when such a measure is not available, a search for it. (Fechner, [1860] 1966, p. xxvii)

That is, he believed that the exact sciences must use mathematics and that the use of mathematics entails measurement. Therefore, the place to begin the new, 'exact science' of psychophysics was with the search for quantitative methods. This search was not seen as containing, as a first step, a test of the hypothesis that the psychological attributes involved are really quantitative. A rejection of that hypothesis would have been taken to mean that psychophysics was not an exact science. For Fechner, this was not possible because the mental and the physical were the same world viewed from different perspectives (the 'inner' versus the 'outer'). If it was accepted that the physical world was subordinate to the category of quantity, then the mental must be as well. Psychophysics was important because it demonstrated 'the common subordination of both the mental and the physical realms to the principle of mathematical determination' (Fechner, [1887] 1987, p. 213). Fechner's metaphysics implied that, despite our inability to judge their additive relations directly, sensations are essentially quantitative and mathematically related to physical magnitudes.[15]

---

[15] Fechner's view about this relation was fairly subtle, as Heidelberger (1994) has pointed out. While the mental and the physical were not thought of by Fechner as different stuff, the mathematical relation between physical quantities and associated mental intensities was not taken to be that of identity because the mental and physical

88   *Early psychology and the quantity objection*

This conception guided his thinking prior to the development of his measurement methods. This is why he overlooked the logically prior issue of determining experimentally that the psychological attributes under investigation are quantitative. His metaphysics inflicted his blind-spot.

Situated in its historical context, Fechner's error was understandable. Not only was Pythagoreanism a widely held, nineteenth-century, metaphysical presupposition, none of his critics brought the specifically empirical character of the quantity objection squarely into the open. Von Kries (1882) was one of Fechner's most forceful critics. However, he also did not see the quantity objection as raising an empirical issue. When he objected that 'One cannot explain what it means to say that one pain is exactly 10 times as strong as another' (p. 12),[16] he was basing this upon the presupposition that it is meaningless to claim that distinct sensation differences are equal. As he put it,

> ... if we load a point on the skin with 2 and then with 3 pounds, and subsequently with 10 and then 15 pounds, then the latter two sensations of pressure are at a completely different position on the total series of sensations as the former two. The one increase is thus something completely different to the others and they allow of no comparison. The claim that they are equal has absolutely no meaning. In fact, it is no different to claiming equality between, for example, a movement of sound and of light. (p. 274)

Von Kries thought that while extensive quantities (by which he meant length, time and mass) are measurable, 'intensive quantities[17] are (theoretically) unmeasurable' (p. 275) because differences between such magnitudes cannot be directly equated. For intensive quantities of a physical kind (e.g., velocity, force, pressure, etc.), he thought that they could in practice be measured by 'fixing' them relative to length, time and mass via a functional relation. For intensive 'quantities' of a psychological kind (e.g., intensity of sensation) exactly the same sort of 'fixing' could not be done. He admitted that Fechner's assumption (that jnds corre-

---

perspectives were not taken to be identical. Hence, identity, or even linearity (according to Scheerer and Hildebrandt, 1988) was ruled out.

[16] As far as I know, von Kries' paper has never been published in an English translation. I am indebted to Julie Hatfield for providing me with one.

[17] By 'intensive quantities' von Kries meant attributes that can only be ordered as opposed to those possessing an additive structure. This was a standard usage at that time.

spond to equal sensation differences) appears to 'fix' a meaning to the concept of equal sensation differences, but it is entirely arbitrary and, so, he thought, there could be no issue of its being correct or incorrect.

Von Kries recognised that there was also an element of arbitrariness in the physical case, as well. The difficulty then, is clearly to expose the difference, if there really is one, between the two cases. This would have required a significant conceptual advance on von Kries' part, one that in fact was not made for almost another century. Thus, his objection to Fechner really established nothing more than that there is an issue to be addressed. No amount of mere assertion by either party could settle the matter. Von Kries was, perhaps, closer to seeing this than was Fechner, for he wrote that 'It is perhaps regrettable, but is a part of nature, that my claims here really cannot be proven' (p. 274). This admission, however, just left Fechner free to ignore the issue.

Objections to Fechner's psychophysics on purely philosophical grounds were the order of the day. Bergson ([1889] 1913) argued that sensations *qua* sensations cannot even be *ordered* according to intensity, much less measured.

If ... we distinguish two kinds of quantity, the one intensive, which admits only of 'more or less', the other extensive, which lends itself to measurement, we are not far from siding with Fechner and the psychophysicists. For, as soon as a thing is acknowledged to be capable of increase and decrease, it seems natural to ask by how much it decreases or by how much it increases. And, because a measurement of this kind does not appear to be possible directly, it does not follow that science cannot successfully accomplish it by some indirect process, either by an integration of infinitely small elements, as Fechner proposes, or by any other roundabout way. Either, then, sensation is pure quality, or, if it is a magnitude, we ought to try to measure it. ([1889] 1913, p. 72)

Bergson's answer was that it is 'pure quality', by which he meant that we can only correctly judge sensations as the same or different. This, he thought, definitely ruled out their measurability. Bergson's claims here are a tangle of misconceptions. First, his suggestion that if sensation intensities are ordinal, then they are measurable was, and still is, a common misunderstanding. Order alone never entails quantity. As we shall see, however, ordinal relations between levels of an attribute under special conditions do entail that an attribute is quantitative. Second, his view that,

90   *Early psychology and the quantity objection*

if sensations are confined to relations of sameness and difference, then they are not measurable was equally mistaken. Hölder's axioms for intervals on a straight line entail that, also, under special conditions, relations of sameness or difference may imply that an attribute is quantitative. The issues in this debate were much more complex than most of the protagonists were then able to see and were deeply obscured by metaphysical presuppositions. The conceptual difficulty of the quantity objection and its implications, allowed Fechner to dismiss it cheaply and, thus, effectively, to ignore it.

APPLYING FECHNER'S *MODUS OPERANDI*

After Fechner, the emerging science forged a compromise between his apparent success in constructing quantitative methods and the reservations induced by the quantity objection. The almost universal failure to see that the quantity objection raises an empirical issue, combined with the almost universal adherence to the quantitative imperative, meant that Fechner's methods were retained. Fechner had bequeathed units in which to count (jnds), and for conformists to the quantitative imperative this legacy was too valuable to sacrifice to philosophical nervousness. Most researchers felt that the quantity objection's force could be met by reinterpreting what Fechner's methods measured. Furthermore, this strategy was generalised: in other areas of quantitative psychology, Fechner's approach (viz., that of finding 'units' of some kind to count) became the established *modus operandi*.

Nineteenth-century psychophysicists reached a consensus. Emerging from the characteristically thorough and meticulous research of Belgian and German psychologists (such as Delbœuf, Ebbinghaus, Höfler, Meinong, G. E. Müller, Plateau, Stumpf and Wundt) was the view that what Fechner's methods measured was, not the intensity of sensations *per se*, but only the magnitude of sensation distances (Titchener, 1905). As William James put it

To introspection, our feeling of pink is surely not a portion of our feeling of scarlet; nor does the light of an electric arc seem to contain that of a tallow-candle in itself ... if we were to arrange the various possible degrees of the quality in a scale of serial increase, the *distance, interval,* or *difference* between the stronger and the weaker specimen before us would seem about as great as that between the weaker one and the beginning of the scale. *It is these RELATIONS, these DISTANCES, which we are measuring and not the composition of the qualities themselves,* as Fechner thinks. (James, 1890, p. 546)

The conviction that sensations were never an additive composite of smaller sensations was the unanalysed, metaphysical premise sustaining the quantity objection, as it was raised against Fechner's psychophysics. Most psychologists agreed that sensations themselves could not be measured because, it seemed, they were conceptually indivisible. However, using methods like the Plateau-Delbœuf method of bisection, distances between sensations seemed to be divisible in practice, if only indirectly (see Titchener, 1905, for a review). Despite the emphasis upon distances, as related to both stimulus differences and differences between the corresponding sensations evoked, there was no recognition of the connection with Hölder's work on intervals within a straight line. Titchener was familiar with German research on measurement theory and alone amongst English-speaking psychologists, provided a detailed bibliography that included important German texts (Titchener, 1905). Hölder's 1901 text was not included. Absent also was recognition of the empirical issue at stake.

Later psychophysicists came tantalisingly close to recognising this issue, but none grasped the nettle. In 1913 the English psychologist, William Brown, participated in a joint symposium of the British Psychological Society, the Aristotelian Society, and the *Mind* Association on psychophysics. Dawes Hicks quoted from Bertrand Russell's *Principles of Mathematics*, a suggestion that in contexts where levels of an attribute are orderable, it is always theoretically possible to order differences between these levels as well (Dawes Hicks, 1913).[18] Brown noted the significance of this for psychophysics in a later publication (Brown and Thomson, 1921): even with just five ordered magnitudes, given the orders between their differences, between differences between their differences, and so on (such orderings the authors call gradings),[19] approximate

---

[18] Russell's views on the concept of measurement are considered in more detail in the next chapter. See also Michell (1993, 1997a).

[19] Such a hierarchy of ordinal relations, if it satisfies certain testable conditions, gives rise to what some psychologists now call an *ordered metric scale*, following Coombs (1950). In the limiting case, an ordered metric scale is an interval scale, i.e., it measures intervals or differences between magnitudes.

92 *Early psychology and the quantity objection*

measures of the magnitudes (actually, measures of the differences between them) follow, so that

> With an infinite number of quantities, and all the gradings of all their differences, we should, it would seem, arrive at an exact solution of the problem, so that grading and measurement are not perhaps so different in their nature as might at first be thought. (Brown and Thomson, 1921, p. 12)

Hence, if it is allowed that in psychophysics subjects can judge the equality or order of differences between sensation intensities, this insight could be applied.

However, it could have been applied in two ways: merely as a method for inferring numerical estimates, or as a basis for addressing the scientific task of quantification. Two conditions had to be satisfied for this insight to be taken beyond the former to the latter: first, the recognition that such a scientific task exists, and second, an understanding of specifically what empirical tests are necessary for the satisfactory investigation of this problem. Unlike most of his contemporaries, Brown satisfied the first of these, for he had earlier written that

> Quantitative relations are characteristics of the real world which are proved to exist by the tentative process of experimenting. Whether forms of measurement other than the physical are possible can only be decided in the same way. (Brown, 1913, p. 185)

However, he failed to satisfy the second, showing no knowledge of the issues taken up in Part II of Hölder (1901). For example, a knowledge of Hölder's axiom 7 for intervals within a straight line might have been applied to the measurement of sensation intensities as follows: if within stimulus pairs the difference in sensation intensity between a and b is the same as that between a' and b', and the difference between b and c is the same as that between b' and c', then if sensation differences are quantitative, the difference in sensation intensity between a and c must equal that between a' and c'. Confirmation of this test (say, by obtaining direct judgments of equality between sensory differences) would support the hypothesis that differences in sensation intensity are quantitative. However, Hölder's paper continued to escape the notice of psychologists, as did other perceptive analyses of the logical problems facing attempts at psychophysical measurement (e.g., Wiener, 1919; see also Fishburn and Monjardet, 1992).

Applying Fechner's modus operandi

The consequences of logical misconceptions in science are not independent of social context. Early in the twentieth century, the social contexts of German and American science were significantly different. The ethos of the German universities, influenced by the Humboltian conception of disinterested inquiry, was more suited to research in psychophysics, an area with minimal relevance to the practical problems of the day. Psychophysics was generally treated with respect by American psychologists,[20] but the social imperatives of the Progressive Era and the native pragmatism of American intellectuals turned attention to areas of psychology promising more direct application to practical problems. They seized the opportunities presented by the development in Europe of methods for assessing intellectual abilities.

In England, Francis Galton's (1869) research into the inheritance of intellectual abilities led to the quantitative research programme of Charles Spearman (1904). Spearman was the first to unify this area conceptually by linking mental tests to mental abilities within a quantitative theory. His contributions gave this area the same kind of mathematical impetus that Fechner's had given to psychophysics. Spearman's contribution also carried the stamp of Fechner's *modus operandi* in its disregard for the fundamental scientific problem at the heart of measurement.

Spearman's quantitative theory was based upon the contributions of Galton and Karl Pearson to the understanding of regression and correlation. Given a set of objects (say, persons) and for each object, i, two numerical scores or measures, x_i and y_i (say, scores on two different mental tests, X and Y), then the Pearson product moment correlation coefficient, r_{XY}, is an index of the degree of linearity between them. If each person's score on test X, x_i, is expressed as a standard score, that is, as a deviation from the mean, μ_X, divided by the standard deviation, σ_X, (i.e., x_i is expressed as $z_i = (x_i - \mu_X)/\sigma_X$) and the same for scores on Y, then r_{XY} is the expected value of the product of the two standard scores in the population. This index may take values ranging from $+1.0$

---

[20] William James, however, was completely disrespectful of Fechner's psychophysics, writing that '. . . it would be terrible if ever such a dear old man as this could saddle our Science forever with his patient whimsies, and, in a world so full of more nutritious objects of attention, compel all future students to plough through the difficulties, not only of his own works, but of the still drier ones written in his refutation' (1890, p. 549). Despite this, reviews of psychophysical research appeared regularly in the American psychological literature (e.g., Jastrow, 1887; Holt, 1904; Titchener, 1905; Rich, 1925).

94 *Early psychology and the quantity objection*

(indicating perfect positive linearity), through 0 (no linearity) to -1.0 (perfect negative linearity).

Spearman took a positive correlation coefficient between scores on two mental tests as indicating that performance was caused, in part, by a common, underlying mental ability. The fact that all mental tests tend to intercorrelate positively he interpreted as meaning that all intellectual performance is caused, in part, by a single, general intellectual ability, which he came to refer to simply as g. As well as g, Spearman postulated specific abilities for each different kind of intellectual task. The 'two factor theory', as it became known, may be expressed as follows;

$$z_{ij} = g_j g_i + s_j s_i$$

(where z_{ij} is the standard score of person i on mental test j, g_j and s_j are the extent to which test j measures general ability and the relevant specific ability, respectively, and g_i and s_i are i's measures of general ability and specific ability). Spearman thought that his theory was very strongly supported by the data he presented, but Brown and Thomson (1921) took considerable pains to show that it was underdetermined by test score data. Despite this, Spearman's theory and its associated method (later called 'factor analysis')[21] continue to influence this area of psychology. The various methods of factor analysis it spawned (e.g., see also Thurstone, 1947), constitute genuine advances in statistical methodology.

Although his theory was quantitative, Spearman ignored the scientific task of quantification. This is all the more striking given that the other great innovator in this area, the French psychologist, Alfred Binet, believed that test scores were not an adequate basis for mental measurement. Binet asserted this quite categorically in relation to his scale of mental age: 'The scale, properly speaking, does not permit the measure of the intelligence, because intellectual qualities are not superposable, and therefore cannot be measured as linear surfaces are measured' (1905, p. 40 (as quoted in Gould, 1981, p. 151)). It is, however, perfectly reasonable to attempt to explain positive correlation coefficients between mental test scores by postulating common underlying causes, it is just that there is no logical necessity for the relevant causes to

---

[21] For a fairly simple and comprehensive introduction to modern factor analysis see McDonald (1985).

Applying Fechner's modus operandi 95

be quantitative. Quantitative effects may have non-quantitative causes. For example, two families may differ with respect to the number of children they contain and this quantitative effect may be due to differences in the contents of beliefs relating to the morality of artificial contraception (a non-quantitative cause). Or, more relevant to abilities, two algorithms for solving intellectual problems (say, for deducing conclusions from syllogisms) may differ in the time taken to reach a correct solution because of non-quantitative differences in the way the problem is approached (say, using Venn diagrams versus using a formal axiomatisation of syllogistic logic). Of course, Spearman's theory that g, and the various specific abilities, are quantitative is a coherent hypothesis and one that ought to be taken seriously. Considerations like that raised by Binet do not, of themselves, refute such hypotheses. Like von Kries' objections to Fechner, they simply raise the issue. However, part of taking Spearman's hypothesis seriously is recognising the contingent character of its quantitative features and, as a consequence, recognising the need to test these experimentally prior to accepting it. The hypothesis that g and s are quantitative attributes of mental functioning is the fundamental issue underlying Spearman's approach to explaining intellectual performance and, as a result of Spearman's influence, the fundamental issue still underlying the majority of theories in this area.

It should be noted that the methods of factor analysis used in this area of psychology do not enable a test of the hypothesis that abilities are quantitative. Instead, they, like Spearman, already presume its truth. Linear factor analysis consists of a set of analytical procedures for reducing a matrix of correlation coefficients to a set of linear relationships between hypothetical attributes (factors) and test scores. The correlation coefficient, r_{XY}, between scores on tests X and Y, is hypothesised to be related to factors as follows:

$$r_{XY} = (f_{X1} \times f_{Y1}) + (f_{X2} \times f_{Y2}) + \ldots + (f_{Xk} \times f_{Yk})$$

(where k is some finite natural number and f_{Xn} ($n = 1, \ldots, k$) is the degree of linear relationship between scores on X and measures on factor n, etc.). The analytical methods used always arrive at a solution to this equation. Hence, the method is insensitive to the truth or falsity of the fundamental hypothesis that the relevant causes are quantitative. If they are all quantitative and if they

96 *Early psychology and the quantity objection*

combine in the fashion displayed above, then the method of factor analysis may help identify them. These are 'ifs' that cannot be taken for granted by the scientist. If the underlying causal factors are not all quantitative, then the method of factor analysis will not help identify them. Indeed, because it delivers a numerical solution regardless, it may mislead us into thinking that these causes are quantitative attributes. The scientific use of factor analysis is premised upon a logically prior commitment to an entirely quantitative causal theory. Within this area of psychology, such theories have simply been assumed and factor analysis has been used in the possibly vain hope of discovering what attributes a given selection of tests actually measures. Pythagorean psychologists are convinced that their tests measure something; they just do not know what.

Spearman studied in Wundt's laboratory at Leipzig, eventually receiving his doctorate there, and spent time with Külpe in Würzburg and G. E. Müller at Göttingen (Spearman, 1930). He had a thorough grounding in psychophysics, contributing to that literature (e.g., Spearman, 1908). Fechner's quantitative *modus operandi* provided a model for him, as Cyril Burt (1960) claimed it did for Galton and Pearson as well. Spearman was later to write that

> . . . great as may be the potency of this [the experimental method], or of the preceding methods, there is yet another one so vital that, if lacking it, any study is thought by many authorities not to be scientific in the full sense of the word. This further and crucial method is that of measurement. (Spearman, 1937, p. 89)

He took measurement to be an essential ingredient of the scientific enterprise and in this he was at one with his German and British mentors. As with them, the quantitative imperative apparently closed his eyes to the empirical issues at stake.

However, in Spearman's writings the emergence can be noted of what was to become a far more potent motive for ignoring the scientific task of quantification: what we might call *practicalism*. This is the view that a science's success resides in its practical applications.

> And, indeed, when we without bias consider the whole actual fruit so far gathered from this science – which at the outset seemed to promise an almost unlimited harvest – we can scarcely avoid a feeling of great disappointment. Take for an example Education. This is the line of prac-

Applying Fechner's modus operandi 97

tical inquiry that more than all others has absorbed the energy and talent of the younger workers and that appears to offer a peculiarly favourable field for such methods. Yet at this moment, notwithstanding all the laborious experiments and profuse literature on the subject, few competent and unprejudiced judges will venture to assert that much unequivocal information of capital importance has hitherto thus come to light. Nor have the results been more tangible in Psychiatry or in any other department of applied psychology. (Spearman, 1904, p. 203)

The scientific task of quantification, like science generally, is logically indifferent to practicalism. Discovering that the causes of intellectual performance are all quantitative (or that some are non-quantitative) is, in and of itself, not something that either should or should not be applied. Spearman, however, reveals an anxiety about the scope of the practical applications of psychological results. There is no necessary link between such an anxiety and neglect of the scientific task of quantification, but they may not be causally unrelated. In circumstances where a scientific issue is difficult, and may even appear unnecessary (as was the case with the scientific task of quantification in psychology), and in circumstances where the social rewards for practical applications are high (as was certainly the case in the application of mental tests), ignoring the scientific issue may be a means of reaping those rewards. In this way practicalism may subvert science.

Practicalism did play this kind of role in the development of the mental testing movement in the United States early in the twentieth century. Here it was the pioneering work of James McKeen Cattell and Edward Lee Thorndike that helped establish applied psychological 'measurement' through the promotion of mental tests within schools, industry and the military.[22] These tests proved useful to administrators in making decisions regarding children, workers and servicemen. Their usefulness, however, did not depend upon the truth of the hypothesis that they measure intellectual abilities. To an extent, their usefulness resided simply in the fact that they produced numerical data and that, therefore, they could be suitably packaged for a public eager to believe that these tests gave measurement. Wise (1995) and Porter (1995) show how what happened in psychology at this time was part of a

---

[22] There were others who played significant roles in this movement, such as Goddard, Terman, Yerkes, etc. (see e.g., Gould, 1981), but these two played an especially important ideological role.

98 *Early psychology and the quantity objection*

much wider social phenomenon in which numerical procedures came to be identified with the values of precision and objectivity, especially in the spheres relating to human organisation or coercion. A quantitative psychology with social applications was a highly marketable commodity and Danziger (1990) has charted elements of the symbiotic relationship between bureaucrats and psychologists which resulted in the widespread acceptance of ability testing in the United States, especially within education.

Brown (1992) shows how Cattell, Thorndike and others in the American mental testing movement promoted psychological tests as measurement instruments by employing easily understood metaphors drawn from the socially valued disciplines of engineering and medicine. Their rhetoric went beyond Pythagorean scientism in likening 'applied psychology' to the applications of quantitative physics and physiology. In promoting the use of psychological tests within the educational system and other institutions, the advantages of this kind of rhetoric are obvious. Its use in this case, however, necessitates turning a blind eye to the scientific issue of whether or not the attributes in question (i.e., the various intellectual abilities) are quantitative. While some argued for restraint in the use of this kind of rhetoric (e.g., Ruml, 1920; McCormack, 1922), American society embraced the message that psychologists offered, despite the lack of scientific credentials. By 1922, three million children per year were subjected to one form or another of mental 'measurement' (Thorndike, 1923) and by 1937, '5005 articles, most of them reports of new tests, which [had] appeared during the fifteen year period between 1921 and 1936' (South, 1937) were available for use by psychologists. A science is vulnerable when its rhetoric outstrips its credentials in such circumstances and its survival may rely upon serving dominant social interests. This sort of complicity has periodically been a source of radical complaint against the mental testing movement (Gould, 1981).

If a psychological test is found useful in some decision-making situation,[23] then that fact does not *settle* a scientific issue, it only

---

[23] Of course, usefulness is an entirely relative notion and Danziger's shrewd observation that 'Not infrequently, administrators simply needed [psychological] research for public relations purposes, to justify practices and decisions they judged to be expedient' (1990, p. 103), supplemented by Porter's message that in the eyes of the public, 'In our own time, measurement means nothing if not precision and objectivity' (1995, p. 23), may

raises one, viz., why are scores on this test usefully related to the criterion? It is perfectly reasonable to speculate that they are so related because the test is deemed to measure[24] some hypothetical quantitative attribute (such as general ability) on which the criterion is causally dependent. However, until that hypothetical attribute is identified and shown to be quantitative, one has here only a theory in need of testing. To the critical, scientific mind, a theory always *raises* questions to be answered by further research; to the uncritical, practicalist mind, a theory is taken to *answer* questions raised. The way in which quantitative psychology embraced practicalism is nicely illustrated via a trajectory through three generations of American psychology, from Cattell, through Thorndike, to Kelley.

Boring (1957) stresses the great influence that Cattell, one of the earliest designated professors of psychology in the United States, had upon the development of American psychology. Cattell, like Spearman, was deeply influenced by both Wundt and Galton, taking his doctorate with the former in 1886 and making contact with the latter in 1888. He wrote a number of early, pivotal papers (Cattell, 1890, 1893a) broadening the scope of quantitative psychology from psychophysics towards the study of intellectual abilities. His brief entry, under the heading *Measurement*, in Baldwin's *Dictionary of Philosophy and Psychology* (1902, vol. 2, p. 57) presents his views succinctly. It expresses his faith in the quantitative imperative ('Exact science consists of measurements and all sciences as they advance become increasingly quantitative') and his commitment to the classical concept of measurement (measurement is the 'determination of a magnitude in terms of a standard unit' and 'a ratio is the basis of all measurement'). Here claims on behalf of psychological measurement were realistic ('The place of measurement in psychology is still an open question'), but confident ('It has been claimed that only physical measurements are made in the psychological laboratory, but it may be replied that at all events mental processes are functions

---

not be too cynical an assessment of precisely wherein the usefulness of psychological tests sometimes really resided.

[24] By the same token, any respect in which test scores are useful as practical tools of prediction is one that can always be described without recourse to the rhetoric of measurement. Unless underlying, hypothetical attributes are shown to be quantitative, talk of tests scores as measurements is a theoretically loaded way of packaging their utility, not a way of explaining it.

100 *Early psychology and the quantity objection*

of the quantities measured'). As he had made explicit earlier (1893b), he thought that mental processes were not just any functions of the physical quantities measured, but quantitative functions. This way of thinking was a consequence of his view, expressed later in *Popular Science Monthly*, that

The mental and the physical are so inextricably interfused that quantitative and genetic[25] uniformities could not exist in the physical world if absent from consciousness. If our mental processes did not vary in number, if they did not have time, intensity and space relations, we should never have come to apply these categories in physics, chemistry or astronomy. (Cattell, 1904, p. 182)

Thus, he concluded, 'Psychology is from the start both quantitative and genetic' (p. 184). In fact, Cattell was totally committed to the development of psychology as a quantitative science. In the same paper he contemplated psychology as an applied science and his discussion entered a grey area where the prospects of practicalism obviously excited his mind. In assessing his response to these prospects we need to keep clearly in mind the fact that if there is no science, in the sense of no body of empirically established results of a general and systematic sort, then there can be no applied science, for there is then no science to apply. Cattell danced on the razor's edge ('It may be true that pure science should precede the applications of science. But of this I am not sure' (p. 185), and 'It may be at present pseudo-science, in the sense that we have drawn conclusions without adequate knowledge, but it is none the less the best we can do in the way of the application of systematised knowledge to the control of human nature' (p. 186)) before yielding to practicalism ('If I did not believe that psychology ... could be applied in useful ways, I should regard my occupation as nearer to that of the professional chess-player or sword swallower than to that of the engineer or scientific physician' (p. 185). Having cast his lot, he disclosed his dream:

I see no reason why the application of systematized knowledge to the control of human nature may not in the course of the present century accomplish results commensurate with the nineteenth-century appli-

---

[25] By *genetic*, Cattell meant here something like *causal*, *deterministic* or perhaps *experimental*, as is indicated in such comments as that made a few sentences earlier, 'The two great achievements of science have been the elaboration of the quantitative method on the one hand and of the genetic method on the other' (1904, p. 182).

Applying Fechner's modus operandi

cations of physical science to the material world . . . We may have experts who will be trained in schools as large and well-equipped as our present schools of medicine, and their profession may become as useful and as honorable . . . in the end there will not only be a science but also a profession of psychology. (p. 186)

That an 'honorable' science of quantitative psychology might require the empirical demonstration that its hypothesised attributes are quantitative as a necessary condition for intellectually responsible applications and that the science ought to come before the profession did not loom large in a mind gripped by practicalist enthusiasms.

Edward Lee Thorndike received his doctorate from Columbia University under Cattell in 1898, then 'took up with the mental test movement and became a leader in it' (Boring, 1957, p. 563). His text, *An Introduction to the Theory of Mental and Social Measurements* (1904) became something of a classic in the area. If anyone was Cattell's spiritual heir it was Thorndike. He welded the various elements of Pythagoreanism, the quantitative imperative and practicalism into his famous 'Credo':

Whatever exists at all exists in some amount. To know it thoroughly involves knowing its quantity as well as its quality . . .
We have faith that whatever people now measure crudely by mere descriptive words, helped out by the comparative and superlative forms, can be measured more precisely and conveniently if ingenuity and labor are set at the task. We have faith also that the objective products produced, rather than the inner condition of the person whence they spring, are the proper point of attack for the measurer, at least in our day and generation.
This is obviously the same general creed as that of the physicist or chemist or physiologist engaged in quantitative thinking – the same, indeed, as that of modern science in general. And, in general, the nature of educational measurements is the same as that of all scientific measurements. (1918, pp. 16–17)

Stripped of its pseudo-scientific, quasi-religious and crypto-metaphysical overtones, Thorndike's confession signalled a potential advance in psychometric thinking. The suggestion that the (educational) measurer attend to 'the objective products produced, rather than to the inner condition of the person', indicated a way of narrowing the focus of psychological measurement. If what one is attempting to measure, be it intensity of sensation or

102 *Early psychology and the quantity objection*

intellectual ability, is a theoretical attribute, then the problems of quantification are compounded. A person's performance on a mental test does not suffer this impediment.

Test performances have many features, some quantitative and some non-quantitative. Thorndike's approach was to focus only on the quantitative. The most obvious quantitative feature of mental test performance is the number of items correctly answered. This is now, almost universally, the only feature of test performance of interest to psychometricians (and is called the person's *observed score*).[26] Observed scores, in and of themselves, are not measures of anything. They may be interpreted as measures of ability, say, within the context of some theory (like Rasch's or Spearman's theories), but then we have reintroduced the theoretical attributes which Thorndike wished, for the present, to avoid. Thorndike mistakenly thought that observed scores count units of variable magnitude:

... the zeroes of the scales for the educational measures and the equivalence of their units are only imperfectly known. As a consequence, we can add, subtract, multiply and divide educational quantities with much less surety and precision than is desirable.[27] (1918, p. 17)

However, an even more egregious mistake was his complete fixation upon observed scores at the expense of other attributes of performance. This sidesteps the issue of whether or not test performance is really measurable. If performances to individual test items are classified as correct or incorrect, and coded as *1* and *0*, respectively, as is typical, then a person's performance on the test as a whole is represented more informatively by an ordered sequence of ones and zeroes than by a single number, the observed score. It is entirely possible for two people to perform quite differently and, yet get exactly the same observed score. Obviously, their performances, as 'objective products produced' are equivalent in one sense (number correct), but not in the more fundamental sense of displaying exactly the same knowledge. *A*'s performance on a given mental test is only at least as knowledgable

---

[26] It should be noted that there has recently been a renewed interest in mental speed, i.e., the time taken to respond to a test item. This feature was also of interest to Cattell in the late nineteenth century.

[27] To his credit, Thorndike here identified a complex and taxing problem, one hinted at by Reid (1748), popularised by Stevens (1946, 1951, etc.) as the problem of *permissible statistics*, and still not resolved to the satisfaction of everyone (Michell, 1986).

Applying Fechner's modus operandi 103

as B's if A also gets correct every item B gets correct (and possibly more as well). What is observed, in terms of this more fundamental relation between people's performances, is not a quantitative relation. It is a mere order relation (i.e., one that is only transitive and asymmetric) and the set of possible performances on any test constitutes only a partially ordered, not a quantitative structure. That is, there will be cases where we cannot conclude that A's performance is more knowledgable than B's or *vice versa* because A gets incorrect items that B gets correct and *vice versa*. As an index of knowledgability, observed score is not even ordinal and, so, it is not a measure of that attribute. Had Thorndike not been obsessed with measurement, he might have been prepared to consider the objectively revealed, non-quantitative structure of mental test performances and, on that basis, to consider the possibility that non-quantitative theories of intellectual abilities are, *a priori*, the most plausible candidates. Instead, he encouraged psychology down a path which, if abilities are not quantitative, was entirely the wrong path for the science to take.

Thorndike's approach to observed scores was to decree by fiat that they were at least an ordinal index of knowledgability (or 'scholarship' as he put it (1904, p. 85)). Thorndike could only justify such a claim by invoking some theory about what observed scores might measure. From that false start he believed he could attempt, what he called *measurement by relative position* (by which he meant something not unlike the modern practices of using percentile scores or standard scores). He claimed that 'Measurement by relative position in a series gives as true, and may give as exact, a means of measurement as that by units of amount' (1904, p. 19). Even if observed scores were an ordinal index of knowledgability, this latter claim would be false. An ordering falls very far short of the level of information given by measurement. 'Measurement' by relative position is merely a monotonic (i.e., order preserving) transformation of observed scores and has no meaning beyond what those scores themselves already possess. The fact that psychologists took Thorndike seriously shows how ready they were to believe that observed scores really do measure something.

The tendency to ignore the scientific issues involved was not a universal one in early American psychology. In one way or another, doubts were raised by critical minds. E. G. Boring, once

Titchener's student and, incidentally, later Stevens' supervisor at Harvard University, took a critical view of measurement in psychology, writing that 'We are left then with the rank-orders of our psychological quantities ... and it is with these rank orders that we must deal. We are not yet ready for much psychological measurement in the strict sense' (Boring, 1920, p. 32). This comment could have been aimed specifically at Thorndike's measurement by relative position. Truman Lee Kelley, 'Thorndike's pupil and for some years America's leading psychologist-statistician' (Boring, 1957, p. 540), published a retort (Kelley, 1923) based on his assessment that 'Boring's conclusions are generally destructive, and tend to leave one with the feeling that there is no sound statistical basis for mental measurement, and little for other psychological measurement' (p. 408). That Kelley saw the problem, at this stage in the history of psychology, as one requiring a 'sound statistical basis', rather than as logical, is interesting. Under the combined influence of Spearman, Thorndike and Kelley, issues to do with psychological measurement gradually became assimilated to statistical issues,[28] and, especially under Kelley's influence, psychometric theory was viewed as a branch of statistics.[29] For psychologists interested in measurement, this had two effects. Quantification was no longer understood in terms of its logical character but, instead, was seen as purely statistical. Given that very few psychologists were competent statisticians, this in turn meant that foundational issues of quantification were no longer much thought about. Psychologists looked to statisticians to resolve measurement problems, much as they did with issues of inference a generation later (Gigerenzer *et al.*, 1989). The questions were in the process of being subtly transformed in ways that pushed the quantity objection to the periphery.

The issue of the unit of measurement, that had bothered Thorndike, was still there. However, Kelley presented an argument intended to remove it:

It might seem axiomatic that there can not be a science of quantitative

---

[28] In this they were also following Fechner, who not only utilised statistical concepts (see Link, 1994) but also made original contributions to probability theory which, in turn, it is said influenced the famous frequentist theorist, Richard von Mises (Heidelberger, 1994).

[29] Kelley also made early contributions to what became known as *classical test theory* (Kelley and Shen, 1929).

Applying Fechner's modus operandi 105

measurement until and unless there is established a particular unit of measurement. This is, however, true only in a limited sense; for it is quite conceivable that one could have a science of physical phenomena in which the units were such that the scale of time intervals was the square of the present intervals measured in seconds, and in which the length scale was logarithmic as compared with the present scale in centimeters. etc. Of course, in terms of these new units, all the laws of physics would be stated by means of formulas different from and in general more cumbersome than our present formulas; but nevertheless we could have an exact science. The existence of the science does not lie in the units employed, but in the relationships which are established as following after the choice of units. (1923, p. 418)

Thorndike's problem had been that because items in a mental test might differ in level of difficulty, the observed score is a sum of units of different magnitude. This had led him to prefer measurement by relative position, which Boring was now classing as a mere 'rank-order'. Kelley's retort was to draw attention to a very subtle and not widely appreciated degree of freedom within quantitative science. His observation about transforming scales for measuring time and length is quite true. What he failed to bring out, however, is that it is really quite a different problem from that facing psychologists. The previous chapter drew attention to the fact that for any two magnitudes of a quantity (say, any two lengths) there is no unique ratio between them. Ratios are tied to relations of additivity. If for any continuous attribute there is one such relation, then there is an infinite number. Replacing our conventional scale of length (which is based upon our conventional view of what it is for lengths to add together) by one which is its logarithmic transform, as Kelley suggests, simply identifies a different relation of additivity between lengths, one which although it seems quite unnatural to us, exists alongside the other. Physics has the luxury of being able to select whichever additive relations best suit (as the case of velocity illustrates), but this is a luxury bestowed in virtue of already having discovered that its attributes possess additive structure. There is no parallel here with the situation then existing in psychometrics and there could be none until it is shown that attributes like ability or knowledgability are quantitative.

Kelley, instead drew the mistaken conclusion that

A parallel situation holds with reference to mental measurement; so that, starting with units however defined, if we can establish important relationships between phenomena measured in these units, we have

106 *Early psychology and the quantity objection*

proceeded scientifically. The choice of the unit is purely a question of utility. (1923, p. 418)

The confusion goes right back to Thorndike's reservation about observed scores being a sum of unequal units. This is not so. In the case of observed scores, there is a fixed, unvarying unit, that of a correct answer. So observed scores are quantitative: they are frequencies. It is only when these frequencies are considered to be indices of some other attribute, such as ability or knowledgability, that an issue of unequal units can be sensibly posed. For this to be meaningful, these attributes must be quantitative. So the same issue, that of whether or not these psychological attributes are quantitative cannot be escaped by those who would invoke the concept of measurement.

Kelley's suggestion then, that psychometricians look for 'important relationships' between observed scores and criteria of interest is valid, but it is a matter that we have already considered. When useful relationships of this sort are found, it does not follow that anything is measured, although quantitative hypotheses might be proposed to explain the relationships observed. If they are, then the problem of testing whether or not the relevant attributes are quantitative returns. The fact that psychologists were satisfied with arguments like Kelley's and thought, as a result, that observed scores must measure something, shows how seriously their critical faculties had been compromised by practicalism.

As a matter of simple logic, the scientific task of quantification cannot be erased by any amount of argument and so those who hope for measurement always invite the quantity objection. Not to face it is to condemn one's discipline to be forever less than scientific. Even if all psychologists agreed to ignore it and made a pact to call their numerical procedures measurement, the reality of the quantity objection would remain.

Up to, say, 1930, an enormous array of mental tests were developed. These were presented as suitable for the measurement of intellectual abilities and educational achievements (for summaries see, for example, Pintner, 1929, and Freeman, 1929). Procedures for their use were standardised in manuals, along with conventions for interpreting the 'measures' arrived at. Considerable attention was paid to the practical issues surrounding the instrumental task of quantification and almost none to the scientific task. Pintner

Applying Fechner's modus operandi

(1929) represented the dominant attitude. Without so much as a nod towards the scientific task, he asserted that 'At present the psychologist has a great number of scales and tests for the measurement of intelligence' (p. 700). He noted, however, that psychologists do not all define intelligence in the same way. Indeed, in 1921, *The Journal of Educational Psychology* had invited seventeen 'leading investigators' to discuss the concept. There was little agreement and most definitions failed: the participants did not know the intrinsic character of intelligence, but each thought he knew what it caused (e.g., learning, cognition, adaptation, etc.). Because of the pressures of practicalism and the quantitative imperative, however, one intrinsic feature was agreed upon: quantitative structure. All thought intelligence measurable. As Kelley later put the matter,

> Our mental tests measure something, we may or may not care what, but it is something which it is to our advantage to measure, for it augments our knowledge of what people can be counted upon to do in the future. The measuring device as a measure of something that it is desirable to measure comes first, and what it is a measure of comes second. (1929, p. 86)

The theory that mental tests are instruments of measurement was accepted because it helped answer the questions raised by the apparent usefulness of such devices. The extent to which the question raised by such a theory (viz., is anything really measured?) was ignored is an index of the triumph of practicalism over critical inquiry in quantitative psychology.

Views critical of this approach to quantification were expressed during the 1930s (e.g., Adams, 1931; Brown, 1934; and Johnson, 1936), but the mainstream of quantitative psychology was unaffected: the quantity objection was buried. Another decisive index of this was the character of psychometrics courses and textbooks, that they dealt only with psychological measurement as a practice based upon an emerging statistical theory: the so-called, classical test theory. This hypothesised that observed scores were a sum of two statistically independent components, true scores and error scores, with the latter being supposedly drawn randomly from a normal distribution of errors. If ever there was, in the history of any science, a theory accepted just because it answered questions rather than investigated because it raised them, this is it. As classical test theory became increasingly entrenched and solidified, this uncritical mass of 'normal science' (Kuhn, 1970) expelled the quantity objection from the dominant paradigm. By the close of the fourth decade of the twentieth century, psychologists' quantitative practices already conformed to the definition that Stevens would soon propose.

CHAPTER 5

Making the representational theory of measurement

The separation between number and quantity is thus complete: each is wholly independent of the other.

(Bertrand Russell)

Measurement is only a means to an end.

(N. R. Campbell)

If, by 1930, the modus operandi of quantitative psychology already anticipated Stevens' definition, by itself this was not sufficient to ensure displacement of the classical concept. However, by 1940 the standing of the classical conception within psychology had altered dramatically. How did this happen? First, whilst most first-generation quantitative psychologists had initial training in established quantitative science (e.g., Fechner in physics, Wundt in physiology), the proportion of quantitative psychologists with such experience diminished as the twentieth century unfolded. Increasingly psychologists were drawn from the humanities, not the sciences. Second, from the turn of the twentieth century, Book V of Euclid's *Elements* exerted a diminishing influence upon the mathematics curriculum and, for the first time since the Dark Ages, central quantitative concepts, such as magnitude, quantity, ratio and measurement, drifted from their traditional moorings. This mattered less in established quantitative science, where measurement practices secured them, than in psychology, where quantitative practices ignored the classical concept.

These factors, however, were alone insufficient. Early this century, more profound changes in the philosophy of measurement encouraged redefinitions. British and American philosophy shifted in an anti-realist direction. As a result, the concepts of number and quantity were prised apart. This forced a reinterpretation of the concept of measurement, one which accommodated the

109

110   *Making the representational theory of measurement*

non-realist views of number then accepted in philosophy of mathematics.[1] The philosophical understanding of measurement came to depend less and less upon the increasingly alien concepts of magnitude and quantity.

The emphasis in philosophy of science upon immediate sensory experience as the bedrock of scientific knowledge and the suspicion of anything beyond hand or eye, put the classical concept on the defensive. In America this spirit was manifest as operationism, in Europe as logical positivism, but, as an intellectual style it was much more pervasive than either of these. The theory-laden concept of continuous quantity was discarded. It was replaced by concepts apparently more firmly located upon the laboratory shelf and requiring for their grasp no exercise of scientific imagination.

So complete was this flight from the classical paradigm that when, in 1966, Ellis's *Basic Concepts of Measurement* was published, virtually all memory of the classical concept in philosophy had been lost. In attempting to describe this concept, Ellis made no mention of the relevant contributions of De Morgan (1836), Helmholtz (1887), Hölder (1901), Frege (1903) and Whitehead and Russell (1913).[2] Quantitative psychologists of the 1940s and 1950s, with little first-hand knowledge of quantitative science, had often studied the philosophy of science from texts such as Cohen and Nagel (1934). They were thereby conceptually closer to Stevens' definition than to the classical. This chapter traces these philosophical changes through the writings of the three most significant measurement theorists of the time, Bertrand Russell, Norman Robert Campbell, and Ernest Nagel.

RUSSELL'S TRANSFORMATION OF THE CONCEPT OF MEASUREMENT

Russell's early interest was in the philosophy of mathematics.[3] Initially, he accepted the classical view of numbers as ratios of

---

[1] The three dominant views were logicism (numerical truths were thought to be derivable from the general laws of logic), formalism (numerical truths were thought to constitute a 'free-standing' formal, axiomatic system, with its own symbols and rules of inference), and intuitionism (numerical truths were thought to be dependent upon fundamental intuitions of human thought). See Benacerraf & Putnam (1983).

[2] This is not to say that Ellis did not refer to some of these authors in other contexts.

[3] See Griffin & Lewis (1990).

Russell's transformation of the concept of measurement 111

magnitudes. Then, still in his neohegelian phase, he rejected it (Russell, 1897).[4] Even though he later described this paper as 'unadulterated Hegel' and 'unmitigated rubbish' (Russell 1959), he never resiled from its main conclusion, that the concept of quantity cannot support that of number. He adjudged the traditional view of quantity incoherent and attempted a reconstruction. Quantity, he argued, reduces to mere order: given any two magnitudes, the most that can be said of them is that one is greater (or less than) than the other. Because quantity reduces to mere order, a relation, and because relations are indivisible, he reasoned that magnitudes also must be indivisible and, so, cannot stand in additive relations. Without additive relations they cannot sustain ratios. This was an explicit rejection of the classical concept: if magnitudes do not sustain ratios, 'The separation between number and quantity is thus complete: each is wholly independent of the other' (Russell, 1903, p. 158) and measurement must be understood anew.

Michell (1997a) analysed Russell's argument (see also Griffin, 1991) and I will ignore its more arcane features here. Russell's central points transcend their Hegelian context and present genuine challenges to the classical view, illuminating features of it. Russell's contention that quantity reduces to mere relation (order, in his view) presents an interesting problem. Likewise, his view that magnitudes are indivisible deserves attention.

The problem of the relativity of continuous quantity

Russell claimed that 'the whole essence of one quantity is to differ from some other quantity' (Russell, 1897, p. 331). Consider a specific magnitude, say, a length of one metre. What can be said about this length other than that it relates to other lengths in certain ways, e.g., it is less than 1 chain, it is greater than 1 foot, etc.? And, likewise, all that can be said about these other lengths, it seems, is how they, in turn, relate to yet other lengths. There seems to be no end to this network of relations and, in particular, no non-relational basis upon which the terms related stand. Since no length appears to be independently definable in terms of its

---

[4] See Griffin (1991) for an account of the development of Russell's views during this period.

own, intrinsic features, the concept of length, and by extension that of any continuous quantity, would appear to involve an infinite regress of relations. If a relation obtains, then there must be *something* standing in that relation (to other things) and that something cannot dissolve into an infinite regress of relations to other things because that would leave nothing definite to stand in any of the relations.

Clarity is attained on this issue by attending, first, to the simpler concept of discrete quantity. Our paradigm of discrete quantity is that of the sizes of aggregates. By this, I mean the attributes that aggregates have in virtue of which they may be the same size as one another. For example, an aggregate of three books and an aggregate of three horses share a common property: that of being three-membered. It can be said of this magnitude that it is less than being four-membered and greater than being two-membered. These are relational characterisations, like those considered above for length. However, these relational characterisations do not entail an infinite regress: they terminate with an obvious basis. For example, an aggregate of Xs is three-membered if and only if it is entirely composed of discrete parts, A and B, where A is a one-membered aggregate of Xs and B is a two-membered aggregate of Xs; an aggregate of Xs is two-membered if and only if it is entirely composed of discrete parts, C and D, where C is a one-membered aggregate and D is a one-membered aggregate; and an aggregate of Xs is one-membered if and only if it is entirely composed of something, E, where E is an X. That is, with the discrete quantity, aggregate size, there is a basis to the network of relations, the property of being one-membered. Since it is only aggregates of finite magnitude that are being considered, every aggregate size is completely definable relative to the unit magnitude, being one-membered. This is what is attempted whenever any magnitude is counted. This unit magnitude is simply a matter of something being a thing of a certain kind and such situations exist, if anything does. That is, for this quantity, the basis, in terms of which every magnitude of the quantity can be defined, is the unit. Is there an analogue for continuous quantities?

Consider length. Given a unit, say, the metre, each other length is defined relative to it by an infinite class of inequalities, as shown by Euclid's *Elements*, Book V. That is, if u is the metre and x any other length, then there will be an infinite set of inequalities of

Russell's transformation of the concept of measurement 113

the form, $nx \geq mu$ (where n and m are natural numbers). So, with continuous quantity, as with discrete quantity, there is a basis relative to which each magnitude is defined and this, in a nutshell, is what is attempted (albeit, generally, only approximately) when any magnitude is measured. It may seem that an infinite set of inequalities relating each magnitude to a unit is not much of an improvement upon the infinite regress of relations mentioned above. This is not so. While it may not be possible for us to specify exactly every magnitude, x, relative to the unit because, potentially, an infinite number of numerical relations is involved, the theory is that x is, in reality, quite definitely, so related to u. That is, the limitation here is human, not ontological.

However, there is another important difference between discrete and continuous quantities. In the case of discrete quantity, the unit (a thing of a certain kind) is, sometimes, directly observable. For example, we can usually see when something is a book or a horse. However, in the case of continuous quantities we cannot literally *see* the unit. One cannot, for example, discriminate exactly one metre from a different length indiscernibly close to it. Even when the standard metre was the bar of platino-iridium alloy at the International Bureau of Weights and Measures at Sèvres, one could not literally see precisely one metre because human perceptual capacities do not permit sufficiently fine visual discriminations. Even then, the concept of a metre was a theoretical concept. This fact is explicit now that the metre is defined as the length of the path travelled by light in a vacuum during a time interval of $1/(299,792,458)$ parts of a second (Jerrard & McNeill, 1992).

Whatever observational difficulties this entails, it does solve the ontological problem raised by the infinite regress of relations to no fixed magnitude. The unit is precisely defined within some theory. Given the truth of that theory, every other magnitude is specified by the infinite class of inequalities relating it to the unit. The concept of continuous quantity is introduced into science by analogy with that of discrete quantity and is a complex generalisation of it. Although it is based upon infinite sets of relations and units are defined theoretically, it remains coherent because at each step of its characterisation, the terms involved are precisely defined.

Observing a metre would mean observing the difference between it and arbitrarily close lengths and this could never be

114   *Making the representational theory of measurement*

done by us, given the finite resolution of our perceptual systems. The real world, with which science deals, is not, in its infinite complexity, defined by its relations with human observers, as positivists and operationists insisted. If the ways of working of natural systems are to be grasped, then the scientific imagination must overcome the limitations of human observation. The concept of continuous quantity shows us just what a blunt sword observation is. Using it effectively requires knowing its limitations rather than treating its limitations as signalling ontological boundaries. Observation is really a form of causal contact between us and the world in which the effect (some state of the observer) is sensitive to the cause (some feature of the observed), in the sense that had the cause been different in relevant ways, then likewise, the effect. In the case where the cause is some quantitative feature, were the effect some continuous function of it, then infinitely fine discriminations could be made and distinct magnitudes, such as the metre, would be directly observable. However, our sensory systems have finite resolution. This is a limitation of the sensory apparatus, not a feature of situations perceived. We can construct a coherent theoretical picture of the structure of continuous quantities by analogy with that of discrete quantity, using concepts clearly articulated by Euclid. Unlike the case of discrete quantity, we have no good reason to suppose that measurable quantities are not continuous and no basis upon which to restrict the class of such magnitudes.

The problem of the indivisibility of magnitudes

Russell's main reason for denying the link between quantity and number was this: on the one hand he held magnitudes of a quantity to be indivisible, on the other he thought that number was divisible, and so, he concluded, number could not be based upon quantity. Division and its obverse, concatenation, are clear enough when applied to the objects that possess quantitative attributes, but not when applied to those attributes themselves. An object, 2 metres in length is divided into two discrete parts, each 1 metre in length: has the length (i.e., the property of being 2 metres long) thereby also been literally divided? Some would say yes (e.g., Armstrong, 1978); Russell asserted no. I know of no way in which this issue can be settled. In this section, I will assume that Russell's intuition is correct and explain how it is no impediment to the classical view.

Even if a magnitude of a quantitative attribute cannot be, itself, literally divided, when an object possessing that magnitude is divided, there is a relation between that attribute and the relevant attributes of the parts of the division. When, for example, a rod, C, is divided into two discrete parts, A and B, the length of C is related to the lengths of A and B. Let us call this relation *additivity*. As stressed in Chapter 3, the additivity of magnitudes is a purely formal matter. That is, any relation between magnitudes satisfying the relevant conditions of Hölder, for example, is one of additivity. Sometimes evidence for the existence of additivity between magnitudes can be obtained by dividing or concatenating objects in appropriate ways. For example, the additive character of length can be tested by concatenating or dividing rigid rods of manageable dimensions. However, one of the most difficult conceptual hurdles in understanding measurement has been that of distinguishing the additivity of magnitudes from the divisibility of objects.

The former is an hypothesis proposed to help explain the latter. If the linear concatenation, end to end, of rigid rods, A and B, exactly spans rod C, then this is partly explained by the fact that their respective lengths, l_A, l_B, and l_C, are such that $l_A + l_B = l_C$. This is not a complete explanation of the outcome of such a concatenation because, as stressed in Chapter 3, additive relations between magnitudes are uniformities of coexistence, not causal laws. The relevant causal law here would need to take account of the other properties (physical, chemical, etc.) of the rods as well as their lengths and, also, of the precise physical character of the concatenation operation.

Numbers are similar. In what sense is the natural number, *3* say, able to be divided into 2 and *1*? The fact that $1 + 2 = 3$ is an additive relation between these numbers, but here additivity does not entail literal divisibility any more than in the case of magnitudes of continuous quantity. Indeed, there is a direct analogy. Discrete aggregates of, say, just two books and of just one book may be concatenated into an aggregate of three books and this operation is explained by the additive relation obtaining between 1, 2, and 3, but not entirely. Discrete aggregates of just two (female) rabbits and just one (male) rabbit may be carelessly

116 *Making the representational theory of measurement*

concatenated into an aggregate of more than three rabbits, as Australian farmers know. The relevant causal law, explaining the outcome of a concatenation operation, must take account of the other properties of the aggregates concatenated and the character of the concatenation.

This matter can be pressed further. The natural numbers are not properties of aggregates. The properties of the aggregates are the aggregate sizes, being one-membered, being two-membered, etc. (see Michell, 1994a). These properties constitute a quantity, as mentioned above. Strictly speaking, it is relations of relative magnitude between these properties that instantiate the natural numbers. Consider, for example, the magnitude of an aggregate of just two books relative to that of an aggregate of just one book: the former's size is twice the latter's. The same relation (being two of) holds between the magnitude of an aggregate of just two rabbits and an aggregate of just one rabbit. It is this relation which is two and, of course, it is, like the real numbers, a ratio of magnitudes of a quantity. Without going into the precise formal details, it can now be appreciated how the additivity of the discrete quantity, aggregate size, connects with the additivity of the natural numbers.

Returning to Russell's claim that magnitudes are not divisible, it is clear that in precisely the same sense, numbers are not divisible either. However, both magnitudes and numbers are additive and, not only is the additivity of number connected with that of quantity, but also the additivity of both can be used to explain partially the results of dividing and concatenating objects.

Russell's new theory of measurement

Russell held that (i) magnitudes are purely ordinal structures and (ii) magnitudes are logically distinct from numbers. He proposed six axioms characterising magnitudes:

1. Every magnitude has to some term the relation which makes it of a certain kind.
2. Any two magnitudes of the same kind are one greater and the other less.
3. Two magnitudes of the same kind, if capable of occupying space or time, cannot both have the same spatio-temporal position; if relations, can never be both relations between the same pair of terms.

Russell's transformation of the concept of measurement 117

4. No magnitude is greater than itself.
5. If A is greater than B, B is less than A, and *vice versa*.
6. If A is greater than B and B is greater than C, then A is greater than C. (Russell, 1903, p. 168)

Axioms 2, 4, 5 and 6 claim that a system of magnitudes is a strict simple order. Axioms 1 and 3 are logical and 3 could be taken as a necessary and sufficient condition for 1. Thus defined, magnitudes seemed incapable of sustaining ratios and, hence, it seemed, numbers could not be introduced into measurement in the classical manner. This left two problems: first, to give an alternative account of number, one independent of quantity; and second, to explain the role of numbers in measurement.

Russell's proposed solution to the first problem is well known (Benacerraf and Putnam, 1983). In brief, it was to define the sequence of cardinal numbers, *1, 2, 3,* . . ., etc., as classes of similar classes, where by similar classes he meant any two classes of the same size.[5] This sequence begins with the class of all singletons, which for Russell was *1*; next, the class of all pairs or *2*; then, the class of all triples or *3*; . . ., etc. He then proceeded to define the integers, rational and real numbers in terms of the cardinal numbers.[6] If this is what numbers really are, then their occurrence in measurement is a mystery. Other definitions of the cardinal numbers (formalist, intuitionist, and set theoretical) were proposed around this time and these made the use of numbers in measurement no easier to understand. Russell's importance for measurement theory resides in his proposed solution to the second problem, for this was a solution equally applicable to any of the other definitions of number.

Since, according to Russell, the series of magnitudes constituting a quantity and the series of real numbers used in their measurement are logically unconnected, their association must be external. Hence, he proposed that,

Measurement of magnitudes is, in its most general sense, any method by which a unique and reciprocal correspondence is established between all or some of the magnitudes of a kind and all or some of the numbers, integral, rational, or real as the case may be . . . In this general sense,

---

[5] Russell avoided mentioning the attribute of class size by defining similar classes as those whose elements correspond one to one.
[6] Russell's approach does not avoid the concept of quantity because, obviously, similar classes are all classes of the same size.

118 *Making the representational theory of measurement*

measurement demands some one-one relation between the numbers and magnitudes in question – a relation which may be direct or indirect, important or trivial, according to circumstances. ... Since the numbers form a series, and since every kind of magnitude also forms a series, it will be desirable that the order of the magnitudes measured should correspond to that of the numbers, i.e. that all relations of between should be the same for magnitudes and their measures. (Russell, 1903, p. 176)

Russell's idea is that measurement involves a one-to-one correspondence between the magnitudes of a quantity and a subset of one or other of the number systems, integral, rational or real, in such a way that the order of the magnitudes is represented by the order of the corresponding numbers. This, as far as I know, is the first explicit statement of the representational view of measurement (Michell, 1993).

What is the difference between this and the classical conception? According to the classical concept, since the ratio of each magnitude to a unit is a real number, for each unit there must be a one-to-one correspondence between all magnitudes and the positive real numbers. So, the difference between the two conceptions is not to be found in the proposition that measurement involves an order preserving isomorphism between magnitudes and numbers. This proposition is a necessary condition for measurement, according to both views but, according to the classical conception, it is not sufficient for measurement. An isomorphism between a purely ordinal system of attributes (as Russell takes magnitudes to be) and numbers is not measurement according to the classical view. Because it shifted the emphasis away from additivity, Russell's new theory possibly accommodated psychological attributes, and Russell emphasised this by using psychological examples. Russell's theory, therefore, differs in two ways from the classical account.[7] First, for him a quantity is not an additive system of magnitudes, it is a purely ordinal one. Secondly, the numbers that magnitudes correspond to are not entailed by the system of magnitudes itself, but are, instead, entirely external to that system.

---

[7] It differs also in another relatively superficial respect, but one that can cause confusion. Russell, somewhat idiosyncratically, used the term *quantity* to refer to objects having magnitudes (Russell,1903). Thus, 'An actual foot-rule is a quantity: its length is a magnitude' (p. 159).

Russell's transformation of the concept of measurement 119

According to the classical view, numbers are already located within a system of magnitudes, as relations of a certain sort (viz., ratios), and, therefore, measurement is the attempt to discover facts about magnitudes. Seen in this way, measurement is continuous with the rest of science: it is part of the process of discovering the way things are. This is not the case with the representational view. According to that view, a complete empirical science could be a 'science without numbers' (Field, 1980). Since numbers are presumed not to be present in the phenomena studied in empirical science, two questions may be asked of representationalists: 'why introduce numbers into science?' and 'why restrict the application of numbers to the representation of ordinal structures?'

Russell attempted neither question. However, he did say that

Without numerical measurement, therefore, the quantitative relations of magnitudes have all the definiteness of which they are capable – nothing is added, from the theoretical standpoint, by the assignment of correlated numbers. The whole subject of the measurement of quantities is, in fact, one of more practical than theoretical importance. (Russell, 1903, p. 183)

So, the imposition of numbers upon magnitudes is for practical reasons. What are the benefits? The answer may seem obvious, as Russell had indicated earlier, 'Number is of all conceptions, the easiest to operate with, and science seeks everywhere for an opportunity to apply it' ([1896] 1983, p. 301). However, such a view trades upon the classical conception, according to which numbers are familiar, close at hand, and instantiated in some way in every situation that we encounter. Russell's numbers (his classes of similar classes) are far from familiar and easy to operate with. Likewise, the numbers of the modern representationalists, the complex constructions out of the empty set (e.g., Suppes, 1960) are neither familiar to us nor are they easy to operate with. Once the concept of number is alienated from the familiar contexts in which ordinary experience finds it, then the measurement theorist is obliged to explain the 'unreasonable effectiveness' (Wigner, 1960) of 'numerical' representation.

There are other unsatisfactory aspects of Russell's account. Having characterised quantities as purely ordinal systems of magnitudes, he had the problem of explaining how it is that the numbers used in physical measurement represent more than merely ordinal structure. Quantitative science relies upon exact numerical relations between magnitudes, relations like, 'this magnitude is double that' (Russell, 1903, p. 178). While he thought that magnitudes are indivisible, Russell did allow that the objects involved may be divisible or stand in other relations that can also be represented numerically. So when, for example, it is said that length a is double b, what is meant is that an object, say a rod, of length a, may be divided into just two discrete parts, each of length b. That is, if the numbers used in measurement represent more than ordinal structure, then the extra relations represented are relations between the objects involved rather than between the magnitudes. The emphasis upon relations between objects later became increasingly important.

In Russell's mind, this distinction between order and other quantitative relations (such as addition) was absolute. However, he also believed that differences between magnitudes (say, differences between lengths) are themselves magnitudes, that is, ordered. Had he been aware of Hölder (1901), he would have seen that if relations between such differences satisfy the axioms for intervals within a straight line, then it follows that the magnitudes possess an additive structure. That is, if Russell's six axioms for magnitudes are supplemented by Hölder's axioms for intervals (with intervals interpreted, more generally than is done by Hölder, as differences between magnitudes), then traditional quantitative structure is implied. Had this aspect been rigorously worked out, then the motivation to remain representational would have been lost. Once quantities entail additive structure, ratios are implied and the most parsimonious approach to measurement becomes the classical.

The most radical features of Russell's account were its new concept of magnitude and its use of the concept of numerical representation. As alternative views of number became accepted within the philosophical community, representationalism became the standard principle for understanding measurement. So this feature of his theory of measurement had enduring and important consequences. The history of measurement theory in the twentieth century is the history of how this principle of numerical representation unfolded. Clearly, because Russell's new theory entailed that some measurable attributes are not quantitative (in the classical sense), it had potential for resolving quantitative psychology's aporia. However, its cost was Russell's view of magni-

Campbell's theory of fundamental and derived measurement 121

tude, a cost too great for some. The first reaction to Russell was an attempt to marry representationalism with a more traditional view of quantity.

CAMPBELL'S THEORY OF FUNDAMENTAL AND DERIVED MEASUREMENT

Campbell's theory was worked out in considerable detail in his influential book, *Physics: The Elements* (1920),[8] and summarised in later works (Campbell, 1921, 1928, 1938). His aim was to present a representational theory of physical measurement. He took physical measurement to be coextensive with measurement generally. Campbell never considered the issues of quantity and measurement as questions of general logic, independently of the circumstances prevailing in physics. This left him inadequately resourced to evaluate psychological measurement.

Measurement was possible, he thought, because certain ranges of physical attributes are similar to numbers: in short, they are additive. Because of this, numbers can be assigned to these attributes in such a way that numerical additivity represents physical additivity. Hence, he thought, demonstrating physical additivity experimentally is the basis of all measurement. The numerical representation of physical additivity he called *fundamental measurement*. The main aim of numerically representing attributes, according to Campbell, was to express their interrelationships as numerical laws. Doing this, he noted, sometimes enables us to identify systems of numerical constants (Campbell's paradigm here was density, which is a different ratio of mass to volume for each kind of substance). Such systems of numerical constants he called *derived magnitudes* and their numerical identification he called *derived measurement*.

Campbell defined measurement as 'the assignment of numerals to represent properties of material systems other than number, in virtue of the laws governing these properties' (1938, p. 126). According to Campbell, the laws required were twofold: (i) the property must be ordered, such that systems[9] having the property

---

[8] This book treats a wide range of issues in the philosophy of science, over and above measurement. It was reissued in 1957 under the title, *Foundations of Science*. See Buchdahl (1964) for a useful summary of Campbell's more general views.

[9] Campbell used the term *systems* to denote objects possessing the relevant magnitudes.

122   *Making the representational theory of measurement*

must be greater than, equal to, or less than one another; and (ii) there must be an operation of physical addition, whereby two systems having the property can be combined to produce a third greater than either and satisfying analogues of the commutative and associative laws of numerical addition. What Campbell had in mind here is illustrated by weight. Objects possessing weight, when placed on the pans of a beam balance, reveal their weight ordering and the weights of two objects placed in the same pan can be shown to be 'added' in the required sense. Whether or not weight or any other property satisfies these laws is a fact revealed by experiment. Once the truth of these laws has been demonstrated, Campbell thought that the measurement of that property could proceed as follows:

All physical measurement depends on the existence of these 'additive' properties, resembling number in this feature. The principle is very simple. We choose some system and assign to it the numeral 1; then we assign the numeral n to the system that results from combining n such systems, or to any system that is equal in respect of the property to that system. Apart from an arbitrary factor depending on the choice of the system to which 1 was assigned, we then have a definite method of assigning numerals which depends on facts; we have *measured* the property. (Campbell, 1938, pp. 126-7)

Campbell's emphasis here on the assignment of numerals (the names of numbers) rather than numbers themselves, derives from his special view of number. Measurement, he thought, was achieved, by analogy with number, but because he thought of numbers as physical properties of collections, he rarely wrote of numbers as being assigned to other properties in measurement. Of course, if there is a one-to-one correspondence between numerals and magnitudes, then there will be a one-to-one correspondence between magnitudes and numbers, so measurement remains numerical representation on his view. Campbell recognised that only a small number of the quantities measured in physics were fundamental: number, mass, volume, length, angle, period, force, electrical resistance, current voltage. All other physical quantities he took to be derived. In elaborating upon the above sketch, I will draw attention to just three features of Campbell's theory: his concepts of number, physical additivity, and derived measurement.

Campbell's theory of fundamental and derived measurement 123

Campbell's concept of number

According to the standard representational view, number is not a physical (or empirical) concept, it is a formal, or abstract concept, and representation is introduced into measurement theory to explain how a non-empirical concept (number) finds its way into empirical contexts (viz., measurement). This was not Campbell's view. According to him, number is a physical concept. He recognised the existence of a purely mathematical concept of number, which he referred to as *Number*. This he identified with Russell's view of numbers as classes of similar classes, but correctly saw that such an esoteric concept was not required to understand measurement. Indeed, he thought it intolerable to contaminate physics with concepts 'so extremely precarious' (1920, p. 338) as that of number. All that measurement required, he thought, was the concept of physical number.

By physical number, Campbell meant a property of physical systems: the property that certain systems (collections or aggregates) have in virtue of which one system is equally numerous to, or more numerous than, another.[10] According to Campbell, physical number is, itself, a fundamental magnitude, similar to other fundamental physical magnitudes, and able to be assessed (or measured) via counting. He sometimes referred to this property simply as 'numerousness', recognising that in assessing it, 'what we are measuring is not simply "number", but "number of something"' (Campbell, 1920, p. 300). He failed to notice that he was confusing *two* physical concepts, what I have called aggregate size, and that of natural number.

Campbell recognised that counting required the specification of a unit, a kind of thing, and that what is discovered as a result is the number of things of that kind in an aggregate. He also recognised that 'in one respect two numbers, one of one thing and one of another, are distinct magnitudes, as distinct as weight and length' (1920, p. 300). However, he also recognised that 'it is possible to attribute a direct physical significance to the statement that numbers of different kinds are equal' (1920, p. 301). In this

---

[10] This view is very similar to that of Mill (1843). Campbell did not acknowledge Mill as an influence and, in general, dismissed 'Mill, whose views are often suggestive just because they are erroneous' (1920, p. 117).

124   *Making the representational theory of measurement*

latter sense, he thought, number, 'unlike all other fundamental magnitudes, is considered to have no dimensions' (1920, p. 301). Here he glimpsed the distinction between aggregate size and natural number, but failed to use it and, confusingly, continued to refer to both concepts as *number*. Aggregate size (the number of things of a kind in an aggregate) is not dimensionless because it is linked to a specific unit. If one concept is dimensionless and the other is not, they cannot be the same concept.

John Stuart Mill (1843) took number to be a property of aggregates. Frege (1884) refuted this suggestion decisively, pointing out that while nothing could be both n and m in number, an aggregate could simultaneously be both nXs and mYs (e.g., a book could be both n chapters and m pages). From this fact Frege correctly inferred that whatever the properties, being nXs and being mYs, are, they are not the same as the natural numbers, n and m. Frege concluded from this that there could be no physical concept of number, and most subsequent philosophers have submitted their critical faculties to his authority. However, all that Frege's argument proves, beyond the fact that being nXs is not being n, is that being n is not a property. It does not follow from this that because being nXs is physical, being n is not. Forrest and Armstrong (1987) suggested that the natural numbers are not physical properties, but physical relations between aggregate sizes. That is, being n is a relation between the properties of being nXs and being an X. This position is not ruled out by Frege's argument.

Campbell made one further observation about physical number that was highly perspicacious. He noted a special feature of truths about number: 'they are assumed to be true by all language' (1920, p. 295). While he took this to be, primarily, a feature of language, he recognised that it reflected a feature of our thought: 'if we talk of objects at all, we unavoidably think of them as permanent and individual' (1920, p. 299). This matter deserves excogitation. Quantity and number (in Campbell's two senses of physical number) enter into every cognitive judgment made. The simplest of judgments, one of the form, This X is a Y, identifies a single, particular thing as an X and, so, introduces both aggregate size and, by extension, natural number. In this sense, they are, as Kant ([1781] 1978) recognised, categories of cognition. If our judgments are at least sometimes veridical, then quantity and number must be features of that which is judged, as well. That is, they

Campbell's theory of fundamental and derived measurement   125

must also be categories of being. Just as the simplest of judgments identifies something as an X, so the simplest of situations judged, likewise, involves a single, particular thing being an X and, so, involves quantity and number. Number is part of the fabric of being. To this extent, the Pythagoreans were correct.

Campbell's concept of physical additivity

The Pythagoreans erred in taking every attribute to be quantitative. While the simplest of situations, this X being Y, involves quantity (in the sense of aggregate magnitude) and number (in the sense of natural number), the character of Y (specifically, whether or not it is a magnitude of some quantity) is always an empirical issue because it is not logically necessary that all attributes be quantitative. While number and quantity are features of every situation, they are not features of every attribute. Some attributes are quantitative, some are not. Campbell was correct, therefore, to insist that there is an empirical issue here. As he saw it, some attributes which are not number are *like* number.

His concept of a quantitative property was similar to the classical concept of a quantity. For example, he claimed that

The difference between those properties which can be measured perfectly definitely, like weight, and those which cannot arises then from the possibility or impossibility of finding in connection with these properties a physical significance for the process of addition. (Campbell, 1920, pp. 277-8)

If by the 'process of addition' is understood the additive relation characterising a quantity and if experimental tests indicating the presence of additive relations between magnitudes are to count as finding 'a physical significance' for it, then the view expressed here is the classical view of Chapter 3. However, Campbell mistakenly concluded that the way in which such physical significance is generally arrived at in the case of physical quantities is the only way.

In his view, for fundamental measurement to be possible there had to be a direct analogy between a physical operation and the process of numerical addition. Consider the two Laws of Addition which he proposed for such a physical operation. His first law was as follows:

126 *Making the representational theory of measurement*

For the process of addition must be such that the system which is produced by adding one body possessing the property in question to another must be greater than either of the bodies added. (Campbell, 1920, pp. 281–2)

And his second was that,

The magnitude of a system produced by the addition of bodies A, B, C, ... depends only on the magnitude of those bodies and not on the order or method of their addition. (Campbell, 1920, p. 284)

Campbell intended his second law to cover physical analogues of the commutative and associative laws of arithmetic. The idea is that there must be some physical operation for combining objects possessing the relevant attribute, the result of which depends only upon the magnitudes of the relevant attribute possessed by those objects. But, if the relationship between the magnitude of the outcome and the magnitudes of the objects combined is analogous to numerical addition and if the magnitude of the outcome depends only upon the magnitudes of the objects combined, then the formal similarity between the physical operation and numerical addition must derive from relations between the magnitudes. This is what 'only' means here. That is, Campbell's view entailed that the additivity of magnitudes is fundamental to understanding the physical operation of addition between objects. If there were no additive relations between magnitudes, the idea of the outcome of the physical operation depending only upon the magnitudes combined would have no content.

Once this is recognised, it is clear that there is at least the logical possibility of detecting additive relations between magnitudes in ways other than by the obvious, direct methods applying to fundamental measurement. Campbell was clearly deflected from considering this because he attended only to physical measurement, but his failure to consider the issue is puzzling, given that he considered derived measurement and that he thought of fundamental and derived magnitudes as quantities in the same sense. It is a very small step from this insight to the recognition of derived measurement as an indirect identification of underlying quantitative additivity. The reason he failed to take this step, I believe, was because he emphasised epistemological issues at the expense of ontological ones. While he did have something like the classical concept of quantity in the background,

Campbell's theory of fundamental and derived measurement   127

influencing his understanding of measurement and guiding his attempt to construct a representational theory, this underlying concept of quantity was never explicitly acknowledged. Instead, his theory of measurement remained a theory about how quantitative attributes are detected and never considered what quantitative attributes are.

Later representationalists (e.g., Stevens, 1951) criticised Campbell because he confined measurement to just the numerical representation of operations of physical addition. Campbell had his reasons. First, he thought of measurement as the numerical representation of quantities, but mistakenly thought that the only evidence for quantity was via the discovery of operations of physical addition. Even if it was wrong on that point, there was some sense to his position. If measurement is the numerical representation of quantity, then it is going to be the representation of additive systems exclusively. Had he developed his implicit concept of quantity, he would have reinvented the classical concept.

Second, non-additive structures (e.g., purely classificatory or ordinal attributes) can be adequately represented by numerals. On the other hand, he thought, the specifically additive structure of quantities cannot be adequately represented by the numerals. The representation of these structures requires numbers. His reasoning here is confused, but contains a germ of truth. Of course, additivity can be represented adequately, if not by the numerals alone, then by the numerals supplemented by other mathematical signs (e.g., '+' and '='), for it is precisely via the numerals plus these other signs that the additive truths of arithmetic are symbolically represented. So strictly speaking his claim is false. However, the germ of truth is this. Quantities are intrinsically numerical in ways that purely ordinal systems are not. Ratios of magnitudes of a continuous quantity possess all of the formal properties of the positive real numbers and this is why numerical concepts (and not just numerals) are implicated in quantitative science.

Third, according to his view, the aim of measurement is the expression of what he called 'numerical laws':

Measurement is only a means to an end; we want to express the properties of systems by numerals only because we are thereby enabled to state laws about them. When we have measured two or more magnitudes characteristic of some system, we can usually find a general numerical

128 *Making the representational theory of measurement*

relation between these magnitudes. The assertion of such a numerical relation is called a numerical law, and it is from laws of this kind that nearly all the advances made in the conscious history of physics have been made. (Campbell, 1920, pp. 328–9)

Now, it is true that if numerical assignments are made to merely ordinal attributes, then numerical relationships will exist between those assignments and other measures and, so, 'numerical laws' could be stated for ordinal attributes. However, even if 'numerical laws' relating ordinal attributes could be expressed as continuous numerical functions, the constants in such 'numerical laws' would have, in Campbell's view, an intolerable arbitrariness. As the matter might now be expressed, the numerical form of such laws would not be invariant under all monotonic transformations of the ordinal 'measurements' involved. Campbell did not develop this point, but his discussion of it anticipated the problem of 'meaningfulness' recognised later within the representational theory of measurement (see Luce, Krantz, Suppes and Tversky, 1990). In terms of this concept, Campbell's point was that with merely ordinal measurement there are no meaningful numerical laws of the sort found in quantitative physics. These are generally laws relating products of powers of physical quantities. Hence, his reasoning could be expressed as follows: if the sole aim of measurement is the expression of meaningful numerical laws and such laws only exist where the numbers assigned represent physical additivity, then measurement must be confined to the numerical representation of additive structures.

Derived measurement

Not all measurement in physics is fundamental measurement. Campbell attempted to accommodate this fact via his concept of derived measurement. Physical quantities in this category, he thought, can be expressed as functions of fundamental physical quantities. For example, the density of a body is a function of its mass and volume. Campbell concluded that the ratio of mass to volume is, itself, a quantity because this ratio is constant for bodies composed of the same substance (e.g., all samples of pure gold have a constant ratio of mass to volume). Since the ordering of substances according to the value of this constant matches the ordering of substances according to density (as determined by

Campbell's theory of fundamental and derived measurement   129

relative buoyancy), the ratio of mass to volume may be regarded as the measure of density. According to Campbell, 'the constant in a numerical law is always the measure of a magnitude' (1920, p. 346).

The relevant numerical laws all turn out to be products of powers of fundamental quantities. For example, density = mass^{+1} × volume^{-1}. In general terms, what Campbell proposed was that if some attribute (possibly hitherto unmeasured) is discovered to be correlated with a product of powers of fundamental quantities, then the numerical value obtained gives a measure of that attribute. Given the wide application of this principle in physics, Campbell inferred that it is generally true as, indeed, later shown in Krantz *et al.* (1971). These authors also display the sense in which numbers so assigned provide a representation of an additive relation within the derived quantity.

While fundamental and derived measurement clearly differ procedurally, it was Campbell's view that they were of quantities in the same sense.

But is there any other difference between fundamental and derived magnitudes other than susceptibility to addition, or rather does this difference indicate any other which is of importance? So far as I can make out it does not; and perhaps the best proof that it does not is obtained from the fact that magnitudes derived from a numerical law are often fundamental magnitudes; they may be fundamental magnitudes well known before the law was discovered, or they may first have been found as derived magnitudes and subsequently discovered to be susceptible to fundamental measurement; the most striking examples of the last possibility is furnished by electrical resistance and capacity. (Campbell, 1920, pp. 346–7)

Whether or not a quantity is susceptible to fundamental measurement, in Campbell's sense, must then be a relation between that quantity and scientists, and is not an intrinsic feature of the quantity. This is strikingly similar to the classical view.

If fundamental and derived measurement involve quantities in the same sense (e.g., as specified, say, in Hölder's (1901) axioms), then it follows that the character of being quantitative resides in an attribute's internal structure and not in its external relations (say, to scientists, via some operation of physical addition which they happen to be able to perform). Hence, any attempt to limit the range of external relations through which scientists can come

130   *Making the representational theory of measurement*

to know quantitative structure (e.g., Campbell's restriction to fundamental and derived measurement), must be accompanied by two demonstrations: first, that these ways are capable of indicating the existence of quantity; and second, that other ways of detecting quantitative additivity are not possible. At best, Campbell only half completed the first task, through his informal demonstration that concatenation operations satisfying his two laws of measurement indicate that the attribute involved is quantitative. Campbell did not complete the other half of the first task. That is, he did not demonstrate that constants in numerical laws must always indicate quantities. Furthermore, he neglected entirely the second task. It is especially important to stress these gaps in his theory because it was at precisely these points that Campbell became most dogmatic in his evaluation of attempts at psychophysical measurement.

As an attempt to establish a rival paradigm, Campbell's theory was inadequate because, first, it focused only upon the special case of physical attributes and neglected the more general issues raised by the logic of measurement and, second, it really presumed the classical theory, anyhow. However, because it appeared to survey ground outside the classical paradigm, it was important. Quite unconsciously, through his neglect of the concept of quantity and his focus upon the experimental identification of physical additivity, Campbell appeared to develop Russell's claim that quantity and number were logically distinct concepts. He showed how much of physical measurement could be understood as the numerical representation of physical operations.

His failure to work out successfully a viable account of number and to explain how derived measurement leads to the numerical representation of quantitative structure was passed over by his contemporaries. Given the commitment of most contemporary philosophers of mathematics to one or other of logicism, formalism or intuitionism, his attempt to construct a physical account of number was ignored. The questions raised by derived measurement for the representational theory were not clearly posed until that theory was articulated more carefully than Campbell had done. Hence, his theory of measurement was not seen as a failure or even as significantly incomplete. Indeed, it came to be seen as especially authoritative. Because Hölder (1901) was neglected, Campbell's representational treatment of physical measurement

Nagel's positivistic representationalism

seemed the best available. It was still a touchstone for Ellis (1966) more than forty years later.

NAGEL'S POSITIVISTIC REPRESENTATIONALISM

Ernest Nagel (1931) was one later measurement theorist who owed a debt to Campbell. In his short, but influential paper,[11] Nagel synthesised contributions of Helmholtz (1887), Hölder (1901), Russell (1903) and Campbell (1920). Nagel chipped away what he considered to be accumulated metaphysical encrustations upon the theories of Russell and Campbell, leaving what later seemed to Stevens to be a conceptually solid bedrock for a better understanding of measurement. Nagel repeated Russell's definition of measurement as 'the correlation with numbers of entities which are not numbers' (1931, p. 313)[12] and his theory is self-consciously located within the representational tradition. Like Campbell (1920), he distinguished between fundamental and derived measurement and characterised the former via a positivist-inspired modification of Hölder's axioms of quantity. Like Russell and contrary to Campbell, he regarded the numerical representation of ordinal structures as measurement, as well, but he rejected Russell's concept of magnitude and, by implication, along with it the classical concept of quantity. Hence, he did not accept Campbell's claim that fundamental and derived magnitudes do not differ, as magnitudes. Finally, these various elements were unified by a philosophical outlook compatible with logical positivism and its American cousin, operationism.

Nagel criticised Russell's concept of magnitude. Remember that Russell thought of magnitudes of some quantity as a strictly ordered range of attributes (e.g., the range of all lengths) which, while sustaining relations of equality and order between objects, did not sustain additive relations. Since, for certain attributes, there are both ordinal and additive relations between objects and since these can be used to provide the conceptual basis for a representational theory of fundamental measurement, as Campbell

---

[11] It provided the basis for the section on measurement in Cohen and Nagel (1934) and was reprinted in Danto and Morgenbesser (1960).

[12] Russell (1903, p. 158) had written, 'Moreover it has appeared that measurement – if this means the correlation, with numbers, of entities which are not numbers or aggregates – is not a prerogative of quantities.'

132   *Making the representational theory of measurement*

had shown, Russell's philosophical agonies about whether or not magnitudes are divisible, must have seemed a nightmare to the positivist mind. Nagel's impatience with Russell's philosophical scruples is not disguised. To the positivist, the question must have seemed all too obvious: Why not define measurement as the numerical representation of empirical relations between objects and be done with it? In dealing with ordinal and additive relations between objects (as opposed to such relations between magnitudes), argued Nagel, we deal with 'a concrete actuality' (1931, p. 323), but Russell's magnitudes reside in 'a realm of essences . . . a domain of immaterial entities having no necessary reference to existence' (1931, p. 323). His argument against them was that they are unobservable and conceptually unnecessary: magnitudes are just reifications of observed relations between objects; 'if Occam's razor still can cut, the magnitudes demanded by the absolute theory may be eliminated' (1931, p. 325).

There are problems with this type of criticism. First, while properties were a familiar target of operationists (see Bridgman (1927)), their supposed logical defects are also shared by relations. If it is held, as Nagel believed, that the same relation can occur in different situations (e.g., the relation of one thing being longer than another), then relations are universals just as much as properties are. Hence, the usual philosophical arguments against properties apply to relations as well.

Nagel's objection to magnitudes, however, was more specific than the usual line. He took the view that what we think of as magnitudes really reduce to relations, i.e., that a magnitude is a mere disposition to relate in various ways to other things.[13] For example, he defined density as 'the capacity of a liquid to float upon other liquids' (1931, p. 317) and he made the general observation that 'when magnitudes, which are always found to be relations exhibited in the physical operations of things, are invoked as the locus of those operations, it seems legitimate to ask what empirical difference their existence or nonexistence as "common essences" would make' (1931, pp. 324–5). But this argument applies to all properties and if all properties are really relations then an object is never a thing of a certain kind, it is just

---

[13] Nagel was not alone in suggesting a dispositional view of magnitudes. See Mackie (1973) for a useful discussion of the issues.

that which relates to other things in various ways. As I argued earlier in this chapter, the idea of things as constituted entirely by their relations to other things, which in turn are likewise constituted entirely by relations, and so on, *ad infinitum*, is an idea that cannot work. It leaves only relations and nothing to stand in them. If there are relations, then there must be things having some sort of intrinsic (i.e., non-relational) character standing in those relations.

Furthermore, the scientific mind recognises a connection between how things behave when treated in various ways and the intrinsic characteristics they possess. So, if it is the case that liquid X floats on liquid Y when both are poured into a common container, it is standard scientific thinking to hypothesise that this is, at least in part, because of different attributes that X and Y possess. Hypothesising thus is not a case of invoking the 'essences' that Nagel feared. It is an example of deterministic thinking, a form of thinking entirely typical of science. Indeed, it is so typical that Nagel himself used it, candidly admitting that 'once having specified the defining operation, whether it is actually performed or not, the things measured have a nature prior to the actual performance which conditions their behaviour in it' (1931, p. 324). Having written this, he immediately attempted to rationalise it as merely a way of speaking:

This observation may be verbal only: if equality is defined in terms of the process, quantities can be called equal prior to the process only proleptically; unless at *some* time the process eventuates, we cannot know that there is such a property as equality. (Nagel, 1931, p. 324)

However, if the character of objects is to condition their behaviour when they are subjected to the relevant operation, then the fact that they possess that character cannot be 'verbal only'. 'Verbal only' characteristics (i.e., characteristics only attributed to and not really located in the objects) cannot condition real behaviour.

What worried Nagel was the fact that we may not know that the objects possess the relevant characteristics prior to performing the necessary operation upon them and, so, in attributing them to the objects after performing the operation, all we appear to be doing is reifying the observed relation. But the characteristics attributed to the objects are not a reification of this relation. The characteristics have an explanatory generality that the observed

134   *Making the representational theory of measurement*

relation lacks. The fact that two objects are both of the same length contributes towards explaining their behaviours in an indefinite number of possible situations, something which their behaviour in a single situation cannot do. To refrain from attributing characteristics to objects because they are only known via some relation, is to sacrifice explanatory power to the scientifically debilitating principle that the world extends no further than we can see.

Nagel's critique of Russell's concept of magnitude fitted the positivistic spirit of the times and it marked the point at which the classical concept of quantity ceased to be seriously considered within measurement theory. Nagel used Hölder's axioms of quantity, but he modified them to apply to *objects*, not *magnitudes*. Hölder's seven axioms for magnitudes of a continuous quantity, at Nagel's hands, became the following twelve conditions for an *approximately* Archimedean set of objects.

1. Either $a > b$, or $a < b$, or $a = b$.
2. If $a > b$, and $b > c$, then $a > c$.
3. For every a there is an a' such that $a = a'$.
4. If $a > b$, and $b = b'$, then $a > b'$.
5. If $a = b$, then $b = a$.
6. For every a there is a b such that $a > b$ (within limits).
7. For every a and b there is a c such that $c = a + b$.
8. $a + b > a'$.
9. $a + b = a' + b'$.
10. $a + b = b + a$.
11. $(a + b) + c = a + (b + c)$.
12. If $a < b$, then there is a number n such that $na > b$ (also within limits). (Nagel, 1931, p. 315)

Note the modifications Nagel made to Hölder's axioms. If a set of axioms relating to objects is to provide a basis for fundamental measurement in Campbell's sense, then replicas of those objects are required for any axiom in which a term is repeated. For example, Nagel's 'axiom' 10, the commutative law, is not directly testable because $a + b$ cannot be directly compared with $b + a$. One way around this is to establish that $b + a = a' + b'$; by using Nagel's 'axiom' 3, then 10 follows by his 'axioms' 5 and 9. So, in part, the increase in 'axioms' is due to those required for replicas (i.e., 'axioms' 3, 4, and 9). Furthermore, Nagel qualified 'axioms' 6 and 12 with the phrase 'within limits', recognising that 'axioms' asserting

Nagel's positivistic representationalism

the existence of objects are not directly testable (3 and 7 should be similarly qualified, as well). Nagel neglected to point out that none of these four 'axioms' (3, 6, 7, and 12) is falsifiable. In addition, he 'axiomatized' > and = and included commutativity as an 'axiom'. 'Axiom' 12 approximates an Archimedean axiom, and is vainly intended to replace Hölder's axiom of continuity. Designed to accommodate positivistic scruples, Nagel's 'axiomatization' is less economical than Hölder's and delivers much less.

Furthermore, it possesses problems intrinsic to this kind of approach. First, Nagel avoided specifying the relevant domain of the 'axioms', that is, the class of objects over which they are thought to hold. If they are intended to apply to length, for example, over what class of objects are the variables, a, b, c, etc., quantified? For any such class to be scientifically interesting, it must be specified via relevant properties. It could be, for example, the class of rigid, straight rods of humanly manageable dimensions. But if it is acceptable to invoke properties in order to specify the relevant class of objects, then why not axiomatise for properties (magnitudes) directly, as Hölder did?

Second, whatever this class is, it must be confined to a class that human scientists can operate upon because the relations, =, <, and +, are required to reflect humanly performable operations. Hence, the class to which the 'axioms' apply will be smaller than the class that scientists will generalise to. For example, having established that Nagel's 'axioms' hold for a specific, finite class of rods between, say, 1 centimetre and 10 metres in length, what can be concluded about rods outside this class, or about lengths outside this range? It cannot be inferred that if operations of the same sort were carried out with objects outside that class similar results would be obtained, because for most of those objects this conclusion would be false (e.g., imagine concatenating the earth and sun to obtain the sum of their diameters: the earth would disintegrate!). However, to even imagine doing this requires thinking in terms of the attribute, length. By way of contrast, Hölder's approach can avoid this defect. The operations upon objects satisfying certain boundary conditions may be taken as telling us something about the structure of length generally, rather than something about just the behaviour of particular objects. There is no long term conceptual gain in 'axiomatizing' only with respect to objects.

136   *Making the representational theory of measurement*

In the same way, Campbell's view of derived measurement retained a coherence that Nagel's lost. Nagel's rejection of the unifying concept of magnitude and his positivistic reduction of concepts to 'empirical' meaning entailed that the meaning of numerical assignments in derived measurement differed from those in fundamental measurement. For example, he claimed that

When one body is said to be thirteen times as heavy as another, a different meaning must be given to such a statement from the meaning of the statement that mercury is thirteen times as dense as water; only in terms of the numerical law connecting mass and volume has the latter proposition significance. (Nagel, 1931, p. 329)

Nagel's problem was to articulate what the meaning of derived measures, like density, then was. Historically, the concept of derived measurement proved to be a difficulty for the representational theory, for it was not clear that empirical relations are numerically represented when numbers are assigned via numerical laws. Hence, it was not clear that derived measurement was measurement in the representational sense.

In axiomatising at the level of operations upon objects and in attempting to reinterpret derived measurement, Nagel indicated the direction in which the representational theory was to develop. He also cleared the ground for Stevens' theory of scale-types. He recognised that numbers could also be used for purposes of identification (i.e., to represent equivalence relations in classification) and to represent merely ordinal relations. While he thought of 'magnitude in the most complete sense' (1931, p. 316) as obtained only when all twelve of his 'axioms' were satisfied, he did not resist thinking of other forms of numerical representation as measurement of some kind, as Campbell did. In this respect, his view broadened Russell's and set a precedent for Stevens.

Despite the above difficulties, Nagel recognised that the logic of the representational theory of measurement requires mathematical relations to be empirically instantiated. He made this point in general terms as follows.

For if mathematics is applicable to the natural world, the formal properties of the symbolic operations of mathematics must also be predicable of many segments of that world. And if we can discover what these formal properties are, since mathematics *is* relevant to the exploration of nature, a physical interpretation *must* be found for them. That physical interpretation will constitute, whenever it can be found, the conditions for measurement of that subject matter. (Nagel, 1931, pp. 314–315)

And he made it specifically in relation to addition as well:

Is it not, however, more perspicacious to think of mathematical "addition" as a *universal*, whose variable empirical content will be *cases* of addition, but which will require further specific definition and experimental proof of the presence of those formal characters which make those empirical contents instances of that universal? (Nagel, 1931, p. 327)

This was an important insight because it was Russell's denial of just this point that caused his escape from the classical paradigm. Unfortunately, it was not a point that Stevens developed and it was one that later representational theorists were slow to run with.[14]

FROM RATIOS TO REPRESENTATIONS

Russell, Campbell, and Nagel all attempted the impossible. Any satisfactory account of scientific measurement must be based upon quantitative concepts as they figure in scientific theories. In such theories, quantitative attributes are hypothesised to stand in continuous functional relations to one another, relations that depend upon additivity (i.e., that are invariant with respect to the choice of unit). It follows that quantitative attributes must also be continuous and additive in structure. Attributes of this form sustain ratios of magnitudes which in turn have exactly the structure of the positive real numbers. The classical paradigm is part of the same conceptual package as the concept of quantity presumed within scientific theories. If scientists think quantitatively, then they think within that paradigm. Any attempt to break away from it, combined with a wish to retain quantitative theories, is thereby doomed to fail.

That which fails logically may still influence uncritical minds. In attempting to transform the logic of measurement from ratios to representations, Russell, Campbell, and Nagel succeeded in loosening the grip of the classical concept of measurement, especially upon the minds of philosophers and those influenced

---

[14] See Narens & Luce (1990).

138   *Making the representational theory of measurement*

by philosophers. Had Hölder encountered Stevens' definition of measurement, he would have seen its poverty and summarily dismissed it. Nagel, however, might have felt able to accept it. The idea that measurement involves numerical assignments (rather than estimations of numerical facts) was common to Russell, Campbell, and Nagel, and each could have interpreted Stevens' non-specific condition, 'according to rule', as necessary but not sufficient. Of course, none of these three would have interpreted Stevens' definition as liberally as he was to do. Properly defined, the representational view is that measurement involves the numerical representation of empirical relations. It was Stevens' unique contribution to argue that assignments made according to rule always represent empirical relations. That was not to be an insignificant step, and it was one that could only be made standing upon the shoulders of earlier representationalists.

Given quantitative psychology's *modus operandi*, such a step had to be taken. Liberal as Nagel's representational concept was, in itself it was of little use to psychologists. A representationalism that emphasises the numerical representation of empirical relations between objects, only seems to work if the relevant empirical relations can be first identified experimentally. Even the numerical representation of a classification requires identifying an empirical equivalence relation, one that has the contingent properties of being reflexive, symmetrical and transitive. Psychologists could not claim to have identified even this much structure in relation to attributes like the various intellectual abilities or personality traits they claimed to be able to measure. This is why, prior to Stevens, psychologists showed very little interest in the representational theory (even in Nagel's very liberal version) and those who did (e.g., Johnson, 1936[15]) tended to be highly critical of psychological measurement.

So the representationalists bestowed a double legacy. By introducing the concept of representation they cleared a conceptual path for an even more radical definition of measurement, such

---

[15] Hornstein (1988) calls Johnson's (1936) paper, 'a widely ignored precursor of Stevens' scales' (p. 30). However, as far as distinguishing different kinds of scales of measurement is concerned, there is nothing in Johnson's paper not already in Nagel's. The important difference between their approaches was that Johnson used Nagel's representationalism as a stick to beat psychology with, while Stevens transformed it into a definition that eased psychologists' minds. In the one area in which Stevens followed Johnson (the so-called problem of permissible statistics), his views were controversial.

as Stevens'. However, Campbell and Nagel, in emphasising the representation of empirically discovered relations, prepared the way for a confrontation between the practice of psychological measurement and the quantity objection. Once it was accepted that measurement presupposed the discovery of the right sort of empirical relations, it was inevitable that embarrassing questions would be asked about psychological measurement. Those psychologists who still clung to a combination of the classical concept of measurement and Pythagoreanism (such as Thurstone, 1931, 1937) were becoming a minority. Pythagoreanism could not long survive the broadening of the subject matter of mathematics to include non-quantitative structures, structures which were finding applications even in physical science. Adherents to the classical concept in psychology were diminishing. Campbell and Nagel had lit a fuse.

CHAPTER 6

The status of psychophysical measurement

You will not find the boundaries of psyche by travelling in any
direction, so deep is the measure of it.

(Heraclitus)

The scientific experimenter ... need not be in the least concerned with methodology as a body of general principles.

(Sir Frederic Bartlett)

If what Kuhn (1970) said about the way that science works is
correct, then the fuse lit by Campbell and Nagel was in danger
of being snuffed out. Quantitative psychologists now possessed a
paradigm of measurement, one almost universally accepted
throughout the discipline. This was that standardised psychological procedures for making numerical assignments yield measurements. The strength of this paradigm was not just that it sustained a thriving 'normal science' (in Kuhn's sense), but equally
important, it would never meet with any 'anomalies' or unsolvable
puzzles. Because every situation involves quantity and number
(i.e., there are always aggregates to count), numerical assignment
procedures can always be contrived for any psychological attribute.
Furthermore, cases of genuine measurement, should they ever
arise in psychology, could also be thought to fit this paradigm. It
stood almost invulnerable.[1]

The fact that relative to the classical paradigm, or even Nagel's
representationalism, quantitative psychology's *modus operandi* was
itself an anomaly, could be ignored by an established science of
psychology, one securely located within the university system, with

---

[1] Which is not to say that it might not degenerate as a research programme, with its
endless array of tests for measuring every conceivable psychological attribute, scores on
none of which contribute to an understanding of how the causal systems producing
behaviour actually work.

The status of psychophysical measurement 141

its own journals and research conventions, attached to an expanding profession. This was certainly the case in the United States where, even by 1912, eighty-three American cities had recognised psychology clinics (Resnick, 1982); by 1917, seventy-four universities and colleges supported psychological laboratories; and there were already twenty-one journals in psychology or cognate disciplines (Canfield, 1973). Nagel's reconstruction of measurement theory did impinge upon American psychology, but the response was entirely consistent with Kuhn's picture.

E. G. Boring, whose doubts about psychological measurement were mentioned earlier, had considered the relationship between measurement theory and psychophysical measurement in his 1934 seminar at Harvard University (Newman, 1974). A paper by McGregor (1935) was an outcome. It was written from the perspective of Campbell (1920) and Cohen and Nagel (1934), requiring that numerical representations only be of operationally identified, empirical relations, and yet it concluded that 'Psychological measurement, understood in operational terms, is a *fait accompli*' (McGregor, 1935, p. 265). How had McGregor managed to deflect the obvious charge that psychologists had not identified additive relations for numerical representation?

First, he confined himself to psychophysics, thus not attending to intellectual abilities, personality traits, or other psychological attributes. Second, he proposed an operational reinterpretation of psychophysical measurement, whereby what was measured was no longer psychological, but physical. According to this reinterpretation, the subject in a psychophysics experiment is regarded as a measuring instrument and the investigator compares physical measures of the physical attribute (say, length) with measures obtained from the subject (say, judgments of equality or inequality of individual lengths or sums of lengths, etc.). As McGregor put it,

We have understood $S = f(R)$ and yet have avoided the Cartesian dichotomy. It is true that we have measured distances under a different set of operational conditions than those chosen by the physicist, but our measurement is no less 'physical' because of that. What we *have* done is to shift the focus of attention from the measured *magnitude* to the operating *organism*. We have examined the relationship between a magnitude measured in the usual way and one measured under special operational conditions which are specially designed to shed light upon the functioning of the organism. But S is as physical, or as psychological, as R. (1935, p. 263)

142 *The status of psychophysical measurement*

It was his reinterpretation of psychophysics that enabled McGregor to slip the representationalist noose. This reinterpretation, however, had been canvassed by Boring (1921)[2] more than a decade before and was as old as Brentano ([1874] 1973). It was aged wine in the new operationist bottle.

The same spirit is present in Johnson's (1936) more thoroughgoing attempt to get to grips with the implications of the representationalism of Cohen and Nagel (1934). Johnson distinguished nominal, ordinal and cardinal applications of numbers: nominal apply to classifications, ordinal to mere orderings, and cardinal only to attributes with demonstrable additive structure. Only the latter is measurement and no psychological attributes fit this category, in Johnson's view. He uncritically included intelligence amongst his list of ordinal attributes, concluding that observed scores on intelligence tests correspond to an ordinal scale of intelligence because equal differences between such scores have not been shown to correspond to equal differences in intelligence (i.e., he reasoned that if they are not quantitative, then they must be ordinal). This is not a valid conclusion, for intelligence test scores or any other for that matter. If the proposition that equal differences between observed scores correspond to equal differences in intelligence is doubtful, then the proposition that the order of observed scores corresponds to the order of intelligence can likewise be doubted. Both are empirical hypotheses in need of testing. Too generous with respect to ordinal scales, Johnson was niggardly with respect to the concept of measurement, where his insistence upon the direct empirical demonstration of additivity outdid even Campbell. Despite this defect in his treatment, Johnson bit the bullet, drew the correct conclusion (viz., no psychological attributes have been shown to be measurable) and drew a sensible, anti-Pythagorean moral: 'Those data should be measured which can be measured; those which cannot be measured should be treated otherwise' (Johnson, 1936, p. 351). For all its toughness and good sense, Johnson's paper stirred barely a ripple. It was, as Hornstein (1988) understated, 'widely ignored' (p. 30).

What Kuhn (1970) has labelled 'normal science' is not normal. If scientists want to discover the hidden ways of working of natural

---

[2] See footnote 12 in Chapter 4. Boring added a footnote to McGregor's paper indicating his complete agreement.

The Ferguson committee 143

systems, ignoring valid criticism is an abnormal way of proceeding. Science is a cognitive enterprise: its pursuit is generally difficult and its practitioners are fallible. Hence, it only works reliably when its method is critical inquiry. Critical inquiry is the common core of scientific method, a core that takes various forms in different disciplines. Critical inquiry, because it is inquiry premised upon its own fallibility, involves seriously questioning the most cherished of assumptions. If critical inquiry characterises normal science (correctly understood), then Kuhn's 'normal science', the sort that existed in quantitative psychology in the 1930s, is gullible inquiry. Quantitative psychologists believed what they wanted to believe with respect to the measurability hypothesis and ignored valid criticism.

Psychology in England was more vulnerable than that in America. Although the English could boast of influential names like Galton, Pearson, Spearman, Burt,[3] and even Titchener,[4] psychology did not easily gain a foothold in English universities prior to the Second World War. As late as 1939 there were only six psychology chairs in all England and only about thirty lecturers (Hearnshaw, 1964). Professionally, English psychology was also far weaker than American. Psychologists did not have the respect of the scientific and medical establishments, as in America. 'A combination of academic hubris, intellectual scepticism and professional antagonism persuaded these élites to keep the psychologists out of their charmed circle' (Wooldridge, 1994, p. 153). A hostile scientific establishment might seek to exclude psychology institutionally by attempting to discredit its scientific claims; and an institutionally weak psychology could ill afford to ignore such criticisms. The implications of Campbell's representationalism could be ignored by American psychologists with impunity, even when one of their own forcefully spelt them out; but when levelled in England, a different response was necessary.

THE FERGUSON COMMITTEE

At York, in 1932, the British Association for the Advancement of Science appointed a committee of nineteen to 'consider and report

---

[3] Although Burt's reputation as a scientist was later discredited, he had enormous influence in British psychology.
[4] Titchener was English by birth.

144 *The status of psychophysical measurement*

upon the possibility of Quantitative Estimates of Sensory Events'. The chairman of the committee was A. Ferguson, a physicist. The committee contained the following psychologists: C. S. Myers[5] (as vice-chairman), H. Banister,[6] F. C. Bartlett,[7] R. J. Bartlett,[8] W. Brown,[9] S. Dawson[10] (Dawson was later replaced by K. J. W. Craik[11]), J. Drever,[12] S. J. F. Philpott,[13] L. F. Richardson[14] and R. H. Thouless.[15] Significantly, it also contained Campbell along with other physicists. As an exercise in critical inquiry, the deliberations of the Committee were a sham. Both the interim and final reports (Ferguson *et al.*, 1938; Ferguson *et al.*, 1940) consisted largely of set pieces: the big guns of a confident, intellectually dominant, Campbell camp, and the pea-shooters of an intellectually limp psychophysics camp.

The battle lines were sharply drawn in 1933. In discussions on vision, organised by the Physical and Optical Societies, the issue of the measurement of sensations had been raised. The only

[5] Myers was the grand old man of English experimental and applied psychology. He was appointed director of the Cambridge Psychological Laboratory in 1912 and founded the National Institute of Industrial Psychology in 1921, of which he was the first director (Bartlett, 1965; Hearnshaw, 1964). The term, 'shell-shock' was apparently first used by him (Hearnshaw, 1964) and in Hearnshaw's view, Myers was 'perhaps the ablest and most balanced mind among the British psychologists of this century' (1962, p. 7).

[6] H. Banister did research on the psychology of hearing at Cambridge University.

[7] Sir Frederic Bartlett, a student of Myers at Cambridge, became director of the Cambridge Psychological Laboratory in 1922 and the first professor of experimental psychology at Cambridge in 1931 (Broadbent, 1970). He achieved international repute as a cognitive psychologist, popularising and adapting Head's concept of 'schema' (Hearnshaw, 1964).

[8] R. J. Bartlett taught experimental psychology at London University and later worked in clinical psychology.

[9] W. Brown was a leading British quantitative psychologist, with a broad range of interests covering psychoanalysis and industrial psychology. He held the Wilde Readership in Mental Philosophy at Oxford University from 1921 until 1946.

[10] S. Dawson was an early advocate of Sir Ronald Fisher's statistical methods in psychology (Hearnshaw, 1964).

[11] K. J. W. Craik, a promising student of F. C. Bartlett in the area of visual perception and first Director of the Applied Psychology Unit of the Medical Research Council, was killed early in his career (Broadbent, 1970).

[12] J. Drever became Scotland's first professor of psychology, at Edinburgh University in 1931. He pioneered experimental psychology in that country (Collins, 1951).

[13] S. J. F. Philpott taught psychology at London University (R. J. Bartlett, 1952).

[14] L. F. Richardson did research in psychophysics and pain perception and had participated in the joint discussions (Smith *et al.*, 1932) which resulted in the Ferguson Committee being set up.

[15] R. H. Thouless was a psychologist at the University of Glasgow. He was the first British psychologist to make use of Fisher's work in statistics and pioneered such fringe areas as the psychology of religion and psychical research (Hearnshaw, 1964).

The Ferguson committee 145

speaker who mentioned a particular theory of measurement was Richardson. He mentioned Campbell's theory and 'deliberately rejected it' (Campbell, 1933a, p. 565). Following this, Campbell targeted Richardson's proposed method of psychophysical measurement and the resulting discussion involved some of the Committee members: R. J. Bartlett, J. Guild, T. Smith, J. H. Shaxby and R. A. Houstoun. Campbell (1933b) claimed that 'nothing but confusion and error can result from using "measurement" in any but its accepted sense. I call nothing measurement that does not possess the distinctive features of the processes physicists accept as measurement' (p. 589). Richardson appealed against Campbell's hard line:

A restriction of the meaning of the word "measurement" so that it should apply only to what Dr Campbell has named A-magnitudes and B-magnitudes[16] is recommended by several speakers. Such a conventional restriction might suitably be left to the decision of the Committee appointed by Sections A and J of the British Association in 1932. But I must point out that Dr Campbell formulated his valuable classification of types of magnitude before he had sufficiently considered the existence and properties of mental estimates. Dr Houstoun in this Discussion has mentioned excellent reasons for not thus restricting the meaning of "measurement". Might we not suitably say that mental estimates are "C-magnitudes", and that all magnitudes are measured? (Richardson, 1933, pp. 587–8)

This revealed a deep misconception of the issues. Richardson thought that the extension of the concept of measurement was simply a convention and he wanted the physicists to alter the convention. Possibly sensing the weakness of his own position in the face of Campbell's critique, he embarked upon a boundary dispute about the denotation of the word "measurement", as if no factual issue was involved. He was prepared to accept that Campbell's theory of fundamental and derived measurement suited the quantitative practices of physicists and wanted quantitative psychology recognised as a new form of measurement. Given the unspoken premise behind Richardson's plea, the Campbell camp would have sensed that they had already won the debate and, so, had no reason to shift their view. Their line was solid from start ('If we wish to talk about measurement in connexion with sensations,

---

[16] Campbell (1928) had called magnitudes open to fundamental measurement, A-magnitudes, and those open to derived measurement, B-magnitudes.

146 *The status of psychophysical measurement*

then measurement must *mean* measurement' (Guild, 1933, p. 576)) to finish ('Measurement is not a term with some mysterious inherent meaning, part of which may have been overlooked by physicists and may be in course of discovery by psychologists ... To use it to denote other ideas does not broaden its meaning but destroys it' (Guild, 1940, p. 345)). The psychologists' best hope of success would have been to propose a new conception of measurement, one not only manifestly superior to Campbell's, but also one that could salvage their own quantitative practices. This the British psychologists could not do, not because they did not have able minds in their midst, but because of a curious indifference to methodological issues.

This attitude is exemplified in F. C. Bartlett's later remark that

The scientific experimenter is, in fact, by bent and practice an opportunist ... The experimenter must be able to use specific methods rigorously, but he need not be in the least concerned with methodology as a body of general principles. (1958, pp. 132, 133)

According to the British historian of psychology, L. S. Hearnshaw (1964), this attitude characterised, not just Cambridge, but also British psychology.[17] Of course, the critical scientist will always sit loose upon methodological rules, adapting them to suit the main scientific game, the discovery of underlying structures and the ways of working of things. Even though, superficially, methodology appears to be just a set of rules, it is really concerned with factual issues, as much as science is in general. In the case of measurement, these facts are those dealt with in Chapter 3. Scientific method has its necessary conditions in the general structure of the subject matter under investigation. If, for some method, such as measurement, these conditions do not obtain in some field, then the method is inappropriate in that field. The purely instrumental attitude to method, in which the scientist simply learns to apply 'specific methods rigorously', leads to methodological rigidity and to the application of inappropriate methods.[18] If Hearnshaw is cor-

---

[17] This is a remarkable attitude towards method in a scientist, especially in a psychologist. Psychologists study not only one of the most complex of natural systems, they study a process, cognition, which no one has yet even successfully conceptualised. These facts should at least raise the question of to what extent the quantitative, experimental methods of physical science can meaningfully apply.

[18] Outside the example of psychological measurement, the best example of rigid thinking in the methodological area is the case of significance testing in psychology (see Gigerenzer, 1993).

rect, and this attitude characterised British psychology, then it explains the bewilderment of the psychologists on the committee in the face of the criticisms of the Campbell camp. Those who are trained to use methods rigorously, but who decline to understand the logic of what they are doing, must inevitably respond to deep methodological criticism with inflexibility and incomprehension. More than one British psychologist missed the point of the Campbellian critique, unable to doubt that what psychologists were doing was the only available scientific option, viz., simply applying the method of measurement to their subject.

In the two published reports (Ferguson, *et al.*, 1938; Ferguson, *et al.*, 1940), Campbell kept a low profile and the case opposing the measurement of sensations was formulated in detail by Guild. Guild's (1938) case was the centrepiece of the Committee's work: it was the largest, most closely argued piece; and discussion revolved around its claims. Guild began with an interpretation of Campbell's theory of fundamental and derived measurement (or, as Guild consistently called them, the measurement of *A-magnitudes* and *B-magnitudes*). This interpretation was faithful to Campbell in its relevant essentials: the measurement of A-magnitudes involves the numerical representation of an experimentally determined analogue of numerical addition; and the measurement of B-magnitudes, the discovery of constants in numerical laws involving A-magnitudes. It differed from Campbell (1920) in what in this context were inessentials: for example, Guild rejected Campbell's physical concept of number; and he thought of B-magnitudes as completely defined by their functional relations with A-magnitudes, so that 'Strictly speaking, therefore, the only measurable magnitudes are A-magnitudes' (p. 299).

Guild's treatment of temperature as an example of a B-magnitude was not as sure-footed as it should have been and Campbell (1940) had to correct a misleading impression inadvertently given. Guild wrote that

The fact that there is no operation of addition applicable to temperature qua temperature, prevents it from being measurable in the true sense of the term. All we are able to do, however we are able to disguise it by theoretical considerations, is to assign numerals to temperatures in accordance with an arbitrary postulated relation to some measurable property of some specified substance or piece of apparatus. When once we have defined some such scale of temperature, temperature becomes

148 *The status of psychophysical measurement*

'measurable' in the broad sense in which the word is generally used; and the laws relating other physical variables with temperature as so defined become open to empirical investigation. (1938, p. 304)

In writing of arbitrary postulated relations as a basis of measurement, Guild had opened a gate wide enough to accommodate Fechner's proposed logarithmic function between sensation intensity and stimulus magnitude. Campbell (1940) firmly shut it, reminding the Committee that

Within a certain range, temperature can be measured by the simple indirect process described above,[19] in virtue of Boyle's Law, pv = constant. The order of this constant is the order of temperature defined as a property such that, if the temperature of A is greater than that of B, A in contact with B will become lower and B of higher temperature. If, then, a value of the constant were assigned to one body, the value to be assigned to any other within the range would be determinate. (p. 341)

That is, Campbell argued, temperature measurement is a genuine case of derived measurement, dependent upon the discovery of constants in a numerical law and not dependent upon an arbitrary postulated relation.

In its essentials, Guild's critique of psychophysical measurement was straightforward: in their experimental work, psychologists have not discovered an analogue of numerical addition, and so sensations do not involve A-magnitudes; without A-magnitudes of a psychological kind, there are no B-magnitudes of that kind (B-magnitudes being defined entirely by their relation to A-magnitudes); therefore, sensations do not involve magnitudes at all and, hence, there is no such thing as psychophysical measurement. Guild applied this form of argument not just to Fechner's sensation intensities but, also, to the later concept of sense-distances.

We have already seen in Chapter 4 how Fechner's attempt to measure the intensities of sensations using his method of jnds is open to the sort of objection put by Guild. If a series of stimuli, each separated from its immediate predecessor by one jnd, was constructed experimentally, then there was no evidence that the increments in sensation intensities corresponding to steps in the stimulus series were equal to one another, nor that any sensation was measured by the number of jnds between the stimulus produc-

---

[19] Campbell is referring to his discussion, a page earlier, of derived measurement.

The Ferguson committee

ing it and the first in the series. R. J. Bartlett spoke for the other psychologists when he said that 'The Committee are on safe ground ... in agreeing that the arguments of Fechner are fallacious: that has been accepted by psychologists from an early date' (1940a, p. 343–4). However, the psychologists were not so ready to give ground when attempts to measure sense-distances were considered.

At this point, the force of Guild's arguments faltered. He considered a particular kind of example:

> The observer is presented with a series of patches of light, all of the same colour, whose intensities are under his control, and is asked to adjust their brightnesses until they form a series so that the 'seeming disparity' between each one and the next in the series is the same. ... The results of experiments of this kind for vision and other senses are usually interpreted as establishing a relation between a psychological magnitude – sense-distance – and stimulus intensities. The grading is supposed to consist of equal sense-distances and the relation found between these equal sense-distances and the corresponding stimulus intervals is regarded by most psycho-physicists as providing a basis on which a quantitative relation between sensation intensity and stimulus intensity may be constructed. (1938, p. 311)

Now, as stated in Chapter 4, if one is prepared to accept that there are sensations, then it is possible to test the hypothesis that sense-distances are quantitative by exploiting an analogy between sense-distances and intervals within a straight line, applying Hölder's axioms for the latter to the former. Guild, like other psychologists of this time, appears to have known nothing of Hölder, but as we have seen, there was at least a recognition by psychologists (e.g., Brown and Thomson, 1921) that an ordering of distances can provide a method for making numerical estimates of magnitudes of a quantity, even if it was not recognised that such an ordering allowed a test of the hypothesis that sense-distances are quantitative. So, what were Guild's objections to the measurability of sense-distances?

First, he argued that sense-distances are not levels of the same attribute as sensation intensities. That is, for example, a difference between the intensities of two sensations of brightness is not the same attribute as intensities of the brightnesses themselves. This is a complex point, but even if true, it does not by itself refute the claim that sense-distances are quantitative. If distances

150   *The status of psychophysical measurement*

between levels of an attribute are quantitative, then so is the attribute itself, even if the distances and the attribute are distinct quantities. Hence, this objection has no force.

Second, he claimed that there is, as a matter of logic, no transitive and symmetrical relation of equality for sense-distances. Guild was not claiming that the available evidence contradicted transitivity or symmetry but, rather, that these properties could not even be tested. He thought this was so because each particular sense-distance can only be specified operationally on any occasion relative to a particular pair of dissimilar stimuli and from this he inferred that each particular sense-distance must, therefore, somehow be linked conceptually to its specific stimulus pair. Given this presumption, there can be no equality between distinct sense-distances because each sense-distance is unique. That is, the sense-distance D_{ij} (between sensations elicited by, say, stimuli, S_i and S_j) and the sense-distance D_{hk} (between sensations elicited by, say, stimuli, S_h and S_k) cannot be equal because D_{ij} cannot be specified relative to S_h and S_k and D_{hk} cannot be specified relative to S_i and S_j. This is a curious argument which, if generalised beyond sense-distances, would make impossible equivalence relations in any domain. A psychophysicist could plausibly argue that just as the same length can be instantiated in two different rods, so the same sense-distance can be instantiated in the relation between the sensations elicited by two quite different stimulus pairs, and so the properties of transitivity and symmetry can be tested. Again Guild's argument is less than compelling.

Third, Guild argued that instructing subjects to perform tasks like setting a variable stimulus, S_j, so that the intensity of the sensation it elicits bisects the sense-distance between sensations elicited by stimuli, S_i and S_k, already presumes that sense-distances are quantitative because bisection is a quantitative concept. One cannot deny that this criticism has force: just because subjects in a psychology experiment respond, it does not follow that the task was meaningful. A psychology experiment is a social situation, the dynamics of which constrain compliant subjects to attempt to please the experimenter by responding, to the best of their understanding, appropriately. Hence, the fact that a subject responds by setting S_j to a value between S_i and S_k does not mean that the intensity of the sensation elicited by S_j bisects the intensities of those elicited by S_i and S_k. However, as Guild acknowl-

The Ferguson committee 151

edged, the experimenter in this sort of psychophysical experiment is not required to use quantitative concepts like that of bisection. The subject's task can be specified purely in terms of relations of equality between sensation differences and neither equality nor difference is a uniquely quantitative concept. That is, the subject only has to recognise sameness of a particular kind of a relation between sensation pairs. While Guild made a valiant attempt to rule this out on philosophical grounds, in the end his argument against the measurement of sense-distances did not have the force of his argument against Fechner's measurement of sensation intensities.

Consequently, Guild had left an opening that the psychologists could have exploited had they been prepared to think about the foundations of quantitative methods. Indeed, the opening was wider than yet indicated. Campbell, who in the published proceedings of the Committee remained silent on the issue of sense-distances, had previously made a pertinent observation:

> Almost everyone will agree, not only that a buttercup is yellower than milk and milk than snow, but also that the difference between a buttercup and milk is greater than the difference between milk and snow. Now it can easily be shown that if we could order in this way all of the differences between sensations, that is to say not only first differences, but also second differences, third differences, and so on indefinitely,[20] then a process of measurement would be possible by means of which we could assign numerals quite uniquely. . . . Here is a system of measurement theoretically possible; the algebra of it is simple, but need not be elaborated. For as a matter of fact, we can rarely, if ever, order any differences higher than the first or second. (Campbell, 1933a, p. 571)

Obviously, when Campbell referred to this as a process or system of measurement, he was unaware that it enabled an indirect test of additivity and was only thinking of it as a means of making numerical assignments to a pre-established quantity (i.e., as a way of solving the instrumental, not the scientific task of quantification). It is a sad irony that he was so near to a more complete understanding of quantification and one that could have been usefully extended to psychophysics. One cannot help but feel that Campbell was so entrenched in his prejudices, first, that

---

[20] By first differences, Campbell meant differences between sensations, by second differences, differences between differences between sensations, and so on.

'physics is the science of measurement' (1928, p. v) (and therefore psychological attributes are necessarily excluded) and, second, that his processes of fundamental and derived measurement were the only possible routes to quantification, that in his mind there was no possibility of defending psychophysical measurement. From Campbell's point of view, the only task of the Committee was to convince the psychologists of this.

The psychologists, for their part, lacked the resources to exploit the deficiencies in Guild's critique. What Campbell had failed to recognise in his discussion of the ordering of differences were two important facts. First, there is a trade-off between the number of first differences and the need for higher order differences, so that given even a modest number of first differences, higher order differences are not required in order to obtain relatively good estimates of the measures of the elements (e.g., sensations) involved (Krantz, *et al.*, 1971). Second, quite independent of that issue, with just a small number of different stimuli (say, at least six) and attending only to first differences between sensations, tests of additivity can be undertaken (i.e., tests of Hölder's axioms for intervals within a straight line). Had these facts been known to the psychologists, both Guild's critique and the generality of Campbell's theory of measurement could have been resoundingly refuted.

The one psychologist whose background qualified him to carry the debate to this level was Brown, for he had dealt with the concept of orders upon differences in earlier publications (e.g., Brown and Thomson, 1921). However, Brown's contribution to the published reports only amounted to about 150 words (Brown, 1938a) and, while he was 'not satisfied that he [Guild] has demolished the case for the direct measurement of *contrastes sensibles* (Delbœuf), commonly translated as "sense distances"' (p. 330), and that 'a very much fuller discussion of the problem is needed, in the light of recent experimental work' (p. 330), he did nothing to advance the discussion. It should be noted, of course, that Brown was at this time nearing sixty years of age and had for the preceding twenty years diverted his energies from quantification to the practice of psychotherapy. He had arrived at the view that 'the observations of psychology are primarily qualitative, not quantitative' (1938b, p. 51). Brown's comments were those of a scientist no longer deeply interested in the issue of psychophysical measurement.

So, how did the other psychologists respond to Guild's critique? It completely overwhelmed one. Thouless, said of it that 'This account of what is meant by "measurement" is excellently clear. I think "measurement" is primarily the physicist's term and I am willing to accept what they say as to what the word means' (Thouless, 1938, p. 328). However, Thouless's capitulation was not typical. Most who made comments wished to find a place for psychophysical measurement but, in the light of Guild's critique, had no idea how. Opposing Guild's critique, Drever had been assigned the task of presenting the case in defence of psychophysical measurement. He correctly understood Guild as arguing that

... In order that we may be able to establish a quantitative relation between the intensity of the physical stimulus and the intensity of the sensation, we must be able to measure not only the physical stimulus in physical units but the sensation in sensation units. (Drever, 1938, p. 332)

Beyond that, however, he was out of his depth. Drever thought that it was theoretically possible to hypothesise that sensation intensity is measurable and because, even in physical measurement, 'for practical purposes all measurement is ultimately in terms of space' (p. 333), he reasoned that it is not necessary that sensation be measured in sensation units. Thus, he concluded,

... in order to relate quantitatively stimulus intensity and sensation intensity, it is not necessary that we should be able to measure each in units of the same kind, but merely to measure the one – the stimulus intensity – and determine the manner in which the other – sensation intensity – varies in dependence upon the former. (Drever, 1938, p. 333)

Those for whom this seems an adequate response to Guild have already assumed that the procedures devised by psychophysicists to measure sensation can be taken as doing just that. In other words, Drever begged the question. It is not surprising that in the Final Report, Drever was not called upon again to give the case for the measurability of sensation. It was left, separately, to Craik and R. J. Bartlett.

Craik (1940b) and Bartlett (1940a) expressed the view, put earlier by Richardson (1933), that a more liberal understanding of

154 *The status of psychophysical measurement*

measurement was required to accommodate psychophysics. Craik wrote that

It is important not to base the definition of measurement only on the most stringent instances, such as length; for 'measurement' is applied also to scales of temperature, density, time, etc., which fail to fulfil one or other of the conditions which are fulfilled by length. (Craik, 1940b, p. 343)

Having said that, one might have expected Craik to set about the difficult task of 'finding a definition of measurement which fits its use in other sciences' (Craik, 1940b, p. 343) and then proceed to inquire 'whether the facts obtained by psycho-physical experiments entitle the estimation of sensation magnitude to be subsumed under this definition' (Craik, 1940b, p. 343). Craik knew what was needed but declined to attempt the hard intellectual work. Instead, he offered the opinion that if the assumption of psychophysical measurement 'can help to co-ordinate the data . . . I feel much in favour of giving such measurement a chance' (Craik, 1940b, p. 343), as if there was no underlying question of the truth or falsity of the assumption. Bartlett wanted, like Brown, the concept of measurement to cover procedures based upon judgments of sameness of sense-distances. As noted already, such suggestions are not without merit, but the entire matter needed much more rigorous development than the psychologists gave it and the issue needed addressing in a systematic fashion, one that attempted to come to grips with the logic of measurement. Nothing short of that could, at this stage, satisfy the critical mind. Unfortunately, the psychologists' 'English' methodological attitude proved too strong.

The psychologists on the Ferguson Committee failed the interests of critical inquiry and the scientific interests of their discipline. They failed because when confronted with the challenges inspired by Campbell's theory of measurement they made no attempt to address the relevant issues in a disinterested, systematic fashion. In general, their approach was dominated by an interest in defending psychophysics as a form of measurement, rather than by addressing the methodological issue dispassionately. Furthermore, they made no serious attempt to understand the general features of measurement prior to addressing the issue of the specific conditions necessary or sufficient for psychophysical measurement.

The response to the Final Report

Although the Campbell camp easily won the debate, the case against the measurement of sense-distances was, objectively, not conclusive and Campbell's attitude revealed serious blind-spots. Nonetheless, the physicists were right to raise the issues they did. They were really doing nothing more than raising the quantity objection within the framework of Campbell's theory of measurement. It was up to the psychologists to examine their quantitative practices in the light of this. Had the psychologists been more interested in the logic of quantification, as a purely methodological issue, the interests of psychology as a science would have been better served.

THE RESPONSE TO THE FINAL REPORT

The first response to the Final Report was by a committee member, R. J. Bartlett, who perhaps, as president of section J (psychology) of the British Association for the Advancement of Science, felt a duty to comment. What he offered (R. J. Bartlett, 1940b) was a review of the current state of quantitative psychology. He provided examples of the variety of numerical data collected in psychology sandwiched between expressions of pious hope. Bartlett noted the criticisms of the physicists on the Ferguson Committee, expressed again the view that Campbell's theory of measurement currently set the hurdle too high for quantitative psychology, and quoted Spearman to the effect that 'the path of science is paved with achievements of the allegedly unachievable' (Bartlett, 1940b, p. 423). He concluded by asking

... does it matter much if some continue to believe ... that our data contain nothing 'that can properly be called measurements' and that it is presumption for us to think that, in any reasonable sense, our data, theories, methods and results constitute 'a systematic science'? After all there is a sense in which logical and mathematical proofs are what the psychology of advertising has called 'rationalisation copy'. (Bartlett, 1940b, p. 441)

Bartlett apparently could not see that the issue of whether or not psychology was a 'systematic science' was logically distinct from the issue of whether or not psychological attributes are quantitative. However, there is no doubt a causal connection between the manner in which these two issues are addressed: a science that refuses to consider the latter issue scientifically, may damage its credentials to be any kind of science at all. Bartlett's attitude is a

156 *The status of psychophysical measurement*

fair summary of what Hearnshaw (1964) describes as the 'English' attitude to methodology: the real work of science goes on in the laboratory and methodological discussion is a mere rationalisation of laboratory results. Hence, Bartlett recommended that quantitative psychologists proceed as usual, describing their procedures as measurement, despite the Campbellian critique, in the confident hope that others outside the discipline would eventually describe them in the same way. Bartlett, like most of his colleagues, still apparently declined to recognise that measurement presumes quantitative attributes and the distinction between quantitative and non-quantitative attributes is an empirical distinction. He also declined to recognise that scientists who consistently presume answers to empirical questions thereby bring science itself into disrepute.

The effect of the two reports of the Ferguson Committee upon psychology was to indicate the importance of the definition of measurement. In contrast to the English, the Americans displayed a refreshing intellectual boldness in their approach to this problem and a willingness to meet Campbell on equal terms. Other than Stevens, there were two American psychologists who attempted to think through the implications for psychological measurement of the Ferguson Committee's Final Report. These were Thomas Reese and Andrew Comrey.

Reese's response to the Campbellian critique of psychological measurement was a model of scientific sanity (Reese, 1943). He accepted a general statement of Campbell's definition of measurement as 'the assignment of numerals to systems according to scientific laws' (Reese, 1943, p. 43), but interpreted it, like Nagel, as including 'ordinal measurement' because establishing an order requires discovering scientific laws as well. In this he may not have differed much from other psychologists but, practically alone amongst his peers, he did not flinch from what such a definition implies. It implies that measurement of all forms must be based upon the experimental demonstration of the relevant empirical relations, ordinal and/or additive: 'the physicists do not demand that psychologists immediately cease demonstrating those relations which they are able to demonstrate; but they do point out that the psychologists should not interpret their data on the basis of undemonstrated relations' (1943, p. 43). According to Reese psychologists needed to commence an experimental research programme, testing for the existence of the relevant relations. As he so aptly put it,

> It is true that no subjective magnitude has been measured fundamentally. The belief of the author that they may be so measured is an hypothesis. Only experimentation can give the answer. But it seems that the major objections of the physicists have been answered. There are no a priori reasons why psychological magnitudes may not be measured fundamentally. Measurement in psychology and physics are in no sense different. Physicists can measure when they can find the operations by which they may meet the necessary criteria; psychologists have but to do the same. They need not worry about mysterious differences between the meaning of measurement in the two sciences. (Reese, 1943, p. 49)

One can only speculate about why the psychologists on the Ferguson Committee could not see with equal clarity. Was it the force of the measurability thesis, the 'English' methodological attitude, or some combination of both? Reese's words deserve to be quoted in every text on psychological measurement. His own experimental work was not without its serious limitations, but its importance lay in the direction it pioneered. It is of the first importance to note that, at the time, no psychologists followed where Reese led. In the immediate aftermath of the Ferguson Committee, the measurability thesis came to be protected by construction of a defensive ideology.

Signs of its emergence are in the approach that Comrey offered. He saw ordinal attributes, on the one hand, and additive attributes, on the other, as constituting opposite poles of a continuum. Between these extremes, he believed, lay most instances of psychological measurement, better than ordinal but not satisfying Campbell's conditions for fundamental measurement. As noted in the discussion of Johnson (1936) above, this was a very generous assessment of most forms of psychological measurement. Comrey (1950, 1951) and Guilford and Comrey (1951) meticulously set forth the empirical conditions necessary for an ordinal structure, but at no time mentioned relevant experimental evidence for any psychological attributes. A consensus had developed, unsupported by serious research, that psychological measurement was at least ordinal scaling. Comrey also set forth empirical conditions of the kind described by Campbell for fundamental measurement. In Comrey's view, these latter conditions were never satisfied by any natural attributes, be they physical or psychological: there are just approximations to them, with physical attributes like length approximating them much better than other physical attributes (like temperature) and, of course, all physical measurable attributes approximating them much better than any psychological attributes. Now, in so far as, in the testing of these conditions, one considers objects and operationally definable relations between objects, Comrey's assessment is correct. The Campbellian conditions for fundamental measurement are too stringent if they are expected to hold for humanly manageable operations and discriminations upon objects. This observation provided Comrey with an interesting defence against Campbell. What Campbell thought of as a dichotomy (measurement vs non-measurement), Comrey saw as a matter of degree (approximations to an idealised set of conditions). Seen from this perspective, the gulf between psychological and physical measurement no longer seemed unbridgeable.

In both cases (i.e., ordinal attributes and those closely approximating fundamental measurement), thought Comrey, the numbers assigned to objects take their empirical meaning from the operationally defined relations between objects. Hence, he inferred, the general principle, of which both the numerical representation of ordinal attributes and fundamental measurement are but two instances, is this: *the meanings given numbers assigned in any type of measurement are merely an expression of the operations performed* (Guilford & Comrey, 1951, p. 525; italics in original). On the basis of this principle, any instance of the use of numbers in psychology is able to be interpreted by considering the operations performed in assigning the numbers. Comrey consistently declined to offer a general definition of measurement. However, he thought that what most instances had in common was this: *numbers are used to represent the results of certain operations that have been performed* (Guilford and Comrey, 1951, p. 507; italics in original). This, together with the above principle, gave Comrey's conception great scope, even if very limited theoretical value. Almost by definition, any procedure for assigning numbers to objects or events involves operations of some kind, and so the numerical assignments are able to be interpreted via these operations. However, this approach is of very limited theoretical value in so far as it is supposed that the attribute measured is a theoretical construct whose meaning transcends the operations involved.

The response to the Final Report   159

For example, if a psychologist supposed, as Spearman for example had, that general ability was an attribute of a person's intellectual functioning (a force driving the engines of the mind as Spearman (1923) believed) which could, in turn, be used to explain that person's performance on an ability test, then a measure of general ability derived from that performance could not, without circularity, be defined by the operations of test performance. If all that a particular level of general ability means, employing Comrey's principle, is a performance of a certain class, then the concept of general ability cannot be invoked to explain performance of that kind because the explanation and what is to be explained are the same. In so far as a scientific explanation of some effect identifies causes and in so far as cause and effect must always be logically distinct occurrences, theoretical quantities defined by Comrey's principle fail as explanatory concepts.

Comrey would not have been greatly troubled by this kind of criticism because he was more concerned with the practical utility of psychological measures than with their value as explanations. As he put the matter,

> If numerical methods of description can be applied which aid in describing and predicting human behavior, then it is absurd to object to their use on the basis of a failure to satisfy a set of conditions designed for a different context. In evaluating methods of measurement in psychology, and in devising new ones, the practical purposes which these methods are to serve must be considered. (Comrey, 1950, p. 222)

Comrey was especially keen to press this point regarding mental tests: 'It seems reasonable to assert that mental testing is and will be for some time essentially an empirical science with certain rather well-defined practical objectives rather than primarily a theoretical scientific enterprise' (1951, p. 330). What Comrey's thinking betrays here is a serious confusion concerning the practical usefulness of certain procedures and the aims of science. As Cronbach[21] and Gleser (1957) later came to acknowledge, the usefulness of tests in predictive or decision-making contexts is an issue independent of whether or not tests measure psychological attributes. Cronbach and Gleser advocated replacing the 'measurement model' by the 'decision theory model' and, while

---

[21] It is interesting to note that in his 1951 paper Comrey acknowledged the critical input of L. J. Cronbach.

160 *The status of psychophysical measurement*

this recommendation may have value in specific, practical contexts, the issue of whether or not such tests measure anything remains a genuine scientific issue. As already noted, discovering that a particular mental test is useful in a particular context raises the scientific issue of why that should be so, but in and of itself, it does not contribute towards settling that scientific issue and, certainly, does not imply that anything is measured.

In fact, in his thinking on these issues, Comrey had brought quantitative psychology to a crossroads: psychologists could treat their quantitative procedures as purely practical tools designed for specific tasks such as prediction (in which case the issue of their status as instruments of measurement could be realistically recognised as presently unknown and the rhetoric of measurement could be dispensed with); or quantitative psychologists could continue to employ the rhetoric of measurement in describing their procedures, interpreting what was measured via the principles of operationism. The fact that Comrey had declined to redefine measurement reveals how fluid the concept had become in psychology. There was now conceptual space for a redefinition and Stevens' approach systematically developed the second of the above alternatives.

Stevens' sone scale (Stevens and Davis, 1938) for the measurement of loudness had been considered by the Ferguson Committee in its final report (Craik, 1940a), which gave Stevens a special interest in the reports of that committee. Stevens' response was to propose a new definition of measurement (1946). It was a definition entirely consonant with the operationist spirit then dominant in psychology. If measurement involves making numerical assignments to things (as the representational view has it) according to definite operations then, in accordance with operationism, measurement itself is operationally defined by the general features of this process. In total disrespect of Campbell's pretensions to have delivered the last word on measurement, Stevens wrote, 'Paraphrasing N. R. Campbell (Final Report, p. 340), we may say that measurement, in the broadest sense, is defined as the assignment of numerals to objects and events according to rules' (1946, p. 677).

Stevens knew that while Campbell often used similar turns of phrase (e.g., 'Measurement is the assignment of numerals to represent properties' (Campbell, 1920, p. 267)), there could be no

The response to the Final Report   161

ambiguity about Campbell's view that 'not every assignment of numerals is measurement' (Campbell, 1938, p. 122) and, so, what Stevens wrote was in no way a paraphrase of Campbell's intention. Indeed, what Campbell had written was that 'Measurement in its widest sense may be defined as the assignment of numerals to things so as to represent facts or conventions about them' (Campbell, 1940, p. 340) and had immediately begun to sketch what, according to his view, the relevant facts and conventions are. Stevens knew this because he quoted it on the final page of his article, attributing it to 'one of its [the Ferguson Committee's] members' and calling it 'the most liberal and useful definition of measurement' (1946, p. 680). What Stevens was doing was implying that the major proponent of the representational view, Campbell himself, had failed to understand his own definition of measurement.

Stevens' reference to Campbell, here, was doubly cheeky because Stevens proceeded to unfold his own theory of the different kinds of measurement scales, the now famous nominal, ordinal, interval, and ratio scales, as if it was a simple derivation from Campbell's own definition. Clearly, Stevens was playing a game, the subtext of which was that Campbell had spent the seven years of the Ferguson Committee's life arguing to exclude psychophysical measurement when in fact his own definition of measurement already entailed the contrary conclusion. Even if both attitudes were out of place, Stevens' confidence was a good match for Campbell's smugness.

CHAPTER 7

A definition made to measure

The number system is merely a model, to be used in whatever way we please.
(S. S. Stevens)

Measurement is the business of pinning numbers on things.
(S. S. Stevens)

The claim to be able to measure psychological attributes was thought to conflict with the Campbellian version of the quantity objection. Almost alone of his generation, Reese sought to defend the measurability thesis by a programme of empirical research. Instead of joining him, mainstream American quantitative psychologists responded in the tradition of Fechner: criticisms were deflected, not faced. Even Comrey's proposal that psychology's quantitative procedures be regarded simply as practical tools was unacceptable to those benefiting by the rhetoric of measurement. Deflecting the quantity objection required neutralising the representational theory's emphasis upon empirical tests of quantitative structure. Operationism provided the key. As a result of the recent revolutions in physics,[1] operationism enjoyed considerable vogue within psychology, where it was interpreted by Stevens as a radical, liberating intellectual force. In Stevens' hands, it seemed to liberate modern psychology from the quantity objection.

Coming at a time of postwar expansion within the discipline, the *Handbook of Experimental Psychology* (1951), edited by Stevens, was very influential.[2] Chapter 1, entitled 'Mathematics, Measure-

---

[1] Those ushering in Relativity and Quantum Theories.

[2] The speed and the extent of the influence of Stevens' views on measurement within American psychology was really quite remarkable. One factor contributing to this was Stevens' membership of the 'Psychological Round Table' (see Benjamin, 1977) from its foundation in 1936 until 1946, the period during which his theory was formed. This highly select group of young American experimental psychologists met annually to dis-

162

A definition made to measure 163

ment, and Psychophysics', was written by him. It was the most complete exposition of his theory of measurement. A reviewer warned that 'Some students may be lulled into a false sense of security, thinking that they now know the essential relations of numbers and mathematics to the psychologist's operations' (Grant, 1952, p. 159). 'Lulled' was right. Stevens' message eased the minds of psychologists unlike anything they had heard about measurement before. His views dovetailed so neatly with the needs of the time that earlier conceptions of measurement were rendered inoperative and largely forgotten. His definition was absorbed so smoothly into psychology's storehouse of conventional wisdom that he had cause to complain that 'many authors feel no need to cite the origin' (Stevens, 1974, p. 409).

Stevens' theory of measurement was integral to his psychophysical research programme. He wrote: 'My own central problem throughout the 1930s was measurement, because the quantification of the sensory attributes seemed impossible unless the nature of measurement could be properly understood' (Stevens, 1974, p. 409). Located at Harvard University, he was exposed to a range of new ideas deriving from the physicist P. W. Bridgman, the philosopher A. N. Whitehead, the mathematician G. D. Birkhoff, and, importantly, members of the Vienna Circle, then arriving from Europe, including Herbert Feigl and Rudolph Carnap.[3] Stevens assumed the role of mediator between the new philosophical trends and psychology. It was a shrewd strategy, for his audience not only received an account of measurement that indulged their illusions, they were also given a stiff dose of 'up to date' philosophy into the bargain.

For psychologists Stevens' definition had the ring of an obvious truth. When a person performing a psychophysics task adjusts one stimulus magnitude to what is judged to be half the intensity of another, and the experimenter assigns corresponding numerical values to the sensations, there is a sense in which this is the assignment of numerals to events. Or when, for example, in

cuss new ideas in psychology, and the list of members included many who were to become important leaders in psychology in the 1950s and 1960s. Stevens certainly promoted his ideas on measurement with this group, as is evident from the programme given for the 1941 meeting (Benjamin, 1977).

[3] According to Still (1997), Stevens belonged to a group that met regularly to discuss the philosophy of science, including Bridgman, Carnap and G. D. Birkhoff.

testing the intellectual abilities of a person, the number of correct answers is transformed into an IQ or some other kind of score, there is a sense in which the numeral expressing that score is assigned to that person (an object). Stevens' definition was tailor-made for both the nature and circumstances of quantitative practice in psychology and it excluded nothing that psychologists called measurement. However, face validity is insufficient, especially when the proposed definition could be construed as opportunistic. A methodological rationalisation was required to legitimise its currency. Supplying this was Stevens' genius. He drew upon three sources: representational measurement theory, Bridgman's operationism, and the logical positivist view of mathematics.

STEVENS' THOROUGHGOING REPRESENTATIONALISM

For Russell and Campbell, the logic of measurement was that of representation. However, Russell thought of it as the numerical representation of ordinal structures only, because he thought that measurement was only of magnitudes and magnitudes were, by definition, ordinal. In this respect his representationalism was compromised by an unexorcised ghost of the classical paradigm, viz., order as a feature of quantity. Likewise, Campbell's theory, that measurement required additive empirical structures, was also adulterated by classical residues. Even more liberal theorists, such as Cohen and Nagel (1934), distinguished measurement 'in the strict sense' (p. 296) from the numerical representation of non-quantitative structures. Half-heartedness always invites the possibility of being thoroughgoing. Stevens accepted the challenge and proposed that the numerical representation of any kind of empirical relation is measurement.

For Stevens, measurement is possible only because there is an isomorphism between features of numerical structures and empirical relations among objects and events. He amplified this thesis as follows:

. . . in dealing with the aspects of objects we can invoke empirical operations for determining equality (the basis for classifying things), for rank ordering, and for determining when differences and ratios between the aspects of objects are equal. The conventional series of numerals – the series in which by definition each member has a successor – yields to analogous operations: We can identify the members of the series and

A definition made to measure   165

classify them. We know their order as given by convention. We can determine equal differences, as $7 - 5 = 4 - 2$, and equal ratios, as $10/5 = 6/3$. This isomorphism between the formal system and the empirical operations performable with material things justifies the use of the formal system as a *model* to stand for aspects of the empirical world. (Stevens, 1951, p. 23)

According to Stevens, any numerical modelling of empirical systems is measurement.[4] He believed that Russell and Campbell had taken specific features of ordinal and additive models as definitive, rather than making numerical representation alone the essence of measurement. Stevens proposed an uncluttered view that reduced measurement to a single, simple concept.

However, at first sight,[5] it appears that Stevens' representationalism does not entail his definition of measurement. It seems to entail a much narrower definition than the one he is famous for, something like, *measurement is the assignment of numerals to represent empirical relations between objects and events*. Of course, if, in his definition, Stevens meant by *rule* an exclusively representational rule, then his definition would have been entirely representational. Stevens made it clear, however, that he did not just mean this when he stressed that 'any rule' would do and that 'provided a consistent rule is followed, some form of measurement is achieved' (Stevens, 1959, p. 19).

An indisputably representational rule for the making of numerical assignments to objects or events is one in which the structure of some attribute of the objects or events is identified independently of any numerical assignments and then, subsequently, numerical assignments are made to represent that attribute's structure. For example, consider hardness. Minerals can be ordered according to whether or not they scratch one another when rubbed together. The relation, x scratches y, between minerals, is transitive and asymmetric and these properties can be established prior to any numerical assignments being made (as, for example, Mohs' scale of hardness (Jerrard and McNeill, 1992). I call this *external* representation because the attribute represented exists externally to (or independently of) any numerical

[4] Stevens (1968) broadened his conception of measurement to include not just numerical modelling but the modelling of empirical systems by any abstract system.

[5] For example, Michell (1986) thought he detected a hiatus between Stevens' theory and definition of measurement.

166   *Stevens' thoroughgoing representationalism*

assignments, in the sense that even if the assignments were never made, the attribute would still be there and possess exactly the same structure. This is the kind of representation that Campbell thought was involved in fundamental measurement and which, he argued, psychophysics lacked with respect to additivity.

Other kinds of consistent but less obviously representational rules are possible. The opposite of external representation is *internal* representation. This occurs when the attribute represented, or its putative structure, is logically dependent upon the numerical assignments made, in the sense that had the numerical assignments not been made, then either the attribute would not exist or some component of its structure would be absent. An extreme case would be that of assigning different numbers to each of a class of identical things (say, white marbles) and on that basis defining an attribute. The attribute represented by such assignments would not be logically independent of them and, so, had they not been made, the attribute would not exist. A less extreme case is where an independent attribute may exist, but the structure that it is taken to have depends upon numerical assignments made. For example, people may be assigned numbers according to nationality (say, Australian, 1; French, 2; American, 3; Belgian, 4; ..., etc.) and then the attribute of nationality may be taken to have the ordinal structure of the numbers assigned. In this case, had numerical assignments not been made, the attribute (nationality) would still exist but the supposed ordinal structure would not. No representationalist explicitly recommends internal representation, although Rozeboom (1966), without calling it by the same name, has drawn attention to it as a logical possibility.

Between these poles lie the cases of most interest to psychologists, what we might call *ambiguous* representation. In such cases it is not known whether or not the attribute or its putative structure exists independently of the numerical assignments made. Mental test scores provide a good example. Suppose two people, i and j, get the same score on test X and that another person, k, gets a different score on X. Then, in the most straightforward, error-free sense,[6] if these test scores externally represent an attri-

---

[6] I discuss only the most straightforward sense here. Obviously, most psychometricians would favour a less straightforward sense of representation, one in which sameness or difference of test scores only indicated sameness or difference of the attribute represented with a specified probability. For example, Rasch's theory of test scores,

A definition made to measure

bute, then i and j will share a level of that attribute, one which k lacks, and this attribute will be identifiable independently of the test scores assigned. No one knows whether or not scores on any psychological test represent levels of an independently identifiable attribute because, as yet, no such attribute has been independently identified. It is not unreasonable to hypothesise that such an attribute exists. Against this hypothesis, it is known that distinct causal systems (as persons i and j must be) can systematically produce the same effect (the same score on a test) under similar conditions because of the action of quite different internal causes. In the case of performances on mental tests, this alternative is *prima facie* plausible because exactly the same test score can result from quite different patterns of right and wrong answers, indicating the possibility of causal processes involving different attributes resulting in the same score. All hypotheses in this area require rigorous testing before any are accepted. Despite this, persons i and j have an attribute in common (the attribute defined by the fact of their obtaining the same test score) and there is a trivial sense in which the number assigned (the test score) represents that attribute, but the issue of whether or not anything over and above that is represented is not obvious. Furthermore, if something is externally represented by test scores, the issue of precisely what sort of structure is represented (e.g., nominal, ordinal, interval or ratio) remains.

The fact that Stevens' definition of measurement subsumes all three cases under his concept means that, something which for earlier representational theorists was a most important issue, is obscured. As the representational theory had been understood by Russell, Campbell, and Nagel, the existence of the empirical relations numerically represented must be logically independent of the numerical assignments made. That is, these empirical relations must be such that it is always possible (in principle, at least) to demonstrate their existence without first making numerical assignments. To do this, it is necessary to give an adequate characterisation of the formal (i.e., topic-neutral) properties of the relations involved. For example, classification (the empirical basis

---

mentioned in Chapter 1, allows people of the same ability to obtain different scores and people of different levels of ability to get the same score on particular occasions.

of a nominal scale) requires a relation possessing the formal properties of transitivity, symmetry and reflexivity (i.e., an equivalence relation). For the scientific mind, the issue of whether or not an empirical relation has these properties can only be assessed by scientific investigation. Simply to presume that a consistent rule for assigning numerals to objects represents an empirical relation possessing such properties is not to discover that it does; it is the opposite. Whenever a transitive, symmetric and reflexive relation is discovered by observational methods, independently of any numerical assignments, then numerals can be assigned to the objects or events involved to represent this equivalence relation. For example, humans can be classified according to nationality by a set of well-defined procedures that is logically independent of any numerical assignments that might subsequently be used to code (or represent) that attribute.

Likewise, an empirical relation only qualifies as an order, if it is transitive and asymmetric, properties which also will not be taken for granted by the scientific mind. The empirical characteristics necessary for fundamental measurement in Campbell's sense are even more demanding and so even less able to be presumed. The precise definition of the empirical conditions necessary and sufficient for various kinds of numerical representation was not rigorously systematised until Suppes and Zinnes (1963). However, enough work (including that of Hölder (1901)) had been done on this matter by the time Stevens was writing for it to be apparent that if measurement is the numerical representation of independently existing empirical relations, then measurement involves demanding necessary and sufficient empirical conditions. Stevens was quite deliberately departing from that view and invoking a much wider concept.

This wider concept depended upon the idea that the existence of relations between things is not logically independent of the operations used to identify those relations. Thus, Stevens could also write that measurement was possible not simply because of an isomorphism between numerical and empirical relations but, also, 'only because there exists an isomorphism between the properties of the numeral series and the empirical *operations that we can perform* with the aspects of objects' (Stevens, 1951, p. 23; my italics). According to his view, it is not the 'aspects of objects' (i.e., the independently existing properties of or relations between objects) that are represented in measurement, as representationalists like Russell and Campbell had thought. Strictly speaking, from the operational perspective, there are no such properties or relations and numerical representation can only be of relations defined via the operations performed upon these objects. This distinction is vital for a correct understanding of Stevens' position. The concept of operation, for Stevens, was science's fundamental category.

STEVENS' OPERATIONISM[7]

In 1927 P. W. Bridgman's *The Logic of Modern Physics* was published.[8] According to Bridgman, earlier physicists, such as Newton, had made the mistake of defining physical concepts via properties; however, in Bridgman's view, 'the proper definition of a concept is not in terms of its properties but in terms of actual operations' (1927, p. 6). Indeed, he thought that 'we mean by any concept nothing more than a set of operations; *the concept is synonymous with the corresponding set of operations*' (1927, p. 5). For example, according to Bridgman, the length of an object is not a property it possesses independently of us (such as its extension in space) but is, instead, constituted by our operations of length measurement (such as bringing the object into the appropriate relation to a tape measure). This now famous slogan embodied Bridgman's philosophical nihilism: there is no nature beyond our knowledge of nature and no knowledge of nature beyond our operations. It also expressed his optimism: he thought he had found the key to doing science, the use of which would 'render unnecessary the services of unborn Einsteins' (1927, p. 24) by eliminating the possibility of future scientific revolutions. It was the promise of this key that attracted psychologists.

While Bridgman argued his case in simple, non-technical terms, giving the impression of presenting a common sense, home spun, grass-roots philosophy of science emerging from the laboratory practices of a successful scientist, the fact is that his views were closely informed by turn-of-the-century positivism and

---

[7] Stevens' attempt to construct an operationist philosophy of science has recently been discussed in some detail by Hardcastle (1995).

[8] Bridgman was a leading American physicist, professor at Harvard University and winner of a Nobel Prize for research on high pressure phenomena.

170 *Stevens' thoroughgoing representationalism*

pragmatism (Moyer, 1991a, b). It is not surprising then that his views were enthusiastically endorsed by like-minded philosophers and scientists and, especially, by psychologists, already under the influence of behaviourism. The leader of the Vienna Circle,[9] Moritz Schlick, deeply impressed by Bridgman's book, wrote to him on behalf of Herbert Feigl about the possibility of postdoctoral research at Harvard under Bridgman. Feigl arrived in 1930 and introduced 'the university's psychologists more fully to Bridgman's operational approach' (Moyer, 1991b, p. 392). A few years later, Stevens (1935a, b, 1936a) presented his own version of operationism.

Operationism was invariably characterised as empiricism, indeed, as 'pure empiricism' (Bridgman, 1927, p. 3). Empiricism,[10] it may have been, but it is more closely related to the anti-realist 'empiricism' of Berkeley[11] than to the natural empirical realism of most scientists. Just as Berkeley thought of reality as entirely constituted by our perception of it, so the operationists thought of scientific reality as completely defined by repertoires of scientific operations. Just as perception is the process by which a perceiver is acquainted with whatever is perceived, so an operation (in Bridgman's sense) is the process by which a scientist identifies something (as an instance of some concept). Furthermore, just as with a perceives x, the fact that x is perceived does not entail that x cannot exist without being perceived (as Berkeley mistakenly thought); so, with a identifies (via operation o) x, the fact that x is identified does not entail that x cannot exist without being identified (via operation o). But if x can exist without being identified via operation o, then x and o cannot mean the same thing (i.e., they must be logically distinct). Hence, operationism is false. In their own ways, both Berkeley and Bridgman confused the knowing of something, with the thing known. Egregiously, each treated

---

[9] The Vienna Circle were scientifically minded philosophers who met in Vienna throughout the 1920s and 30s developing the doctrines now called logical positivism. Some (e.g., Rudolph Carnap and Herbert Feigl) later became significant philosophers in America.

[10] Empiricism is the view that knowledge derives only from our sensory experience of things. However, if empiricism is also that at least some knowledge is of independently existing situations, then operationism is *not* a form of empiricism.

[11] Linking operationism to the British empiricist, Bishop Berkeley, is not far-fetched. The intellectual impulse underlying operationism is clearly evident in Berkeley ([1721] 1951).

Stevens' operationism 171

his own special confusion as if it was a revolutionary philosophical insight.

According to Stevens' version of operationism, 'A word or statement means something . . . only if the criteria of its applicability or truth consist of concrete operations which can be performed' (1936a, p. 94). This sounds as if Stevens thought that the meaning of a concept is not synonymous with the operations involved but rather, the existence of these operations only provides a necessary condition for meaning and truth. This, however, is not the case. Stevens held that the basis of scientific concept formation was classification, that 'Classification can proceed only when we have criteria defining the conditions of class-inclusion, and these criteria are essentially operational tests' (1939, p. 233) and that 'the concept of that class *is defined by* the operations which determine inclusion within the class' (1939, p. 234, my italics) (see also Stevens (1942)). In this respect his position did not differ from Bridgman's.[12]

In reshaping the understanding of measurement, Stevens' problem was this. He had to find a way of relaxing the requirement, prescribed by earlier representationalists, that measurement always involves external representation. However, he had to find a way of doing this that (i) avoided the obviously indefensible excesses of internal representation, and yet (ii) could be given a methodological defence. His understanding of measurement as the numerical representation of operationally defined empirical relations, gave representationism the new twist required for it to entail his definition of measurement, and thereby for it to include not just his psychophysics, but all psychological quantitative procedures, past, present and future. A rule for assigning numerals to objects or events could always be taken as representing empirical relations if those relations were understood as operationally defined by that rule itself. If objects do not possess properties or stand in relations which are logically independent of scientists' operations (as operationists held), then the earlier distinctions made between external, internal and ambiguous representations

---

[12] Stevens' view of science differed from Bridgman's in at least one respect. Stevens thought science was a 'social convention' (1935b, p. 327). His view that 'from the social criterion of truth there is no appeal' (1936a, p. 97) should warm the heart of modern social constructionists (like Lovie, 1997) who otherwise, inexplicably, want to disown their philosophical harbinger.

collapse. From the operational point of view, these three forms of representation are not three, but one. In all cases of measurement, from the operational perspective, the numbers assigned represent nothing that is not completely defined by the operations involved in the rule for making the assignments.[13] Any such rule must always deliver at least a nominal scale (in Stevens' terms): assigning numerals to objects or events according to that rule indirectly classifies them as the same (in the sense that they are assigned the same numeral) or different (if they are assigned different numerals). Hence, at least a nominal scale is always defined by every consistent assignment rule. This is a way of thinking which non-operationalists would adjudge viciously circular, but that is because they presume the existence of independent attributes and regard as trivial those which can *only* be defined via rules for making numerical assignments. The operational interpretation involves no such presumption. If the numerical assignment rule linked numerical ratios to the operationally defined empirical relations, then the resulting scale would be called, by Stevens, a ratio scale. This is the kind of thinking that lay behind Stevens' attempts at psychophysical measurement.

Prior to the publication of his influential measurement paper, Stevens had established a reputation within psychophysics. In fact, it was his sone scale (Stevens, 1936b) that the Ferguson Committee's Final Report (Ferguson *et al.*, 1940) singled out for special attention. Stevens claimed that certain psychophysical methods produced scales of 'true numerical magnitude' (1936b, p. 406), that is, scales of the sort that he was later to call ratio scales. The procedures considered by Stevens in this early paper required subjects to make direct judgments of numerical relations between the loudness of tones. For example, the subject was instructed to 'make a direct estimate by varying the intensity of one tone until it sounds half as loud as another' (1936b, p. 408). These methods anticipated the more general (direct) psychophys-

---

[13] Stevens was not so blatant as to say that once numbers have been assigned to objects or events according to a consistent rule, any properties of the numbers could be used to define 'empirical' relations. In fact his strictures on permissible statistics (see Michell, 1986) contradict such a position. Although, he never explicitly stated anywhere precisely what his view really was, looking through the lens of his practice he seems to have believed that 'empirical' relations could be defined via properties of the numerical assignment rule itself.

Stevens' operationism 173

ical methods of magnitude estimation and cross-modality matching later used by Stevens (e.g., Stevens, 1956).

Stevens applied his operationism to the interpretation of these methods. By a subjective scale or a scale of sensation, Stevens did not mean what Fechner and most subsequent mentalists had meant. Stevens denied that there was an inner, private world of experience that could be studied scientifically. He proposed another interpretation of the subject-matter of psychophysics.

Any attempt to define the term experience operationally or point out what, concretely, is meant by the philosopher's 'given' discloses at once that the discriminatory reaction is the only objective, verifiable thing denoted. Scientific psychology is operational and as such can have nothing to do with any private or inner experience for the simple reason that an operation for penetrating privacy is self-contradictory. Therefore, we need no longer think of immediate experience as the subject-matter of psychology. (Stevens, 1936a, p. 95)

Since he thought that what was really observed in the study of sensations was the discriminatory reactions of the subject, he concluded that 'a subjective scale is a scale of response' (1936b, p. 407), that is, a scale of discriminatory responses. Thus, for Stevens there was no hiatus between the discriminatory judgments made by the subject and the sensory intensities of which they had been taken to be judgments by an earlier generation of psychophysicists.

In this sense then, subjects' judgments could be taken at face value. Fechner had not thought that subjects could make direct, quantitative judgments of sensory intensity accurately enough, and so had resorted to his indirect psychophysical methods. If sensory intensity is intensity-as-judged, as Stevens contended, then there is no obstacle to eliciting direct judgments from subjects. Stevens also concluded that such judgments could be taken at face value as measurements of true numerical magnitude: '... the response of the observer who says "this is half as loud as that" is one which, for the purpose of erecting a subjective scale, can be accepted at its face value' (1936b, p. 407). This conclusion followed from his operationism: one tone's being half as loud as another may be operationally defined by the operation used to determine it, i.e., by the subject judging it to be so. As Stevens put it: 'With such a scale the operation of addition consists of changing the stimulus until the observer gives a particular

174   *Stevens' thoroughgoing representationalism*

response which indicates that a given relation of magnitudes has been achieved' (1936b, p. 407). The relation of magnitude between sensations was seen as being defined by the judgment operation itself. On this basis, Stevens proposed that

A scale, then, which would enable us to designate the *numerical* as well as the *intensive*[14] magnitude of an attribute of sensation can be constructed according to the criterion that, having assigned a particular number N to a given magnitude, the number $N/2$ shall be assigned to the magnitude which appears half as great to the experiencing individual. (Stevens, 1936b, p. 407)

The operationist concludes that a ratio scale is obtained because of the character of the assignment rule, viz., the subject is instructed to judge ratios. For such a procedure to count as ratio scale measurement, according to the non-operationist, subjects' responses must manifest a special sort of empirical structure. Just as a nominal scale requires a transitive, symmetric and reflexive empirical relation and an ordinal scale requires a transitive, asymmetric empirical relation, so a ratio scale requires empirical relations of a definite character.[15] Thus, to take numerical judgments as constituting measurements at face value, in accordance with operationism, is to resort to postulating what one wants instead of looking to see what is the case.[16]

Ironically, Stevens liked Russell's maxim: 'The method of "postulating" what we want has many advantages; they are the same as the advantages of theft over honest toil' (Russell, 1919, p. 71; quoted by Stevens, 1951, p. 14, 1958, p. 386). In this vein, he candidly conceded that (i) 'We postulate, among other things, that the subject knows what a given numerical ratio is and that he can make a valid judgment of the numerical relation between two values of a psychological attribute' (Stevens, 1951, p. 41); and (ii) 'If this postulate is thievery, it is certainly no petty larceny' (Stevens, 1951, p. 41). In admitting this, Stevens momentarily shifted from operationist to realist ways of thinking, but his

---

[14] Stevens is here using the term *intensive* to mean *ordinal*, a typical usage at that time (see, e.g., Cohen & Nagel, 1934).

[15] See Gage (1934a, b) and Fagot (1961) for an indication of these in the sort of context that Stevens' research fell into.

[16] Considering Stevens' more general direct psychophysical methods, later measurement theorists, such as Krantz (1972), Luce (1990) and Narens (1996), have made the relevant experimental tests explicit.

realism was not very serious. Stevens' writings reveal no meaning-ful engagement with the relevant empirical issues in the sense of attempting to formulate testable conditions necessary and sufficient for responses of this kind to be representable as a ratio scale. Indeed, Stevens wrote that 'the early loudness scale had become a scientific reality before a measurement theory capable of designating what kind of scale it was' (Stevens, 1975, p. 50). In science, there is nothing wrong with postulating what we want in a provisional sense. All scientific research involves assumptions of some kind. Properly understood, postulation in science need not be theft. It may be more like taking out a loan. However, just as borrowing becomes theft if repayment is declined, so conclusions conditional upon postulations cannot be claimed as scientific knowledge if no attempt is ever made to check the truth of the postulations. This means that Stevens' proposed psychophysical scales of measurement could never have been taken as a scientific reality while the underlying, empirical issue of quantity was neglected.

Given Stevens' injunction to one of his later critics ('attend to what I do and not to what I say' (1966b, p. 33)), his operationist psychophysics provides the primary basis for understanding his theory of scales of measurement. This theory is as widely accepted within psychology as is his definition, although its presentation by Stevens contains a convenient ambiguity. Even though Stevens never resiled from his operationism (see for example Stevens, 1966a, b), he never advertised it in his most influential papers on measurement theory (especially his 1946 and 1951 papers). A reader who knew nothing of his operationism might misinterpret the scope of Stevens' representationism, thinking that his theory of measurement scales was intended to apply only to external representation. The fact that Stevens believed that proponents of external representation (such as Suppes and Zinnes (1963)) had drifted 'off into the vacuum of abstraction'(Stevens, 1968, p. 854) because they attempted to specify the formal properties of empirical structures, adds weight to my rejection of such an interpretation for Stevens and, indeed, there are other considerations supporting this rejection.

If Stevens had intended his theory to apply only to external representations, then some of his examples were exceedingly ill-considered. When Suppes and Zinnes came to present their theory

176   *Stevens' thoroughgoing representationalism*

of scales of measurement (1963), they introduced the concept of an empirical relational system. This is an empirical structure, the relations within which are defined quite independently of any numerical assignments. Given Stevens' conceptual resources, he could have pursued a similar approach. He declined, making pronouncements such as 'most of the scales used widely and effectively by psychologists are ordinal scales' (1951, p. 26) without giving even one instance of a psychological relation known to be both transitive and asymmetric.[17] In another example, he (1951) considered a set of non-additive procedures for making ratio scale assignments to weights without considering the issue of why the empirical structure involved sustained this level of numerical representation. This failure, together with the fact that this latter set of procedures was workable, simply confirm the impression that for Stevens the key feature determining scale type was the character of the rule for making numerical assignments and not the structure of any independent empirical system which might be involved.

This impression is even more strongly confirmed by Stevens' discussion of the subject of admissible scale transformations. This concept was actually a valuable addition to representational measurement theory. Admissible scale transformations refer to the classes of mathematical transformations that can be made to numerical assignments without altering the type of scale involved. It is known that with nominal scales, the class of admissible transformations include all one to one transformations; with ordinal scales, the class of all increasing monotonic (i.e., order preserving) transformations; with interval scales, the class of all positive linear transformations (i.e., adding a positive or negative constant to all numerical assignments or multiplying them all by a positive constant, or both); and with ratio scales, the class of all positive similarities transformations (i.e., multiplying all numerical assignments by a positive constant). In the case of external representation, these classes of transformations are largely determined by the structure of the empirical relations numerically represented. While admissible scale transformations alter the specific numbers used in the numerical representation, they leave unchanged the empirical information numerically represented.

---

[17] In this he was doing no more than giving vent to a typical misunderstanding.

However, in Stevens' presentation the emphasis is upon transformations that 'leave scale form invariant' (1951, p. 26) which, in the absence of a commitment to external representations only, does not necessarily mean transformations that leave invariant the empirical features represented.

Both giants of psychophysics, Fechner and Stevens, each mistakenly thought that their psychophysical methods could be taken as methods of measurement without any further scientific justification. In doing this first, Fechner established the psychological tradition of regarding number-generating procedures as measurement procedures and Stevens translated that tradition into a definition of measurement. Stevens may have wanted to repeal Fechner's psychophysical law and legislate his own (1961), but his definition of measurement legitimised Fechner's quantitative *modus operandi*, in the minds of psychologists. This *modus operandi* was Fechner's most enduring legacy to psychology and Stevens made it seem scientifically respectable. Although completely anachronistic, Adler's comment that 'Fechner understood the essential nature of measurement as "the assignment of numerals to objects or events according to rule" ' (Adler, 1980, p. 14), perhaps points to the truth that Stevens' definition made explicit, in operationist concepts of mid-twentieth-century psychology, Fechner's *modus operandi*.

Operationism commits an elementary confusion: it confuses 'the act or process of measuring with the object of the act, namely the quantity in question' (Byerley, 1974, p. 376). Once this confusion is exposed, Stevens' definition of measurement is revealed for the charade it is. In general, psychologists have declined to acknowledge this. Stevens had given them what they wanted: a definition which, if accepted, made the quantity objection magically invisible. Mainstream interest in the definition of measurement effectively ceased with receipt of that 'gift'.

STEVENS' CONCEPT OF NUMBER

Having stretched the representational theory to the span of his definition, Stevens remaining problem was to explain the concept of number in a way that would forestall return of the classical concepts of quantity and number. He might have been expected to pioneer an operational concept of number. However, Stevens'

178   *Stevens' thoroughgoing representationalism*

was not a creative mind. His genius lay in synthesising others' contributions. Thus, he borrowed a version of formalism from the logical positivists. According to the formalist view, mathematical concepts are devoid of any content external to the abstract system within which they are defined and their meaning derives solely from interrelationships within that system. In its most extreme version, a mathematical system is thought of as one composed of (uninterpreted) symbols, rules for constructing well-formed formulas out of those symbols, strings of symbols called 'axioms', and 'inference' rules for deriving 'true theorems' from axioms via a finite number of steps. If the symbols are thought of simply as ciphers of a certain shape, then mathematics is understood as merely a 'game' played with strings of symbols according to explicit rules. Thus conceived, mathematical concepts are devoid of empirical content.

The influence of positivism upon psychology was at its height in the immediate pre- and postwar decades and this fact aided the reception of the formalist view of number. Stevens, therefore, could assert with impunity that 'mathematics is a game of signs and rules, man-made and arbitrary, like the game of chess' (Stevens, 1958, p. 383) and explicitly align his exposition with formalism ('The present account of things is more in line with the formalist tradition' (Stevens, 1951, p. 5)), confident that the majority of psychologists would not baulk at this contemporary conventional wisdom. However, his exposition of formalism was amateurish and, at times, deeply ignorant. For example, when explaining why he defined measurement as the assignment of numerals, rather than numbers, to objects and event, Stevens wrote

In using two different words, 'numeral' and 'number', for what gets related to objects by means of semantical rules, Campbell and Russell probably both intend the same meaning. Elsewhere I have sided with Campbell's usage because the meaning of the term 'number' is often ambiguous: among other things, it refers sometimes to a physical attribute of a collection of discrete objects (a number of peanuts), sometimes to Frege's class of isomorphic classes (cardinal number), and sometimes to Russell's relational expressions (relation numbers, of which the ordinal numbers are a subclass). My guess would be that the numbers Russell intends for measurement are the relation numbers.

The term 'numeral' has the defect that it sometimes means the physical ink mark on a piece of paper and it sometimes means the essentially *logical* relation that a numeral may stand for. This second meaning is in line with the formalist's view of mathematics, according to which arithmetic is regarded as the rules of a game played with numerical symbols 'whose shape is recognizable by us with certainty independently of space and time, and of the particular conditions of their manufacture, and of the trifling differences in their execution' (quoted from Hilbert by Weyl [1949], p. 35). Campbell seems to have this second meaning in mind, which is probably also Russell's meaning. (Stevens, 1951, p. 22)

Here, Stevens is bluffing. Had he ever actually read Russell and Campbell in detail? The former, while notorious amongst philosophers for changing his views, was unwavering in his opposition to the formalist view of mathematics.[18] Campbell, on the other hand, took great pains to explain that numerals were the names of numbers and that numbers, in the sense of physical properties, were all that were needed in measurement.[19] This, of course, was exactly what Russell denied in his account, wherein the logicist (i.e., Fregean) concept of number was presumed. Campbell, on the other hand, was deeply suspicious of this concept of Russell's.[20] Ignorant of these facts, Stevens wove their names together with those of Frege (the foremost logicist) and Hilbert (the foremost formalist), as if distilling a canonical essence from their conjoined eminences.

Formalism has serious problems and these were widely known at this time. Perhaps, the most important derives from Gödel's (1931) *incompleteness theorem*. This theorem is that any consistent, formal system entailing arithmetic is incomplete and, so, the truths of mathematics must exceed the theorems of mathematics provable within any formal system. Interestingly, the implications of Gödel's theorem for Hilbert's formalism were discussed in some detail by Weyl (1949), the reference cited by Stevens in the paragraph quoted above. Weyl concluded with the following anti-formalist prescription: 'A truly realistic mathematics should be conceived, in line with physics, as a branch of the theoretical

---

[18] Of formalism Russell wrote: 'The theory is perfectly adequate for doing sums, but not for the applications of number. Since it is the applications of number that make it important, the Formalists' theory must be regarded as an unsatisfactory evasion' (1959, p. 110). This critique of formalism is typical of his position after his adoption of logicism, sixty years earlier.

[19] This is a matter discussed at length by Campbell (e.g., 1920, pp. 303–5).

[20] He adjudged Russell's logicist view of number 'extremely precarious' (Campbell, 1920, p. 338).

180 *Stevens' thoroughgoing representationalism*

construction of the one real world' (1949, p. 235). Stevens did not distract his readers with this alternative! Formalism is now not only thought to be logically inadequate, it is also considered psychologically inadequate in the sense that 'many mathematicians retreat to a nihilistic formalism–"We are just playing meaningless games with empty symbols"–but none of us really believes that' (Hirsch, 1995, p. 137). Furthermore, if formalism is true, then 'the enormous usefulness of mathematics in the natural sciences is something bordering on the mysterious and there is no rational explanation for it' (Wigner, 1960, p. 2).

Stevens addressed this last problem by suggesting that some formal mathematical systems have been deliberately constructed to match the kinds of empirical structures identified in the natural sciences. As he put it:

Of course the rules for much of mathematics (but by no means all of it) have been deliberately rigged to make the game isomorphic with common worldly experience, so that ten beans put with ten beans to make a pile is mirrored in the symbolics: $10 + 10 = 20$. (Stevens, 1951, p. 2)

Ignoring the fact that for many kinds of thing, X, putting $10X$s with $10X$s does not always precisely mirror this arithmetic proposition, this sort of response does appear to provide a way out for the formalist. It seems not unreasonable to propose that, say, the formal system characterising the truths about natural numbers arose via a process of abstraction from ordinary human experience with aggregates of things and that, for this reason, true sentences within that formal system reflect some of our common observations. This was essentially Stevens' proposal: 'Striving somehow to count his possessions, ancient man seems destined in the nature of things to have hit upon the concept of number and to have made therein his first triumphant abstraction' (Stevens, 1958, p. 384). This process of abstraction is repeated, thought Stevens, in the child learning arithmetic:

He learns his first arithmetic with the aid of fingers or buttons or beads, and only with great labour does he finally, if ever, achieve the reoriented view that mathematics is an abstract game having no necessary relation to solid objects. (Stevens, 1958, p. 384)

This 'reoriented view' is that pure mathematics involves only 'syntactics'.

Syntactics refers to the formal disciplines of logic, mathematics, and syntax, where the relations among signs are *abstracted* from the relation of the signs to objects and to the users or interpreters of signs. The propositions of syntactics are devoid of empirical content. They say nothing about the physical world. They are statements like the laws of algebra, which set the rules for the combining and arranging of the signs of algebra. In short, abstract mathematics is a branch of syntactics. (Stevens, 1951, p. 2)

Stevens neglected to discuss the philosophical commitments entailed by this way of looking at the matter. Once acknowledged, they make formalism less plausible.

If, for example, the strings of symbols that can be used to express the truths of the arithmetic of the natural numbers mirror certain empirical facts to do with aggregates of things of some kind, then there are already numbers of things in the world, including amongst others, numbers of symbols. Stevens accepted this (empirical) fact quite happily, identifying this as 'number in the layman's sense' and calling it 'numerosity' (1951, p. 22). If there are numbers of things, say, twenty beans in a heap, then there are facts of the following kind: this aggregate of twenty beans is entirely composed of two discrete parts, each an aggregate of ten beans. If there are aggregates, then there must be aggregate sizes (e.g., the property of being an aggregate of ten beans, etc). When the theory of aggregate sizes is developed in detail (Michell, 1994a), it can be seen that the range of all aggregate sizes constitutes a discrete quantity. If there are aggregate sizes, then there will be relations of ratio between them (e.g., the size of an aggregate of twenty beans is ten times the size of an aggregate of two beans). In developing the theory of such relations (Michell, 1994a) an empirical structure (empirical in the sense of being present in the spatio-temporal world) is identified having exactly the structure of the natural numbers. This much Stevens might have been happy with, because he tacitly admitted the existence of such structures, even though he declined to think of these empirical structures as instantiating the system of natural numbers.

However, in admitting this much, Stevens was admitting as much as an account of the natural numbers requires. There are relations between quantities (be they discrete or continuous) and the enterprises of counting and measurement are the attempt to

182 *Stevens' thoroughgoing representationalism*

identify them and the theory of counting and measuring can be worked out exclusively in terms of them. Recognising that in theorising about such relations, it is useful to devise a set of special symbols, Stevens wished to treat these symbols, together with their associated syntactic rules, as the exclusive subject matter of mathematics. This is the logical equivalent of treating the symbols used to designate physical quantities (say, m for mass, v for velocity, etc.), together with the syntax of physical theories, as the exclusive subject matter of physics. But no sane scientist would think of physics as just the study of the language of physics. This would be recognised as a superficial confusion, one not worthy of serious refutation. What then is the merit of regarding what is seen as a confusion elsewhere, as being a virtue when applied to mathematics?

The benefits that Hilbert wished to derive from his formalist approach were twofold: (i) the establishment of a distinctive subject matter for mathematics (i.e., it was to become the study of formal, axiomatic systems); and (ii) the establishment of a distinctive method (formal proof) whereby (a) all of the truths of mathematics could be derived and (b) the system itself could be proved logically consistent. While Gödel's incompleteness theorem entailed that for most of mathematics, if it is consistent, (a) and (b) are impossible, (i) and (ii) are still worthwhile aims. However, they do not require the extreme formalism that Stevens proposed.

If the view is taken that relational structures constitute the distinctive subject matter of mathematics (as is sometimes variously advocated today (e.g., Parsons, 1990; Resnik, 1981)), then a different kind of formalism can be defended. Ignoring the sorts of things that any empirical structure is composed of, considering structures only as characterised by their relations, and relations only as characterised by their topic-neutral (i.e., formal) features, then mathematics may be understood as the study of such structures. Given that structures may be not only natural (e.g., quantitative structures) but also conventional (e.g., linguistic structures), then the syntactic structure of mathematical theories may still be included within its subject matter (the theory of formal languages), but only as a small part. Furthermore, since there is no necessity that all of the logically possible sorts of structures are instantiated in the world, mathematicians may explore the character that other sorts of structures might have were they to exist. Seen this way, mathematics has a distinctive subject matter.

Turning to Hilbert's second benefit, that of establishing a distinctive method for mathematics, this also does not depend upon a formalism of the kind advocated by Stevens. Hilbert thought that in mathematics the validity of proofs within an axiom system should be entirely logically independent of any extraneous content associated with any symbols. For example, considering geometric axiom systems, 'It must be possible to replace in all geometric statements the words *point, line, plane* by *table, chair, mug*' (quoted in Weyl, 1970, p. 264). This is simply the familiar fact that validity depends upon the form of the argument and not its material. For example, the valid conclusion that *Socrates is mortal* from the facts that *All men are mortal* and *Socrates is a man* depends not upon the content of the specific terms in the propositions (*Socrates, men,* and *mortal*) but upon the topic-neutral, *Barbara,* form of this syllogism (Thom, 1981). Now, while logic is the science of formal implication, and so mathematics presupposes logic, implication itself is a relation (a formal relation between kinds of situations), and so the structure of valid-argument forms may be studied mathematically, which is really what logic is. That is, on this structuralist view, logic (the science of implication) is just a special branch of mathematics and Hilbert's desire for a distinctive mathematical method is realised. However, in so far as every situation studied in any science has its (topic-neutral) form, as well as its own material, this distinctive mathematical method is relevant to *all* science.

If mathematics is taken to be the study of form in that sense, then not only can the familiar distinction be maintained between mathematical symbols and the mathematical 'entities' denoted (e.g., the distinction between numerals and numbers) but, also, there is a compellingly simple explanation available for the fact that some mathematics is not just applicable to the real world but is also fundamental to all science. It is applicable to the real world because mathematics studies the formal properties of structures, including the sorts of structures instantiated in the world, and it is fundamental to all science because scientists look for structure in the natural systems they study.

What Stevens actually required, given his commitment to

184   *Stevens' thoroughgoing representationalism*

operationism, was not a formalist view of number at all, but an operationist one.[21] Such an account would be one in which it is revealed how numerical concepts (such as *one*, *two*, *three*, etc.) are constructed out of the operations we perform on things. The operationist might begin by asking what operations are involved in showing that a single X (say, one sheep) is just one X and not two or more. A typical reply to this question would be that the relevant operation for numbering a collection of Xs is just that of coordinating, one to one, the Xs and the elements of the series of numerals, taken in their conventional order and beginning with the first (i.e., *one*). A single X on its own takes us no further along this series than *one*; whereas two Xs takes us to *two*, etc. By this operation two Xs are distinguished from one, three from two, and so on. The obvious problem is that for this operation to work successfully we must already be able to recognise single Xs (including, of course, single instances of the different numerals). As I have suggested in earlier chapters, number and quantity are present in every situation and we cannot conceive of a human operation that does not presume their existence. This is where Stevens' observation, quoted earlier, that 'ancient man seems destined in the nature of things to have hit upon the concept of number' (1958, p. 384) gains its force. It is the nature of things, quite literally, that includes the concept of number. If there were no individual things, separate from other things but, also, arranged with them as aggregates, there would be no nature of things involving the concept of number.

The character of numerical assignment procedures is such that they always presume that the world has sufficient structure for numbers to be real features (Michell, 1997a). Therefore, not every application of numerical concepts to the world requires the concept of representation. Because there are finite aggregates, there are numbers. In the counting of things aggregated, numbers are discovered (as ratios between aggregate sizes), not assigned. Likewise, in measuring magnitudes of continuous quantities, numbers are discovered or estimated (as ratios between magnitudes), not assigned. The logic of counting and measuring is not representation, it is instantiation. In both practices, instances of number

---

[21] In this respect Bridgman was a more consistent operationist than Stevens, taking the view that mathematics was 'just as truly an empirical science as physics or chemistry' (1964, p. 52).

are located in the world. However, there are applications of numerical concepts with a different logic. Chief amongst them is numerical coding. When structures (such as classifications or orderings) are coded numerically, the numerals are not used in those situations to name numbers instantiated therein. Then the logic of numerical application is not instantiation, it is representation. It is to the context of representation that Stevens theory of nominal and ordinal scales scales and scale transformations has valid application.

STEVENS' 'REVOLUTION'

Prior to 1951, measurement was defined within psychology in ways reflecting the classical paradigm. As already noted, Fechner ([1860] 1966) had written that 'Generally the measurement of a quantity consists of ascertaining how often a unit quantity of the same kind is contained in it' (p. 38). In Baldwin (1902), an entry under *measurement* states that

> In order that a concept may be measured as a mathematical quantity without ambiguity, it is essential that the special attribute by which we measure it should be conceivable as made up of discrete parts, admitting of unambiguous comparison *inter se*, with respect to their quality or difference of magnitude. (p. 58)

Titchener (1905) wrote that 'When we measure in any department of natural science, we compare a given magnitude with some conventional unit of the same kind, and determine how many times the unit is contained in the magnitude' (p. xix). Brown and Thomson (1921) held that

> The preconditions of measurement in any sphere of experience are (1) the homogeneity of the phenomena, or of any particular aspect of it, to be measured, (2) the possibility of fixing a unit in terms of which the measurement may be made, and of which the total magnitude may be regarded as a mere multiple or submultiple. (p. 1)

The entry in Warren (1934) under *measurement* defines it as 'the comparison of a quantitative datum of any sort with a fixed, enduring datum or standard of the same sort' (p. 161); and that in Harriman (1947) defines it as 'the application of temporal or spatial units to psychological events or functions' (p. 215). These quotations are just examples and while they differ in adequacy,

186 *Stevens' thoroughgoing representationalism*

emphasis and detail, what they have in common is the view that measurement involves comparison with a unit, the implication even where not explicit being that of numerical comparison. This idea connects easily with the classical view of measurement.

The contrast with most definitions offered within the psychological literature after 1951 could not be more dramatic. Stevens' definition occurs (with and without acknowledgment) regularly and across the discipline (Michell, 1997b). Even when it is not quoted verbatim (or with the minor substitution of *numbers* for *numerals*), its form is utilised and measurement is defined as *the assignment of X to Y according to Z* (where X may be numerical values, scores, other symbols or abstract systems; Y, attributes, behaviour, characteristics, individuals, observations, persons, properties of experimental units or of objects, responses, situations, or things; and Z sometimes specifies a particular kind of rule (e.g., numerical representation).

As noted in Chapter 1, this situation within psychology contrasts sharply with the definitions given in the physical sciences. Modern authors of works in the physical sciences who provide a definition of measurement are rare, but those I have found who do (e.g., Beckwith and Buck, 1961; Massey, 1986; Terrien, 1980) invariably present the classical concept.

What this literature shows is that after 1951, the majority of psychologists came to accept Stevens' definition of measurement, but this was never the case within mainstream quantitative disciplines. To call this a revolution within psychology would be to go too far. The theories and practices of psychologists were unchanged by acceptance of this definition. However, acceptance of Stevens' definition within the discipline made the policy of ignoring the quantity objection socially acceptable. That is, after 1951 this policy was sanctioned by the methodological principles accepted as normative within the discipline. This allowed those interested in the measurement of psychological attributes to proceed as if the practices long employed actually did measure those attributes.

In a variety of research contexts (for the most part, what are called psychophysics and psychometrics), psychologists have developed a wide range of procedures for collecting numerical data. These procedures have been standardised, theorised about in quantitative terms, and in some practical contexts they have proved remarkably useful. Most undergraduate students of psychology are educated in these theories and techniques in courses variously called 'psychophysical measurement', 'psychological scaling', 'psychometric methods', 'psychological measurement', etc. That is, this body of procedures and theories is 'packaged' under the label of 'measurement' or cognate terms. This is standard practice in the education of psychologists. However, in so far as it is held that these procedures measure psychological attributes, there has been little serious scientific research undertaken to show that the relevant attributes are really quantitative and, therefore, that the relevant attributes are measurable. If they are not, then their character and their relationship to the standard number-generating procedures that psychologists use needs to be investigated. Despite this lack of attention to the scientific issues involved, psychologists treat these methods as measurement. The principal difficulty involved in maintaining this misconception is the obvious objection that in the physical sciences measurement is typically understood classically. Psychologists have overcome this difficulty by persuading themselves that both within psychology and within the physical sciences, measurement simply means 'pinning numbers on things' (Stevens, 1958, p. 384). Since very few quantitative psychologists ever have any serious engagement with quantitative science, this illusion easily survives.

The manner in which Stevens' definition has been institutionalised within psychology is very interesting, because what in reality is a debilitating conceptual weakness has been mythologised as a strength. Most attributes that psychologists believe they are able to measure are not attributes open to direct observation. This, as already noted, was seen by generations of psychologists prior to Stevens as a source of serious difficulties. Since Stevens, psychologists claim to have solved this problem via the conceptual device of operationalising their theoretical attributes. In reality, this amounts to no more than stipulating that certain numerical assignment procedures measure theoretical attributes. However, this combination (Stevens' definition and operationist philosophy) is packaged as a major conceptual breakthrough in scientific method.

In Kerlinger's (1979) words, the standard line is as follows:[22]

---

[22] Views similar to these of Kerlinger are ubiquitous in psychology. The most up-to-date texts on research methods in psychology still recite Stevens' definition and invoke the mantra of operationism (e.g., Heiman, 1995; Whitley, 1996).

An *operational definition* assigns meaning to a construct or variable by specifying the activities or 'operations' necessary to measure it or to manipulate it. An operational definition, alternatively, specifies the activities of the researcher in measuring a variable or in manipulating it. It is like a manual of instructions to the researcher: It says, in effect, 'Do such-and-such in so-and-so manner.' A well-known though rather extreme example is: Intelligence (anxiety, achievement, and so forth) is scores on X intelligence test, or intelligence is what X intelligence test measures. This definition tells us what to do to measure intelligence. It tells the researcher to use X intelligence test. Achievement may be defined by citing a standardized achievement test, a teacher-made achievement test, or grades assigned by teachers. We here have three distinctly different ways of operationally defining the same construct. The reader should not let this multiplicity of operational definitions bother him; it is part of their flexibility and strength. After all, a construct like achievement has many facets, and researchers can be interested in different facets at different times. (p. 41)

Here, two important empirical issues, that of how a theoretical attribute, such as intelligence, relates to performance on a particular test and that of whether scores on such a test are measures of anything at all, are dissolved into a simple matter of 'operational definition', so-called. That is, stipulation and postulation are substituted for serious scientific investigation into these issues. Yet no psychologist really means by intelligence, scores on an intelligence test, and in believing intelligence to be measurable, psychologists typically theorise about it as a quantitative attribute, one continuously related to other attributes. The ideology of operationalising, therefore, completely obscures what is really going on: psychologists are thereby caused to ignore the distinction in meaning between theoretical concepts, like intelligence, and their observable effects, like test scores; and they are also thereby caused to ignore the conceptual commitments of quantitative theorising in science. The real function of this ideology is to make such arbitrary stipulations and unsupported postulations appear to be both legitimate and debt free. The bottom line is maintenance of the measurability thesis. Without a hint of irony, Kerlinger (1979) believes that this practice is 'a radically different way of thinking and operating, a way that has revolutionised behavioral research' (p. 41); that as a result of this practice, 'the success of behavioral scientists in measuring behavioral variables is remarkable' (p. 142); that 'measurement is measurement in the natural sciences and in the behavioral sciences. The basic definition and the general procedures are the same' (p. 143); and, finally, that *'Measurement* is the assignment of numerals to objects or events according to rules (Stevens, 1951). This is an excellent example of a powerful definition' (p. 129). Powerful indeed!

Stevens broke the nexus between the measurability thesis (some psychological attributes are measurable) and the quantity objection (no psychological attributes are quantitative). It was a two-step process. In the first place, his definition of measurement broke the nexus quite simply by entailing that some measurable attributes are non-quantitative. Stevens' definition not only admits ordinal and nominal attributes to the class of measurables, it entails that all non-quantitative attributes are also measurable. That alone, however, is something of a pyrrhic victory, because it leaves the quantity objection unaffected. Hence, it would not have satisfied those psychophysicists like Stevens, psychometricians like Lord and Novick (1968), or methodologists like Kerlinger (1979), who want to maintain that at least some psychological measurement is on a par with physical measurement. A second step was required to neutralise the force of the quantity objection, without in any way confronting the scientific task of quantification. This is where Stevens' operational interpretation of his theory of measurement scales paid off. Stevens introduction of his own terminology (nominal, ordinal, interval, and ratio scales) effectively removed the term *quantitative* from the psychologists' lexicon. Then, allowing the type of measurement scale to be defined operationally enabled him to conclude that his ratio scales (of sensory intensities) were on a par with measurement scales used in the physical sciences. This way of proceeding became standard practice in psychology, sanctioned under the name of *operationalising*. In this way, the quantity objection was deflected and the nexus broken. The proposition that there now exist interval and ratio scales of measurement for psychological attributes is currently generally accepted within the discipline and most contemporary quantitative psychologists would have great difficulty grasping the force of the quantity objection, were it possible to bring it before their minds. If one has already accepted the operational view, that measurement is the assignment of numerals to objects or events according to rule, then theoretical research showing how to test the hypothesis that attributes are quantitative will seem to be not only irrelevant but also unhelpful, because it raises doubts about matters taken to be already settled.

In order to break the nexus between the measurability thesis and the quantity objection, Stevens stood the classical concept of measurement on its head. According to this latter concept, numerical measurements supervene upon quantitative attributes: if an attribute has the right kind of structure, then numerical measures are implicit in it. According to Stevens, the implication moves in the opposite direction: measurable attributes supervene upon numerical assignments. If a consistent procedure can be devised for making numerical assignments to objects or events, then a measurable attribute is implicated. With the classical concept upturned, the measurability thesis, at long last, looked secure.

CHAPTER 8

Quantitative psychology and the revolution in measurement theory

The revolution that axiomatic measurement theory might have touched off has not yet occurred.

(Norman Cliff)

The only revolution properly so called is an intellectual revolution, 'a revolution in ideas'.

(John Anderson)

The shift from the classical understanding of measurement to that encapsulated by Stevens' definition is unsustainable. Not only does acceptance of Stevens' definition sever connections between mainstream quantitative psychology and the traditions of quantitative science, it blinds those who accept it to the character of quantification, thereby causing them to ignore fundamental empirical commitments of quantitative theorising. Mainstream quantitative psychology is now in the anomalous position of being unable to consider the measurability thesis in the critical manner characteristic of normal science. When a science's institutionalised ways of proceeding impede critical inquiry into some issue relevant to its subject matter, then that science subverts itself as a cognitive enterprise.

As a social movement, science is a complex phenomenon. It always serves diverse social and personal interests. These may sometimes oppose those of critical inquiry. There are dramatic instances of this, like scientific fraud, when scientists claim results which they know they do not have. In general, however, scientific fraud is an aberration of individual scientists, not of entire disciplines. More dramatic still are cases where the scientists of a particular nation are completely overwhelmed by non-scientific interests to the extent that critical inquiry into relevant issues stops, as illustrated by the case of Lysenko and the political domination

192 *The revolution in measurement theory*

of Soviet genetics (Soyfer, 1994). Again, such disasters rarely afflict entire disciplines on an international scale.

There may be less obvious interests at work, however, that can affect entire disciplines. The majority of those participating in a science might be pressed unwittingly by shared philosophical presuppositions to conform to a false idea of science. This is scientism. The historical record shows that endorsement of the measurability thesis and, in turn, Stevens' definition served some such image. Furthermore, many sciences are allied to professions. If the members of a profession are required to sell their services, then they have an economic interest in presenting these services as attractively as possible. The historical record shows that the profession of psychology derived economic and other social advantages from employing the rhetoric of measurement in promoting its services and that the science of psychology, likewise, benefited from supporting the profession in this by endorsing the measurability thesis and Stevens' definition. These endorsements happened despite the fact that the issue of the measurability of psychological attributes was rarely investigated scientifically and never resolved. When the economic and social interests of a 'science-based' profession take precedence over the interests of critical inquiry within a discipline, then this is a form of practicalism.

Of course, to some degree, scientism and practicalism influence most sciences and their effects are not necessarily detrimental. They may even advance inquiry. Furthermore, endorsement of the measurability thesis and of Stevens' definition, taken in isolation, were simply errors. Given our fallibility, error is a normal feature of all cognitive enterprises. Science is subverted, however, when mechanisms for correcting errors go awry. The integrity of individual scientists in endorsing a view, the social conditions favouring such endorsement, and the social interests that such a view might serve are distinguishable. It is possible that all psychologists who endorsed the measurability thesis and Stevens' definition were moved by the highest of personal motives (which, of course, never rules out the possibility of error) and, yet, because of the special social conditions obtaining, acceptance of these views served social interests opposing those of critical inquiry. These social conditions may have caused a breakdown in the science's error-correcting mechanisms. For example, these mechanisms depend crucially on the training of scientists, and both professional institutions and false images of science can influence the syllabus content of university courses, the criteria for assessing the competence of graduates and, thereby, the criteria for the interpretation and acceptance of research results. Defects here may seriously impede critical inquiry.

In order to test the hypothesis that mainstream quantitative psychology works against itself as a cognitive enterprise, evidence is required that quantitative psychology is prevented by its internal ways of working from correcting the errors of accepting both the measurability thesis and Stevens' definition. Suppose that a group of scholars, working outside the mainstream tradition of quantitative psychology, made conceptual breakthroughs in relation to the issue of testing the hypothesis that psychological attributes are quantitative. Suppose they advertised this progress within mainstream vehicles of scientific communication. Then strong evidence of a breakdown in internal, error-correcting mechanisms would exist if mainstream quantitative psychology failed to integrate these developments into its curricula and research programmes, and continued business as usual. Interestingly, this scenario was played out in the history of psychology in the latter half of the twentieth century.

THE REVOLUTION THAT HAPPENED

Book V of Euclid's *Elements* presents the theory of ratios of magnitudes. This theory initiated the conceptual project of understanding measurement. Completing this project requires explaining what magnitudes are (that they should sustain ratios), what ratios are (that they should sustain real numbers), and how to test the hypothesis that attributes are quantitative. If the work of Hölder (1901) and Frege (1903) made progress with respect to the first two of these, what psychology lacked was any understanding of the third. While the second part of Hölder (1901) pointed in the right direction, its significance was not recognised.

The seeds from which a breakthrough developed were sown in the year of Stevens' *Handbook*, 1951: Patrick Suppes, a philosophy graduate of Columbia University, where one of his teachers had been Ernest Nagel, published a paper on extensive measurement (Suppes, 1951). It displayed a number of important characteristics. First, Suppes was not only aware of Hölder (1901), Hölder's

194 *The revolution in measurement theory*

views were debated. Second, Suppes showed an interest in empirically testing the 'axioms' of extensive measurement. In these respects he followed Nagel. He departed from Nagel in the specific mathematical approach employed. Suppes was now at Stanford University and he attended seminars by the Polish logician, Alfred Tarski,[1] at Berkeley (Suppes, 1979). As a result, Suppes' trademark became the axiomatic, set-theoretical analysis of philosophical and scientific problems. This proved to be an extremely productive vehicle for advancing measurement theory.[2] Finally, Suppes' views were contaminated neither by the practicalist/scientistic interests of quantitative psychology in general nor by Stevens in particular.[3]

Suppes (1954) recommended that philosophers of science attempt to 'axiomatize' developed branches of empirical science and, especially, those portions involving scientific measurement. A theory is 'axiomatized' when it is expressed as a set of (ideally, logically independent) propositions (called 'axioms') from which the remainder of the theory deductively follows. These propositions are not 'axioms' in the sense of being self-evident or, even, taken to be true. They are simply the fundamental hypotheses of the theory. An 'axiomatization' is set-theoretic when the entities to which the theory applies are described as members of a set of some kind and the 'axioms' state conditions which this set satisfies (such as, for example, that some relation between members is transitive). In this way Suppes aimed to bridge the gap

between qualitative observations ('this rod is longer than that one,' 'This pan of the balance is higher than the other one') and the quantitative assertions demanded in developed scientific theories ('The length of this rod is 5.6cm.,' 'The mass of this steel ball is 7.2gm.'). (1954, p. 246)

Given the view that numbers are not part of the furniture of the world, this connection can seem to be a problem. Since number systems had already been axiomatized set-theoretically, 'axiomati-

---

[1] Alfred Tarski, professor of mathematics at Berkeley until 1968, had a profound influence upon modern philosophy through his analyses of the concepts of truth and logical implication.

[2] Referring to Suppes' axiomatic, set-theoretic approach, Luce (1979) reports that 'More than any other living person, Suppes has affected contemporary presentations of theories of measurement' (p. 93).

[3] Suppes' undergraduate training was not in psychology but in physics and meteorology (Suppes, 1979), and his eventual interest in psychological measurement developed via decision theory and utility, rather than via psychophysics and ability testing.

zations' of empirical systems might smooth the task of establishing a connection between these so-called 'qualitative'[4] and quantitative domains. A further aim implicit in this programme was, as far as possible, to restrict the axioms of the 'qualitative', empirical structure to those directly testable. The result of this programme was to bring into the open testable, 'qualitative' conditions necessary and sufficient for various forms of numerical representation. Suppes' programme was clearly located within the representational tradition, but it was also firmly realist, as opposed to operationist.

As Luce and Narens (1994) indicate, the application of this programme to any instance of scientific measurement reduces to four steps.

1. A 'qualitative', empirical system is specified as a relational structure, that is, as a non-empty set of entities of some kind (objects or attributes, perhaps) together with a finite number of distinct relations between elements of this set. It is required that these elements and the relations between them be identifiable by direct observation. These are the empirical primitives of the system.

2. A set of 'axioms' (preferably finite in number) is stated in terms of the empirical primitives. So far as possible, they should be directly testable.

3. A numerical structure is identified such that a set of many-to-one mappings (homomorphisms) between the empirical structure and this numerical structure can be proved to exist. This proof is sometimes referred to as the *representation theorem*.[5]

4. A specification of how the elements of this set of homomorphisms relate to one another is given, generally by identifying to which class of mathematical functions all transformations of any one element of this set into the other elements belong. This is sometimes referred to as the *uniqueness theorem* and it makes rigorous Stevens' more informal views about admissible scale transformations.

---

[4] By qualitative, Suppes and associates seem to mean non-numerical and by quantitative, numerical. This differs from my usage throughout this book.

[5] A representation theorem is a purely mathematical result and is therefore logically independent of the representational theory itself and able to be appropriated by any theory of measurement, if needed. A set of mathematical theorems never constitutes a theory of measurement.

196   *The revolution in measurement theory*

Suppes and associates made contributions to this programme during the 1950s (e.g., Suppes, 1951; Suppes and Winet, 1955; Scott and Suppes, 1958), and a range of possible empirical structures relevant to instances of physical measurement and attempts at psychological measurement was presented by Suppes and Zinnes in the first chapter of the first volume of the *Handbook of Mathematical Psychology* (1963). I will illustrate the above four steps via their treatment of extensive measurement.

Suppes and Zinnes defined the relevant empirical relational structure as follows:

An *extensive system* $<A, R, o>$ is a relational system consisting of the binary relation R, the binary operation o from $A \times A$ to A, and satisfying the following six axioms for a, b, c in A.
1. If aRb and bRc, then aRc;
2. $[(a \ o \ b) \ o \ c]R[a \ o \ (b \ o \ c)]$;
3. If aRb, then $[a \ o \ c]R[c \ o \ b]$;
4. If *not* aRb, then there is a c in A such that $aR[b \ o \ c]$ and $[b \ o \ c]Ra$;
5. *Not* $[a \ o \ b]Ra$;
6. If aRb, then there is a number n such that $bRna$ where the notation na is defined recursively as follows: $1a = a$ and $na = (n-1)a \ o \ a$. (1963, p. 42; my square brackets)

The empirical structure is the system denoted by $<A, R, o>$,[6] the non-empty set of entities being A and the relations, R and o. R may be interpreted as the relation, *being at least as great as*. For example, if the entities in A are lengths, then aRb simply means that length a is at least as great as length b. o is a *concatenation operation*. That is, sticking with the length example, $a \ o \ b$ is the length obtained when a is extended by (or concatenated with) b. Strictly speaking, o is a binary *operation*, rather than *relation*, but as Suppes and Zinnes note, 'operations are simply certain special relations' (1963, p. 5). That is, if $c = a \ o \ b$, then a, b, and c are related in a specific way, so corresponding to the concatenation operation there is a relation (of additivity) between lengths. The empirical structure is described as qualitative because the 'axi-

---

[6] The pointed brackets, $< >$, simply indicate that the elements they enclose are taken as ordered. In the case of Suppes' notation for denoting relational structures, the convention is that the set of objects is mentioned first, followed by the relevant relations holding between those objects.

The revolution that happened 197

oms' do not contain any reference to numerical concepts, other than in 'axiom' 6 where, of course, the recursive definition of na shows that n is defined completely by a and o. It is empirical because it is thought to capture the form exhibited by various spatio-temporally located structures, e.g., lengths, as explained, or a set of objects differing in weight, ordered by heaviness on an equal arm, beam balance, upon which the objects may be concatenated.

'Axioms' 1 (transitivity of the order relation), 2 (associativity of the concatenation operation), 3 (monotonicity of concatenation) and 5 (positivity of concatenation) are directly testable. For example, 5 would be false for the case of weight if some object perfectly balanced the combination of itself and some other object. On the other hand, 'axioms' 4 (the solvability condition) and 6 (the Archimedean condition) are not directly testable, although it should be stressed that in combination with the other 'axioms' they entail testable predictions.

Suppes (1951) proved (the representation theorem) that extensive systems of this kind are homomorphic to numerical extensive systems of the sort $<N, \leq, +,>$ where N is a subset of positive real numbers and the numerical relation, $\leq$, is used to represent R and $+$, to represent o. That is, given a set of objects and relations R and o for which the above axioms are true, positive real numbers may be assigned to the objects in such a way that the values of the numbers assigned reflect both the order of the objects and the concatenation relation, that is, if $a = b \, o \, c$ then the number assigned to a is the sum of the numbers assigned to b and c. More formally, for any a, b, and c in A,

$$aRb \text{ if and only if } \phi(a) \leq \phi(b) \text{ and}$$
$$aR[b \, o \, c] \text{ if and only if } \phi(a) \leq \phi(b) + \phi(c)$$

(where ϕ is a homomorphism from A into N). Suppes and Zinnes proved (the uniqueness theorem) that any two such homomorphisms for the same empirical extensive system are related by multiplication by a positive constant. That is, in Stevens' sense, the numerical assignments to an extensive system constitute a ratio scale.

Suppes emphasised the numerical representation of more or less directly observable structures. His emphasis upon numerical representation, meant that he did not link such structures to the traditional concept of quantity.[7] In this respect, Suppes was again following Nagel. However, while Suppes and Zinnes gave attention to purely ordinal structures, later work within this framework has paid increasing attention to possible empirical structures which map into additive substructures of the real numbers (what Stevens would have called interval and ratio scales). 'Hölder's theorem'[8] came to play a central role in this research programme on measurement theory, so much so that it has been caricatured as 'the enterprise of proliferating boring corollaries to Hölder's theorem' (Domotor, 1992, p. 202). The general strategy has been to show that the 'axioms' for certain kinds of more or less directly observable, qualitative, empirical structures enable the definition of an Archimedean, ordered group and, thus, via 'Hölder's theorem', an additive numerical representation.

Suppes and Zinnes (1963) did not advance the substance of measurement theory much beyond Hölder (1901). Their instances of fundamental measurement treated only extensive measurement and difference systems. While there was an array of the latter (including the psychologically interesting cases of semiorders (Luce, 1956) and 'Coombs systems' (Coombs, 1950)), these are all special cases of, applications of, or refinements of Hölder's ideas relating to intervals on a line. The treatment given of derived measurement was especially inadequate given the sorts of problems faced by psychology in attempting to find indirect ways of testing the hypothesis that attributes are quantitative. It failed to bring out the fact that empirical issues are involved and it unfortunately made derived measurement appear to be a matter of stipulation.

However, Suppes' and Zinnes' (1963) paper was significant. First, it demonstrated an approach to fundamental measurement

---

[7] Suppes (1951) used the concepts of quantity and magnitude in a way not unrelated to Russell's (1903) idiosyncratic usage. He did not retain this usage in later publications. Modern representational theories centred upon the concept of quantity are those of Mundy (1987, 1994) and Swoyer (1987).

[8] 'Hölder's theorem', so-called, is not the proposition that ratios of a continuous quantity are isomorphic to the positive real numbers (the main theorem of Hölder, 1901) but, rather, the proposition (e.g., Birkhoff, 1948) that an Archimedean, ordered semi-group is isomorphic to a subgroup of the positive real numbers (a reinterpretation of a footnote of Hölder, 1901). 'Hölder's theorem' is a weaker version of Hölder's main theorem, one in which continuity (or Dedekind completeness) is replaced by the Archimedean condition.

The revolution that happened 199

which required specifying the structure of empirical systems prior to any numerical assignments being made. In this, its approach would have been an antidote to Stevens' operationism had it been adopted. Second, it illustrated the strength of the axiomatic, set-theoretic approach to measurement theory, requiring mathematical proofs that empirical structures were numerically representable and of the uniqueness of proposed representations. In this respect it elevated measurement theory to a level of rigour not attained since Hölder (1901) and Wiener (1919). Set alongside Stevens' main contribution to measurement theory (1951), Suppes and Zinnes (1963) made the quantum leap from informal, 'folk' representationalism[9] to mathematically rigorous representationalism.

In achieving this much, Suppes and Zinnes (1963) provided the methodological basis for the developments that followed, due largely to R. D. Luce and collaborators. Luce (an engineer and mathematician by training) began work in mathematical psychology in the 1950s, having some contact with both Stevens and Suppes (Luce, 1989). He later worked with the statistician, J. W. Tukey, exploring the idea that measurement might be attainable via the discovery of relations of additivity between attributes, as distinct from the more conventional route via relations of additivity within attributes. This led to their revolutionary paper on the theory of conjoint measurement (Luce and Tukey, 1964).

Extensive measurement relies upon locating a concatenation operation the relevant effects of which depend almost entirely upon a single attribute. Every object is complex in the sense of possessing indefinitely many properties and standing in indefinitely many relations to other things (i.e., it has indefinitely many attributes). Any operation of bringing two objects together in some way is an operation which must have effects, but there is no necessity that any of these effects should depend upon just one attribute of the objects involved. Fortunately, it works this way sometimes. For example, in the extensive measurement of length with rigid straight rods, the operation of joining two rods end to end, linearly, is one where an outcome (viz., the length of the

---

[9] To use a term coined by Niederée (1994) with a slightly different meaning. Niederée's category of folk representationalism is wider than mine and Suppes' and Zinnes' 1963 paper would probably fall into it.

200 *The revolution in measurement theory*

joined rods) depends pretty much only upon the lengths of the rods used. Our capacity to locate concatenation operations suitable for extensive measurement of the attributes that interest us depends upon the existence of a very special class of causal relations, as well as upon our sensory-motor capacities and how we, as observers, relate to these attributes. Given the fact that 'nature loves to hide', as Heraclitus aptly put it (Burnet, 1930, p. 133), the amazing thing is not that the prospect of psychological measurement presents enormous difficulties; it is that the accomplishment of physical measurement was so smooth.[10]

The existence of derived measurement in physics implies that for some quantitative attributes there must be ways of identifying the additive structure of quantities other than extensive measurement. The theory of conjoint measurement, as developed by Luce and Tukey (1964), explicates one such other way. Some of the ideas behind the theory of conjoint measurement had been anticipated by Hölder (1901) and others, much later, by Adams and Fagot (1959) and by econometricians (e.g., Debreu, 1960). The mathematical proofs of Luce and Tukey (1964) were improved by Krantz (1964), utilising 'Hölder's theorem', and the account later given in Krantz *et al.* (1971) is perhaps the best mathematical introduction.[11] Here I will simply present the ideas involved without explicating mathematical details and detached from the representational theory.

Hölder (1901) had pioneered the logic of indirect tests of quantitative structure by exploiting the fact that intervals within a straight line are composed additively of discrete parts which are themselves intervals. One of his conditions depended upon the fact that any two intervals, say, that from point A to point C (AC) and that from point A' to point C' ($A'C'$), entirely composed of the discrete interval pairs, AB & BC, and $A'B'$ & $B'C'$ respectively, must equal one another if $AB = A'B'$ and $BC = B'C'$. That is, in the context of discrete adjoining intervals on a straight line, equals plus equals gives equals. What is true of intervals within a

[10] Of course, when inspecting physical measurement in its present state, its accomplishment can seem much smoother than it really was. Consider, for example, the enormous difficulties medieval scientists had in just conceptualising quantities like distance and velocity, a process that took several centuries and was a necessary step for the achievements of Galileo and Newton.

[11] See also Narens (1985). A version written specifically for those with little mathematical background is given by Michell (1990).

The revolution that happened 201

straight line must also be true of differences within any quantitative attribute. The theory of conjoint measurement generalises this idea to combinations of attributes in a context which enables differences within the two attributes to be matched between them relative to joint effects upon a third attribute. If, in some context, attribute Z increases only with increases in attributes X and Y, and increasing X by some specific amount (what I will call a difference within X) has the same effect upon Z as does increasing Y by some specific amount (a difference within Y), then these differences are equal in that sense. The generalisation of Hölder's idea is this: if two discrete but adjoining differences within attribute X can be matched with two discrete but adjoining differences within attribute Y, then if these attributes are quantitative the X-difference entirely composed of the two adjoining differences within X must equal the Y-difference entirely composed of the two adjoining differences within Y (relative to effects upon Z).

The idea of a difference between two levels of X (or Y) having an effect upon Z can be made clearer by taking a hypothetical psychological example. It might be supposed that a person's performance upon an intellectual task (e.g., a test of some kind) is influenced by both ability to do tasks of that kind and level of motivation: increases in ability and increases in motivation each cause increased levels of performance. If an experimental situation can be contrived in which differences in performance are due just to these two attributes and in which levels of each can be identified and manipulated to some extent (although, of course, not initially measured), then the sort of situation exists to which the theory of conjoint measurement applies.

I will develop this example assuming that the way in which ability and motivation combine to produce performance does not differ between individuals. Suppose persons K and L perform at exactly the same level on the test despite the fact that they differ from one another in motivation and ability. K does as well as L because of a higher level of motivation and L compensates for K's higher level of motivation by possessing a higher level of ability. That is, K's level of motivation (M_K) minus L's level of motivation (M_L) equals L's level of ability (A_L) minus K's level of ability (A_K) in terms of effects upon performance. Putting it in quantitative terms, relative to performance, a difference in motivation equals a difference in ability, i.e., $M_K - M_L = A_L - A_K$. The basic idea is that levels within either of the two attributes (motivation and ability) can be 'traded off', as it were, against one another, relative to effects upon a third attribute (performance).

If this is possible for one pair of differences, then it is possible for adjoining differences. Consider persons J and H who also do equally well on the test but better than L and K. Suppose J has K's high level of motivation but does better than K because of more ability. Suppose H has L's high level of ability but does better than L because of higher motivation. Now, $M_H - M_J$ is traded off against $A_J - A_H$, these two differences being equal relative to effects upon performance. However, because $M_J = M_K$ and $A_H = A_L$, if $M_H - M_J = A_J - A_H$, then $M_H - M_K = A_J - A_L$. Since $M_H - M_K$ adjoins $M_K - M_L$ and $A_J - A_L$ adjoins $A_L - A_K$, it follows, if the attributes are quantitative, that the two composite differences, entirely composed of these adjoining components, must likewise be equal, i.e., that

$$(M_H - M_K) + (M_K - M_L) = (A_J - A_L) + (A_L - A_K)$$

and, simplifying, that

$$M_H - M_L = A_J - A_K.$$

Additivity between differences has been indirectly identified via adjoining component differences. This last equality, entailed by the equality of the corresponding components plus the hypothesis that the attributes are quantitative, entails a new prediction. It implies that two people trading off these two differences, must also perform equally well. That is, someone, F, compensating for having only L's level of motivation by having J's level of ability should perform as well as someone, E, compensating for having only K's level of ability by having H's level of motivation. Hence, this prediction provides a specific test of the hypothesis that the attributes are quantitative: if they are, then this prediction follows; if not, then it does not.

This test is called the *Thomsen condition* by Krantz *et al.* (1971) and it is simply, as hinted, a fresh application of the ancient Euclidean axiom that equals plus equals gives equals. If, within it, the equality relation between the terms is replaced by the weak inequality (the relation of equal to or less than), then the condition is known as double cancellation. Double cancellation is a key condition in the theory of conjoint measurement. Krantz *et al.*

The revolution that happened 203

(1971) add two further conditions: solvability and an Archimedean condition. In terms of the above example, solvability just means that for any difference in ability there exists an equal difference in motivation at any point on the motivation attribute, and vice versa. The Archimedean condition amounts to the requirement that differences within the attributes involved cannot be infinitesimally small or infinitely large relative to other differences. That is, given any two differences within one of the attributes (say, within the ability attribute), the smaller of the two multiplied by some natural number will at least equal the larger. The solvability and Archimedean conditions are difficult conditions to test experimentally. However, Scott (1964) proved a result which implies that they can be tested via a potentially infinite hierarchy of cancellation conditions, each similar in form to double cancellation, but most of them involving more terms. The technical details of this are not important to pursue here.[12] The important point is that a way, distinct from extensive measurement, had been specified whereby the hypothesis that an attribute has additive structure could be tested.

Given these conditions (double cancellation, solvability and the Archimedean condition),[13] it not only follows that ability, motivation and performance are quantitative[14] but also that

$$\text{performance} = \text{ability} + \text{motivation}.$$

This last relationship needs commenting upon, for had a different additive relation within the attributes been identified then the functional relationship discovered would have been

$$\text{performance} = \text{ability} \times \text{motivation}.$$

In the example discussed above, a trade-off between an increase in ability and one in motivation identified an equality between

---

[12] For a simplified account see Michell (1990).

[13] I have overlooked two others which Krantz *et al.* (1971) specify: *essentialness* (there must be more than two levels on each of the attributes, ability and motivation); and *weak order* (levels of performance must be ordered in the sense that given any two, one is greater, equal to or less than the other, and if one is greater than another and that greater than a third then the first is also greater than the third).

[14] Strictly speaking, it does not follow that they are quantitative in exactly the sense described in Chapter 3 because these conditions do not entail continuity. However, if the attributes involved satisfy these conditions then their ratios constitute a substructure of the positive real numbers and so the attributes will be measurable.

differences. The same trade-off identifies an equality between ratios. As mentioned in Chapter 3, if there is one relation of addition within a continuous quantity, then there are infinitely many others. As is obviously the case, one relation of addition is identified via differences. When a trade-off between increases in two attributes identifies equal differences, the specific relation of additivity identified within each attribute is one connecting these differences to component differences in the way described above. In turn, via that relation, ratios between differences can be identified and measurement thus achieved.

Alternatively, and, perhaps less obviously in this context, a trade-off between equal increases in two attributes identifies equal ratios directly. An increase from, say, X to Y, within an attribute, not only identifies a difference $(Y - X)$, but also identifies a ratio (Y/X), the factor by which X is multiplied to reach Y. When, for example, the increase from K's ability to L's ability affects performance to the same extent as the increase from L's motivation to K's motivation, then the fact that $A_K/A_L = M_L/M_K$ is identified. The specific relation of additivity identified via such ratios is one between levels of the attribute, rather than between differences as before. These two relations of additivity are totally distinct and so sustain totally different systems of ratios and hence different systems of measurement. However, because it is the case that if

$$\text{performance} = \text{ability} \times \text{motivation},$$

then

$$\log(\text{performance}) = \log(\text{ability}) + \log(\text{motivation}),$$

these two sets of measurements are related mathematically. Identifying ratios directly via trade-offs results in the identification of multiplicative laws between quantitative attributes. This fact connects the theory of conjoint measurement with what Campbell called derived measurement.

Luce and Tukey's (1964) theory of conjoint measurement, reinterpreted as trade-offs between ratios, explained the logic of derived measurement in physical science. Their work made it possible to understand the empirical tests which would validate instances of derived measurement, to understand why attributes quantified via derived measurement are quantitative in the same sense as those quantified via Campbell's notion of fundamental

The revolution that happened 205

measurement, and to understand the precise character of the interlocking between interdependent attributes. Especially importantly, they showed that the measurement of derived attributes did not depend upon the prior measurement of any other attributes, as Campbell had incorrectly insisted. Many matters, hitherto deeply obscure, were made transparent by this work and its later developments. For these reasons, it was a scientific revolution in the strict sense.

Prior to the discovery of conjoint measurement theory it was not clear how derived measurement worked. Consider the case of density. Physicists knew that the density of something was the ratio of its mass to its volume, but what was not clear was the kinds of observations sustaining such a relationship. Campbell (1920) took it that because the ratio of mass to volume is a constant for each different kind of stuff, the constant identifies a quantitative attribute. The theory of conjoint measurement explains why this is so. It is because density and volume trade off against one another relative to mass. For example, if a brick of pure gold weighs exactly the same as a block of pure aluminium, then relative to effects upon mass, the increase in volume between the aluminium block (V_A) and the gold brick (V_G) equals the increase in density between the gold brick (D_G) and the aluminium block (D_A). Identifying equal ratios directly via such trade-offs means that $V_A/V_G = D_G/D_A$. If density is a quantitative attribute, then double cancellation must obtain for sets of such volumes of densities.[15] This means that the known relationship between density, mass and volume is not an arbitrary stipulation, but is a testable, scientific hypothesis. This same logic applies to all instances of derived measurement in physics.

Here was the answer to Craik's request (1940b), mentioned in Chapter 6, that the understanding of measurement be based not just on 'the most stringent instances, such as length', but that it also include 'temperature, density, time, etc.'. The theory of conjoint measurement showed how this could be done without relaxing the classical understanding of quantity and measurement one iota and without resiling from the fact that specific empirical

---

[15] This is, for any three levels of volume, V_1, V_2, and V_3, and for any three densities (as identified, say, via homogeneous substances), D_1, D_2, and D_3, if V_1 of D_2 weighs at least as much as V_2 of D_1 and V_2 of D_3 weighs at least as much as V_3 of D_2, then V_1 of D_3 must weigh at least as much as V_3 of D_1.

206 *The revolution in measurement theory*

tests were at stake. This theory implied that psychologists could not be let off the hook simply because psychological attributes are not amenable to fundamental measurement in Campbell's sense. It scuttled Campbell's attempt to reject the possibility of psychological measurement just as surely as it should have scuttled psychologists' misplaced confidence in the measurability thesis.

Consider, for example, Spearman's two-factor theory of ability mentioned in Chapter 4. It states that performance on a simple intellectual task depends upon two kinds of ability: an ability which contributes only to performance upon tasks of that kind, called specific ability; and an ability which contributes to all intellectual performances, called general ability. On a test, j, composed only of tasks of one specific kind (a *homogeneous* test), Spearman's theory states that

$$z_{ij} = g_j g_i + s_j s_i$$

(where z_{ij} is the standard score of person i on test j; g_i is i's general ability; s_i is i's specific ability; g_j is the extent to which performance on test j is dependent upon general ability; and s_j is the extent to which performance on test j depends upon specific ability). For a fixed homogeneous test, g_j and s_j are constant for all subjects, and so G_i ($= g_j g_i$) and S_i ($= s_j s_i$) are simply rescalings of g_i and s_i. That is,

$$z_i = G_i + S_i.$$

The theory of conjoint measurement applies directly to any theory of this form and, in doing so, brings out clearly (i) that such a theory could be mistaken in its requirement that the relevant attributes be quantitative, and (ii) that, as a consequence, in the absence of relevant evidence, confidence that these attributes are measurable is misplaced.

In this instance there are three further requirements necessary to apply conjoint measurement theory: a theory of problem solving capable of distinguishing homogeneous from non-homogeneous tests;[16] some way of identifying values of general ability that is independent of test scores, some way of identifying values of specific ability, also independently of test scores, and some way of, first, identifying and, then, controlling other relevant causes, so

---

[16] The fact that psychology so far lacks such a theory means that Spearman's later rejection of his two-factor theory (Spearman, 1927) was premature.

that the features of the data diagnostic of additive structure are not swamped by error. These are matters that require the theory to be elaborated well beyond its present state. In requiring these, the theory of conjoint measurement makes explicit a fundamental defect in the exclusively factor analytic study of human intellectual abilities. Not only have quantitative psychologists working within this tradition assumed without adequate evidence that abilities are quantitative attributes, they have also tended to characterise abilities for the most part simply as dispositional concepts. For example, verbal ability is the ability to do well in verbal tasks. Sometimes the best we can do in science is to identify something via its effects, but this never justifies defining it as a disposition to produce those effects, as if absurdly it has no intrinsic character, only effects.[17] A necessary step in applying conjoint measurement theory to Spearman's theory is that of hypothesising more about abilities than just their likely effects upon test performance. Only when theorists in this area are prepared to hypothesise about the intrinsic character of abilities can the issue of whether or not abilities are quantitative be investigated experimentally.

This illustrates the fact that a theory of measurement, like conjoint measurement theory, only takes us so far along the road to quantification. Further progress requires adequately developed substantive theories to which to apply it. Clearly, the successful application of conjoint measurement theory to psychology is never going to be an 'easy fix' for the measurability thesis. Conjoint measurement theory is but one conceptual resource amongst an array. Its significance is that it fills a specific, debilitating gap in the quantitative psychologist's methodological armory. Even applying it, however, the path to evaluating the truth or otherwise of the measurability thesis must be long and difficult, with all of the false leads and discarded ancillary hypotheses that attend any significant scientific advance. It indicates a place to start, but the journey will only ever be completed in conjunction with advances in substantive areas of psychology and a deeper understanding than we have now of how psychological systems

---

[17] Of course, others have drawn attention to this logical defect in the concept of ability (e.g., Passmore, 1935; O'Neil, 1944).

208 *The revolution in measurement theory*

work. As Heraclitus said, those who seek for gold will dig up much earth to find little (Burnett, 1930).

Here is not the place to review all of the advances in measurement theory made by Luce and his associates nor to analyse this movement historically.[18] These developments are covered in detail in the three volumes of the *Foundations of Measurement* (Krantz *et al.*, 1971; Suppes *et al.*, 1989; Luce *et al.*, 1990) and some of them are summarised more accessibly in other publications (e.g., Narens and Luce, 1986; Luce, 1988; Luce and Narens, 1994; Luce, 1996a). From the historical point of view, my interest here is only in the fact that the development of the theory of conjoint measurement enables a test of my hypothesis that something in the internal workings of mainstream quantitative psychology impedes critical inquiry into the measurability thesis.

However, one further development does warrant mention because it reconnects these developments to the concept of quantity. For the most part, Suppes, Luce, and their associates avoided this concept in treating measurement. They theorise at the surface level of the objects or events to which they think numerical assignments are made, rather than at the theoretically deeper level of the quantitative attributes measured. That is, the empirical relational structures considered were generally structures composed of directly observable objects and the empirical relations considered were observable relations between such objects. At their hands, this was a strength because it provided exactly what psychology needed, the surface-level theory of conjoint measurement. However, it raised this question: if extensive measurement yields a ratio scale (in Stevens' sense), if conjoint measurement may also yield ratio scales (given a multiplicative representation of the conjoined factors), and if it is theoretically possible that indefinitely many other kinds of surface-level, empirical structures could also yield ratio scales; what, if anything, do all these different empirical structures have in common sustaining this common form of numerical representation? From the classical viewpoint the answer is obvious: they all involve quantitative attributes. However, these theorists were looking for an answer specifiable via the primitives of the surface structure itself.

Proceeding this way, it was discovered that a relational struc-

---

[18] Díez (1997a & b) attempts this.

The revolution that happened 209

ture rich enough to sustain a ratio scale representation always has the following property: the class of all automorphisms of the structure is an Archimedean ordered group.[19] An automorphism of a relational structure is a function mapping that structure into itself in such a way that its internal structural features are preserved. Automorphisms are familiar enough in science, but sometimes under different names. For example, magnification is an automorphism upon length. When we look through a magnifying glass, small lengths become enlarged in such a way that structural relations are preserved. For example, if length a is greater than b, then a magnified by a specific glass is greater than b magnified by the same glass. Or, if $a + b = c$, then a magnified by a specific glass plus b magnified by the same glass equals c likewise magnified. Of course, a magnifying glass applies typically only to a highly restricted range of lengths, but imagine one that was totally unrestricted and could be applied to all lengths. Such a magnifying glass would be an automorphism upon length. Now, different glasses may differ in strength of magnification, i.e., any specific length is enlarged to different extents by different glasses. Imagine the set of all magnifying glasses with unrestricted application to all lengths. Each glass translates each, specific length into its own, specific enlargement, which, of course, is another length.

By way of contrast, a lens of a different kind may shrink lengths but similarly preserve relevant structural relationships. Likewise imagine the set of all lenses,[20] each able to shrink any length to another, smaller length and each having unrestricted application to all lengths. Now we have the complete set of automorphisms that may be applied to any length. Furthermore, as we know, if we select a length, a, to be magnified or shrunk as the case may be, and another length, b, into which a is to be magnified or shrunk (depending upon whether a is greater or less than b), then these two lengths completely fix the magnifying glass or lens that will do the job. Let us call the set of all such magnifying glasses and lenses the set of automorphic translations upon length. These translations have a quite well defined structure and it is because of this that length is ratio scalable.

---

[19] See Luce (1987) and Luce *et al.* (1990).
[20] For convenience of exposition in this discussion, I will confine the term *lens* to mean only those lenses that shrink lengths.

210 *The revolution in measurement theory*

The structure is this. First, these translations are ordered according to their magnifying or shrinking power. Translation t is greater than or equal to translation s according to whether t applied to any length a is greater than or equal to s applied to a. Second, the translations form a group in the special mathematical sense of that term. In order to see what this means, note first that translations can be combined (a can be magnified to b by glass t and then b to c by glass s which is equivalent to magnifying a to c directly by glass r with the powers of t and s combined) and second that there is the possibility of looking at lengths through a plane glass, one that neither magnifies nor shrinks (this is the identity translation because it 'translates' each length only into itself). The translations are a group because (i) any translation combined with the identity translation equals itself; (ii) for each translation there is another such that the two combined equal the identity translation; and (iii) any three translations combined will result in the same outcome regardless of the order of combination. Third, the set of translations are an Archimedean ordered group, which means that given any two translations which are magnifications (translations greater than the identity), the smaller, when combined some finite number of times with itself, results in a level of magnification at least as great as that of the larger.

If the translations form an Archimedean, ordered group then they have the same structure as a subgroup of the positive real numbers, and so may be given a ratio scale representation. This, of course, is 'Hölder's theorem'. In the forgoing exposition, length has been taken as the example and using somewhat idealised concepts of magnifying glass and lens the concepts of automorphism and translation have been illustrated. To understand the full force of this work in measurement theory, this example must be generalised. Any attribute that can be ordered has its own special analogues of magnifying and shrinking. Of course, it does not automatically follow that these analogues always preserve relevant structural features, whatever these features might be in any specific instance, as idealised magnifying glasses and lenses do for the structural features relevant to length as an extensive structure. Even if they do, it does not automatically follow that the translations so identified constitute an Archimedean, ordered group. But if they do and only if they do, then the empirical structure involved is able to be numerically represented as a ratio scale.

Thus, all ratio scales, no matter what the surface character of the empirical structure involved, share this feature.

However, the fact that this result depends upon 'Hölder's theorem' is significant. Remember that Hölder's main theorem was that the ratios of magnitudes of an unbounded continuous quantity have the structure of the positive real numbers. The restriction to Archimedean structures in 'Hölder's theorem' is a relatively minor one. While in some cases it might be theoretically important, it is not a difference that will ever show up easily, if at all, in empirical tests. Note, also, that the translations discussed above are simply a generalisation of the familiar concept of ratio. Restricted to Hölder's quantities, the translations would be equivalent to ratios. Of course, more generally, as discussed above, they do not appear to be ratios because the concept of quantity has been bypassed and the theory goes directly from the surface, empirical structure to the concept of translations. However, if the translations form an Archimedean, ordered group, then the concept of quantity is, I think, implied. It seems plausible to suggest that the additivity of the translations (which they possess in virtue of being an Archimedean ordered group) reflects back upon the empirical objects involved (or, more correctly, upon their relevant attributes) even when the empirical structure itself contains no directly or even indirectly observable additive relation. Thus, a system of attributes satisfying Hölder's conditions (with the Archimedean condition substituted for his Condition 7) is identified. If this is so, then the representational theory of measurement entails the concept of quantity. However, with quantity comes number, which means that this theory does not escape number as part of the furniture of the world. That is, the concept of representation is redundant as an explanation of measurement (see Michell, 1997a).

ELUDING THE REVOLUTION

The theory of conjoint measurement provides a conceptual basis for testing the measurability thesis. However, Cliff (1992) alleges that mainstream quantitative psychology has declined to exploit this resource. For this reason, he calls it 'the revolution that never happened' (p. 186). In their reply Narens and Luce (1993) pointed to areas such as decision making and psychophysics. These areas of research represent the main empirical interests of these authors and their associates. As a result, research based upon conjoint measurement theory and other, more recent, developments has been conducted in these fields, some of it encouraging (see, for example, Luce, 1996b). However, the fact remains that most research in mainstream quantitative psychology overlooks these revolutionary developments. Those areas of quantitative psychology having the greatest impact upon the lives of ordinary people, viz., those relating to attempts to measure intellectual abilities,[21] personality traits, social attitudes and even most research in psychophysics remain substantially unaffected.

In relation to psychological measurement as understood by most psychologists and by most lay people, Cliff's assessment is correct. This is not to say that all psychometricians have ignored these developments. Ross (1964) had already, apparently independently of Luce and Tukey, anticipated features of conjoint measurement theory and had applied his ideas to issues relevant to psychological testing. Keats (1967), in an article reviewing then recent developments in test theory, mentioned Ross and gave centre place to the contributions of Luce and Tukey (1964), suggesting how they could be applied to Rasch's (1960) item response theory. Furthermore, Volume 1 of *Foundations of Measurement* (Krantz *et al.*, 1971) was reviewed by Ramsay (1975) in *Psychometrika*, the leading journal of mainstream quantitative psychology.[22] Such initial, isolated attention to these developments makes their subsequent absence from mainstream quantitative psychology all the more striking. Levy's otherwise perspicacious commentary on test theory (1973) lists Krantz *et al.* (1971) as a reference, but does not mention conjoint measurement; Lumsden's highly critical review of developments in test theory (1976) referred to no research using these ideas; and works such as Goldstein and Wood (1989), and van der Linden and Hambleton (1997), which review developments in item response theory, make no mention of it (despite attempts by Keats (1967), Brogden (1977), Perline *et al.* (1979) and Andrich

---

[21] Blinkhorn (1997) gives a brief history of developments in test theory over the past fifty years. No mention is made of conjoint measurement theory.

[22] Ramsay (1991) also reviewed in the same journal volumes 2 and 3 when they were published about twenty years later. Interestingly, in that review he recommended that psychologists cease using the term *measurement* to describe their numerical practices. This recommendation goes too far: psychologists' use of the term *measurement* is really hypothetical.

(1988) to relate Rasch's theory to conjoint measurement). One recent publication does highlight the significance of conjoint measurement for psychometrics: Cliff's own (1993).

Confirming Cliff's assessment is the fact that only in very exceptional cases do these developments form part of the standard psychology curriculum. All textbooks on test theory, from Lord and Novick (1968) to the present not only ignore them, they contain no discussion of the more general underlying issues, the measurability thesis and the quantity objection. Aiken *et al.*(1990) surveyed Ph.D. programmes in quantitative methodology in psychology in North American universities. Although the tone was generally critical and programmes in measurement were specifically targeted, no mention at all was made of work in measurement theory. Meier's recent paper on 'revitalizing the measurement curriculum' in psychology (1993), gave no attention to these developments or to the underlying conceptual issues. The measurability thesis, the rock upon which quantitative psychology is built, and conjoint measurement theory, psychology's best chance of checking the foundations upon which this rock stands, are systematically ignored within mainstream quantitative psychology. Cliff (1992) proposed five reasons.

His first proposal is that the mathematics used in modern representational theory is 'foreign to most other quantitatively oriented psychologists' (p. 188). A similar observation was made by Ramsay (1975). While perhaps true, this suggestion does not account for neglect of this work. Scientists seriously researching some issue do not let the fact that a body of knowledge is 'foreign' stand in their way, once its relevance is recognised. As illustrated in the above exposition of conjoint measurement, the conceptual basis is far from foreign and it is easily detached from the abstract algebra and set theory in which it is typically cast. The fact that very little attempt has been made to master even this conceptual basis suggests that quantitative psychologists do not recognise its significance for psychological measurement. That suggestion plus the foreign appearance of the mathematics together might explain this neglect.

Cliff's second proposal is that there has not been enough 'in the way of striking empirical examples of its utility' (p. 188). In their reply, Narens and Luce (1993) again mentioned decision theory as providing such an example. However, applications are

214 *The revolution in measurement theory*

not 'striking' *in vacuo*. Context is crucial. Those already convinced that psychological attributes are quantitative and that existing procedures measure them, will fail to be impressed by demonstrations of what, for them, would be the obvious. On the other hand, any quantitative psychologists for whom the measurability thesis raises empirical issues will not require 'striking' empirical examples before wanting to apply revolutionary ideas.

Cliff's third proposal is what he calls the 'error problem': 'There has been relatively little in the way of answers to questions of how to apply the abstract measurement principles to fallible or incomplete data' (p. 189). Narens and Luce (1993) concede that this is a problem. However, what they do not bring out is that its importance needs to be placed in the context of how the issue of 'error' is dealt with more generally in psychology. What psychologists call 'error' in their data has two sources. The first source resides in the observer or the instruments of observation used. Error deriving from this source is a familiar concept in quantitative science. When not thought to be systematic, it is taken as random and is generally dealt with by averaging. The second source resides in the causal processes underlying the phenomena studied. In psychology it is generally impossible to study specific processes in isolation from wider causal networks. Unwanted factors invariably contaminate observations. Of course, this is a problem in all science, but an especially difficult one in psychology because of the complexity of psychological processes, our general ignorance of them, and the insurmountable difficulties of controlling extraneous factors. The conventional way of dealing with this problem in psychology when hypothetical quantitative attributes are under investigation is to conceptualise error as a random process, described by the 'Normal curve' and added on to the effects of the hypothetical processes of immediate interest. Enough has been written in recent times to suggest that this conventional 'solution' to the problem of error is not free of its own, possibly debilitating, difficulties (e.g., Gigerenzer *et al.*, 1989; Gigerenzer, 1993). However, when all is said and done, the interpretation of data in science is an art (not a mechanical procedure) and it is an art best practised under no illusions regarding its fallible and speculative character. Seen in this wider context, the problem of error for conjoint measurement theory is not diminished, but it is seen to be part of a parcel of problems general to

Eluding the revolution

psychology and, indeed, to a greater or lesser extent, to all science. Those convinced of the importance of conjoint measurement theory regard the problem of error as a challenge, not an obstacle. Those interested in applying this theory have found their various ways (e.g., Falmagne and Iverson, 1979; Michell, 1994b; Pieters, 1979; Rodewald, 1974; Stankov and Cregan, 1993; Tversky, 1967). To those not convinced of this theory's importance, however, this problem could serve as an excuse for continuing to ignore it.

Cliff's fourth proposal for explaining the failure of quantitative psychologists to apply conjoint measurement theory is what he refers to as a difference in 'research styles' between the mathematical psychologists developing this theory and both research traditions (experimental and differential) characterising mainstream quantitative psychology. Experimental psychologists prefer designs amenable to analysis of variance, and differential psychologists prefer multivariate linear methods, such as correlation and factor analysis. Cliff is correct about these different research styles and the deep reluctance of the psychologists involved to depart from their respective traditions. However, the interesting question in this context is what this fact tells us about the attitudes of such researchers to psychological measurement. In so far as the various univariate and multivariate procedures used in these areas of psychology are intended to inform us about psychological quantitative attributes, they presume that such attributes are already known to be quantitative, and so presume the very thing that conjoint measurement theory might be used to test. That is, these research styles are really theoretically loaded packages already tilted against conjoint measurement theory. Those committed to these styles have first accepted, perhaps without noticing it, the very proposition conjoint measurement theory is designed to test.

Cliff's final proposal is that quantitative psychologists were 'distracted by separate developments that took place at about the same time' (1992, p. 189). He refers, on the one hand, to 'the striking work of Sternberg' and, on the other, to 'Jöreskog's ... solution, at a stroke, of a multitude of computational and, at least indirectly, conceptual problems' (p. 189). Now, whatever the merits of this other work, it is not the case that it dealt with the issue of showing how the conflict between the measurability thesis and quantity objection could be resolved. To propose that these

216 *The revolution in measurement theory*

separate developments could have distracted quantitative psychologists from this issue for almost thirty years, had they recognised its importance, is implausible to say the least. If a fundamental issue is recognised as unresolved, it does not normally lie fallow for that length of time if the means to investigate it are available. Cliff's proposal also presumes, rather simplistically, that both these developments and conjoint measurement theory could not have been taken up at once.

Considered in the light of the fundamental empirical issues raised by the measurability thesis, Cliff's proposed reasons alone are not adequate to explain the failure of quantitative psychologists to exploit conjoint measurement theory. Only if the measurability thesis is understood as already accepted, and accepted free of qualms, are any of Cliff's reasons plausible. In turn, the widespread acceptance of Stevens' definition of measurement explains how it is that the measurability thesis can be accepted within quantitative psychology in the face of the otherwise obvious quantity objection.

IN FINE

Failure to investigate the measurability thesis, by itself, of course, is not an error. Such failure implies, however, that attempts to measure psychological attributes do not yet stand as scientific results. They remain hypotheses, the truth of which have not been adequately tested. Instead of candidly admitting their ignorance, quantitative psychologists promote their attributes as quantitative and their procedures as instruments of measurement. They may be right: the attributes may be quantitative and the procedures may measure them. However, the point is that in the absence of experimental tests known to be specifically sensitive to the hypothesised additive structure of the attributes studied, it is not known whether or not these attributes are quantitative and thus it is not known whether or not existing procedures measure them. The error committed, therefore, is that of accepting hypotheses prior to possessing adequate evidence. This error has been further compounded by another: an understanding of measurement which hides the first error has become institutionalised. This, in turn, has had the consequence that when a way of possibly correcting the first error was discovered, it was largely ignored because its significance could not be appreciated. Thus, a necessary component of normal science, viz., science's error-correcting mechanism, has been subverted.

Does this tissue of errors matter? Of course, it matters to the extent that scientists who overstate their findings, even unwittingly, may bring science into disrepute. It matters as well to the extent that those whose lives are affected by scientific claims have a right to be assured that these claims are warranted by sufficient evidence. But do these errors matter in the more fundamental, scientific sense of possibly interfering with the progress of psychology as a science?

Some quantitative psychologists with whom I have discussed this question console themselves by pointing to the history of quantitative physics. Physics became a successful quantitative science before anyone had anything like the insights into the logic of quantification reported in Chapter 3 and certainly well before the theory of conjoint measurement was articulated. If this lack did not in the end harm physics, the paradigm of quantitative science, why should it harm psychology? Some think that psychology's progress thus far confirms the view that it is well on the way to becoming a successful quantitative science, although that is a matter of opinion. At least one wise mind has his doubts (Meehl, 1991) and another thinks that psychologists cannot at present do any better than order levels of their attributes (Cliff, 1996). Psychology might be on the way to becoming a successful quantatitive science, but as a body of workable, quantitative theories and laws, it is so far short of the example set by physics that no one yet has a clear idea of what a successful quantitative psychology would look like. The history of science teaches us many things, but I do not think that one of them is that we can expect to make progress by ignoring pertinent matters.

If it does teach us one thing, it is that the acquisition of scientific knowledge does not always travel in straight lines. The route to scientific understanding is sometimes circuitous, even chaotic. Only the reckless would attempt to predict the future of psychology from the history of physics. The differences between the circumstances of the two sciences are significant enough to make such extrapolation tenuous in the extreme. First, physics began its history in the fortunate position of being able to isolate a range of attributes separately (the geometric attributes), the

218   *The revolution in measurement theory*

quantitative structure of which was directly evident. Indeed, length provided the paradigm of continuous quantity for millennia and the logic of quantification was developed with the example of length uppermost. Psychology differs from physics in that no hypothesised psychological attributes are obviously quantitative in the manner of the geometric attributes.

Second, when the range of known physical quantities was extended via the application of the experimental method, physicists again were fortunate in being able to isolate and control independent variables in a way that is presently impossible in psychology. Under certain conditions it is highly plausible to conclude that a theoretical attribute is quantitative. For example, if it is found that an observed continuous quantity (say, mass) varies, so far as we can tell, continuously with a theoretical attribute (say, density), which corresponds to a directly observable attribute (say, kind of substance), while a third (say, volume) is held constant, then the most economical explanation of this relationship is that the theoretical attribute (density) is likewise, a continuous quantity. Quantitative effects typically require quantitative causes because the level of complexity of the causally relevant attribute must match the level of complexity of the attribute involved in the effects. This sort of principle sustained the expansion of quantitative physics in a way that it cannot yet do with psychology. Psychologists have not yet devised ways of isolating their relevant theoretical attributes. Behaviour is always a function of more than one attribute and these cannot be controlled separately. This fact itself is further complicated by the possibility of individual differences in causal processes between subjects (they are distinct causal systems, after all) and by the ubiquitous problem that error (in the sense of effects caused by 'unwanted' factors) masks structure in psychological data much more than it does in physics. While quantitative effects require quantitative causes, they do not require, *a priori*, that all of their causal conditions must be quantitative. Because causal processes can never be manipulated as cleanly in psychology as in physics, it is never clear in psychology that all of the relevant causes must be quantitative even when the effects studied are quantitative (e.g., reaction times or observed scores). Also, exclusively quantitative theories can never be considered as the only possible candidates in psychology because we have models of less complicated causal systems (e.g., computer models of problem solving) in which

In fine 219

quantitative effects can be produced by a confluence of quantitative and non-quantitative causes. Furthermore, the one distinctive process that psychologists study, and the one that is causally relevant in most psychological experiments, cognition, does not have an obviously quantitative structure. Indeed, behaviour, in so far as it is infused with cognition, has structural features which are definitely non-quantitative (e.g., semantic and grammatical structures). This fact makes exclusively quantitative theories unlikely, *a priori*, to be adequate in giving causal accounts of behaviour. Of course, exclusively quantitative psychological theories can be hypothesised and, to an extent, can be tested experimentally, but without a clear idea of how the structure of the hypothesised underlying attributes may be reflected in behavioural data, the scientist does not have a clear idea of what to look for in order to distinguish quantitative from non-quantitative causes. These differences between psychology and quantitative physics are significant and it is obtuse to ignore them.

The only reliable way forward in science is by subjecting all empirical hypotheses to empirical test, and not by protecting hypotheses in which we have a vested interest. This is the normal way for science to proceed. It cannot ensure success, because nothing can. And the possibility of quantitative psychology achieving success in some way via its present uncritical route cannot be ruled out. However, a science that ignores a body of theory which is relevant to the testing of some of its hypotheses is denying itself an opportunity. Science is not so easy that opportunities can sensibly be passed up. Most scientists recognise this fact and the situation is only different in psychology because a body of theory is not recognised for the opportunity it is.

If, despite this error and neglect, quantitative psychology has a claim to be seen as a normal science, it is in large part because of the trajectory of critical thought extending from Helmholtz and von Kries to Suppes and Luce. This trajectory delivered a revolution in ideas about measurement. If it can be accepted that some of psychology's cherished attributes, such as the intellectual abilities, the personality traits, the social attitudes, might not be quantitative, indeed, if it is even possible that some of the psychological attributes listed at the beginning of this book might not in fact be quantitative, can quantitative psychology, as a science, afford not to grasp this opportunity?

Glossary

abilities hypothetical properties of, states of, or processes within a person which are supposed to sustain cognition and cause performance on intellectual tasks, for example, verbal ability or spatial ability.

additivity a relation between levels of a quantitative attribute. For any two distinct levels of a quantitative attribute, a third always exists such that the greater of the two is the sum of the third and the less. These three levels are related additively. Additive relations must be commutative and associative.

Archimedean condition a condition satisfied by a quantitative attribute if and only if the magnitude of any level relative to each other is finite.

associativity a property possessed by a form of combination if and only if the combination of one term with the combination of a second and third is equivalent to the combination of the third with the combination of the first and second. The relation of additivity between magnitudes is associative.

asymmetry a property of binary (i.e., two-term) relations. A relation is asymmetric if and only if whenever it holds between one thing and a second, it does not hold between the second and the first. For example, the relation of *being the mother of* is asymmetric because if one person is the mother of a second, the second is never the mother of the first.

attribute a range of properties (e.g., lengths or colours) or a range of relations (e.g., velocities or kinships) that are mutually exclusive in the sense that (i) if properties, then nothing can possess more than one property within the range at any one time, or (ii) if relations, then no ordered class of entities (of the appropriate number) can stand in more than one relation within the range at any one time.

categories sometimes called the 'categories of existence'. They are features common to all situations (and so to those that might be studied scientifically), for example, quantity, generality and spatio-temporal location. That is, every situation involves *some number* of

Glossary 221

things of *some general kind*, located *somewhere* at *some time*. The logic of science requires investigation of the categories.

causality a relation between events: an event of kind X, occurring in a context (or 'causal field') of kind C, causes an event of kind Y if and only if in the context of C, X is necessary and sufficient for Y. If to *be* is to have effects (that is, to make some sort of difference), then causality is one of the categories.

commutativity a property possessed by a form of combination if and only if the combination of every pair of terms is independent of order. The relation of additivity between magnitudes is commutative because if one magnitude is the sum of another two in one order, it remains their sum in the other.

concatenation operation a humanly performable operation which, when carried out upon objects manifesting different levels of a quantitative attribute, directly displays the additive structure of the attribute, at least for a limited range. For example, the operation of combining rigid, straight rods lengthwise linearly.

conjoint measurement a way of identifying the additive structure of attributes indirectly, via trade-offs in the way that two attributes relate to a third. For example, in the way that differences in density can be traded off against differences in volume to keep mass constant, the otherwise hidden additive structure within the attribute of density is revealed.

connexity a property of some binary (that is, two-term) relations. A relation is connected if and only if it holds between any two things which stand in that relation to other things. For example, the relation of being *not older than* is connected.

continuous quantity a quantitative attribute that contains no gaps in its order. It is not just that between any two distinct magnitudes there is a third, less than the greater and greater than the less, but that for any subset of the magnitudes containing all those less than some other specific magnitude, there is a magnitude no less than any in the set and no greater than any not in the set. Technically put, its order is not just *dense*, but *Dedekind complete*.

extensive quantity a quantitative attribute, the additive structure of which is manifest via a concatenation operation for some range of its magnitudes, for example, length.

homomorphism the same as an isomorphism except that one structure has more objects in it than the second, to which it is otherwise similar in form. As a result objects in the first are matched, many to one, with those in the second. If measurement is understood as the numerical representation of objects, then because more than one object can be assigned the same number, the representation is a homomorphism, rather than an isomorphism.

222 *Glossary*

intensive quantity a quantitative attribute, the additive structure of which is not open to direct test via human sensory/motor capacities. For example, we are only able to show that attributes like temperature and density are quantitative indirectly (e.g., by conjoint measurement).

isomorphism two distinct relational structures are isomorphic if they are identical in form. That is, the objects in the two structures can be matched, one to one, in such a way that corresponding to any situation in one structure, involving some of its objects, there is an analogous situation in the second involving the matching objects. For example, there is an isomorphism between the *Titanic* as she was, say, in March 1912, and an exact scale replica constructed now.

magnitude a specific level of a quantitative attribute (or quantity). For example, each specific length that any object might have is a magnitude of the attribute, length.

measure an estimate of the ratio of a magnitude of a quantity to a unit of the same quantity.

measurement the discovery or estimation of the ratio of a magnitude of a quantity to a unit of the same quantity.

metaphysics the branch of philosophy concerned with the study of the most general features of existence (the categories of being).

number the ratio of a magnitude of a quantity to another of the same attribute. If the quantity is discrete then the number is *rational*; if the second magnitude is an aliquot part of the first, then the number is *natural* and if either is a difference, then the number is *integral*. If the quantity is continuous, then the number is *real*.

numeral a conventional sign for a number. The Arabic numerals, *1, 2, 3, ...*, are those most commonly used, although Roman numerals, *I, II, III, ...*, have a ceremonial function. Signs should never be confused with what they signify.

practicalism the view that the success of a science depends upon the extent to which it has practical applications.

property an attribute that something has intrinsically, that is, logically independently of anything else. For example, if a person is male, then his being male logically implicates no other object. Thus, *being male* is a property. However, if a person is a parent, then there must be something else (viz., a child). Thus, *being a parent* is not a property.

psychological attribute an attribute of a person (or, more generally, of an organism) that is logically dependent upon cognition.

psychophysics the study of the relationship between physical attributes and the sensations or judgments of them.

Pythagoreanism the thesis that all attributes are quantitative.

quantification the process of (i) showing that an attribute is quantitative and (ii) devising procedures to measure it.

Glossary 223

quantity an attribute possessing ordinal and additive structure. For example, length is a quantity because lengths are ordered according to their magnitude and each specific length is constituted additively of other specific lengths.

ratio the magnitude of one level of a quantitative attribute relative to another of the same attribute. If the quantitative attribute is continuous, then the ratios are real numbers and they are always relative to a specific relation of additivity.

relation an attribute that is not intrinsic to something, that is, not logically independent of other things. It is the way in which something is *vis-à-vis* one or more other things. For example, *being a parent of* is a relation, for it is how one person is *vis-à-vis* another and no one can be a parent without there being another person, a child of the first.

scientism the view that a method successfully employed in one or more sciences must apply to others, for example, the view that because measurement is successfully employed in the physical sciences it must apply to others, such as psychology.

sensations the immediate objects of sensory perception according to the school of thought that locates these objects in the mind or brain of the perceiving person.

situation a state of affairs. It is always a matter of something's having a property or standing in relation to one or more other things.

symmetry a property of some binary (that is, two-term) relations. A relation is symmetric if and only if whenever one thing stands in that relation to a second thing, the second thing also stands in that same relation to the first thing. For example, the relation of *being a sibling of* is symmetric.

transitivity a key property of ordinal relations. A binary (that is, two-term) relation is transitive if and only if whenever one thing stands in that relation to a second thing, and the second to a third thing, then the first also stands in that relation to the third. For example, the relation of *being heavier than* is transitive.

unit a specific magnitude of a quantity relative to which measurements are made.

References

Adams, E. W. and R. F. Fagot, 1959, A model of riskless choice, *Behavioral Science*, 4, 1–10

1975, On the theory of biased bisection operations and their inverses, *Journal of Mathematical Psychology*, 12, 35–52

Adams, H. F., 1931, Measurement in psychology, *Journal of Applied Psychology*, 15, 545–54

Adler, H. E., 1980, Vicissitudes of Fechnerian psychophysics in America, in R. W. Reiber and K. Salzinger, (eds.), *Psychology: Theoretical–historical Perspectives*, New York: Academic Press, pp. 11–23

Aiken, L. S., S. G. West, L. Sechrest, and R. R. Reno, 1990, Graduate training in statistics, methodology, and measurement in psychology, *American Psychologist*, 45, 721–34

Anderson, J., 1962, *Studies in Empirical Philosophy*, Sydney: Angus and Robertson

Andrich, D., 1988, *Rasch Models for Measurement*. Newbury Park, CA.: Sage

Armstrong, D. M., 1968, *A Materialist Theory of the Mind*, London: Routledge and Kegan Paul

1978, *Universals and Scientific Realism*, Cambridge University Press

1989, *Universals: An Opinionated Introduction*, Boulder: Westview Press

1997, *A World of States of Affairs*, Cambridge University Press

Bairati, E., 1991, *Piero della Francesca*, New York: Crescent Books

Baker, A. J., 1986, *Australian Realism: The Systematic Philosophy of John Anderson*, Cambridge University Press

Baldwin, J. M., 1902, *Dictionary of Philosophy and Psychology*, Vol. 2, London: Macmillan

Bartlett, F. C., 1958, *Thinking: An Experimental and Social Study*, London: Unwin

1965, Remembering Dr Myers, *Bulletin of the British Psychological Society*, 18, 1–10

Bartlett, R. J., 1940a, In defence of the measurability of sensation intensity, *Advancement of Science*, 1, 343–4

1940b, Measurement in psychology, *Advancement of Science*, 1, 422–41

1952, Obituary: S. J. F. Philpott, *Quarterly Bulletin of the British Psychological Society*, 3, 114

References 225

Beckwith, T. G. and N. L. Buck, 1961, *Mechanical Measurements,* Reading, MA: Addison-Wesley

Benacerraf, P. and H. Putnam, 1983, *Philosophy of Mathematics: Selected Readings,* 2nd edn, Cambridge University Press

Benjamin, L. T., 1977, The psychology round table: revolution of 1936, *American Psychologist,* 32, 542–9

Bergson, H., [1889] 1913, *Time and Free Will,* trans. by F. L. Pogson, London: George Allen and Co

Berkeley, G., [1721] 1951, De Motu, in A. A. Luce and T. E. Jessop, (eds.), *The Works of George Berkeley Bishop of Cloyne,* Vol. 4, London: Thomas Nelson, pp. 31–52

Beveridge, E., 1924, *Fergusson's Scottish Proverbs,* Edinburgh: Blackwood

Bigelow, J., 1988, *The Reality of Numbers: A Physicalist's Philosophy of Mathematics,* Oxford: Clarendon Press

Binet, A., 1905, *L'Étude éxperimentale de l'intelligence,* Paris: Schleicher

Birkhoff, G., 1948, *Lattice Theory,* New York: American Mathematical Society

Blinkhorn, S. F., 1997, Past imperfect, future conditional: fifty years of test theory, *British Journal of Mathematical and Statistical Psychology,* 50, 175–85

Bock, R. D. and L. V. Jones, 1968, *The Measurement and Prediction of Judgment and Choice,* San Francisco: Holden-Day

Boring, E. G., 1920, The logic of the normal law of error in mental measurement, *American Journal of Psychology,* 31, 1–33
  1921, The stimulus error, *American Journal of Psychology,* 32, 449–71
  1957, *A History of Experimental Psychology,* New York: Appleton–Century Croft

Bostock, D., 1979, *Logic and Arithmetic,* Vol. 2: *Rational and Irrational Numbers,* Oxford: Clarendon Press

Brentano, F., [1874] 1973, *Psychology From an Empirical Standpoint,* trans. by Antos C. Rancurello, D. B. Terrell and Linda L. McAlister, New York: Humanities Press

Bridgman, P. W., 1927, *The Logic of Modern Physics,* New York: Macmillan
  1964, *The Nature of Physical Theory,* New York: Wiley

Broadbent, D. E., 1970, Sir Frederic Bartlett: an appreciation, *Bulletin of the British Psychological Society,* 23, 1–3

Brogden, H. E., 1977, The Rasch model, the law of comparative judgment and additive conjoint measurement, *Psychometrika,* 42, 631–4

Brooks, G. P. and S. K. Aalto, 1981, The rise and fall of moral algebra: Francis Hutcheson and the mathematization of psychology, *Journal of the History of the Behavioral Sciences,* 17, 343–56

Brown, F. G., 1996, Measurement, in R. J. Corsini and A. J. Auerbach, (eds.), *Concise Encyclopedia of Psychology,* New York: Wiley, pp. 546–8

Brown, J., 1992, *The Definition of a Profession: The Authority of Metaphor in the History of Intelligence Testing, 1890–1930,* Princeton University Press

226 *References*

Brown, J. F., 1934, A methodological consideration of the problem of psychometrics, *Erkenntnis*, 4, 46–61

Brown, W., 1913, Are the intensity differences of sensation quantitative? IV, *British Journal of Psychology*, 6, 184–9

1938a, Notes on Mr. Guild's statement, *British Association for the Advancement of Science*, 108, 328–9

1938b, *Psychological Methods of Healing: An Introduction to Psychotherapy*, London: University of London Press

Brown, W. and G. H. Thomson, 1921, *The Essentials of Mental Measurement*, Cambridge University Press

Brozek, J. and H. Gundlach, 1988, *G. T. Fechner and Psychology*, Passau: Passavia Universitätsverlag

Buchdahl, G., 1964, Theory construction: the work of Norman Robert Campbell, *Isis*, 55, 151–62

Burnet, J., 1914, *Greek Philosophy: Thales to Plato*, London: Macmillan

1930, *Early Greek Philosophy*, London: Macmillan

Buroker, J. V., 1991, Descartes on sensible qualities, *Journal of the History of Philosophy*, 29, 585–611

Burt, C., 1960, Gustav Theodor Fechner Elemente Der Psychophysik, *The British Journal of Statistical Psychology*, 13, 1–10

Byerley, H. C., 1974, Realist foundations of measurement, in K. F. Schaffner and R. S. Cohen, (eds.), *P.S.A. 1972*, Dordrecht: Reidel, pp. 375–84

Campbell, N. R., 1920, *Physics, the Elements*, Cambridge University Press

1921, *What is Science?* London: Methuen

1928, *An Account of the Principles of Measurement and Calculation*, London: Longman, Green and Co

1933a, The measurement of visual sensations, *Proceedings of the Physical Society*, 45, 565–71

1933b, Reply, *Proceedings of the Physical Society*, 45, 588–90

1938, Measurement and its importance for philosophy, *Aristotelian Society, Supplementary Volume 17*, 121–42

1940, Physics and psychology, *British Association for the Advancement of Science*, 2, 347–8

Canfield, T. M., 1973, The professionalisation of American psychology, *Journal of the History of the Behavioral Sciences*, 9, 66–75

Cattell, J. McK., 1890, Mental tests and measurements, *Mind*, 15, 373–80

1893a, Mental measurement, *Philosophical Review*, 2, 316–32

1893b, On errors of observation, *American Journal of Psychology*, 5, 285–93

1902, Measurement, in J. M. Baldwin, (ed.), *Dictionary of Philosophy and Psychology*, Vol 2, London: Macmillan, p. 57

1904, The conceptions and methods of psychology, *Popular Science Monthly*, December, 176–86

References   227

Clagget, M., 1968, *Nicole Oresme and the Medieval Geometry of Qualities and Motions*, Wisconsin: University Press

Cliff, N., 1992, Abstract measurement theory and the revolution that never happened, *Psychological Science*, 3, 186–90

    1993, What is and isn't measurement, in G. Keren and C. Lewis, (eds.), *A Handbook for Data Analysis in the Behavioral Sciences: Methodological Issues*, Hillsdale, NJ: Erlbaum, pp. 59–93

    1996, *Ordinal Methods for Behavioral Data Analysis*, Mahwah, NJ: Erlbaum

Clifford, W. K., 1882, *Mathematical Papers*, London: Macmillan

Cohen, M. R. and E. Nagel, 1934, *An Introduction to Logic and Scientific Method*, London: Routledge and Kegan Paul

Collins, M., 1951, Obituary notices: Emeritus Professor James Drever, *British Journal of Psychology*, 42, 311–14

Comrey, A. L., 1950, An operational approach to some problems in psychological measurement, *Psychological Review*, 57, 217–28

    1951, Mental testing and the logic of measurement, *Educational and Psychological Measurement*, 11, 323–34

Coombs, C. H., 1950, Psychological scaling without a unit of measurement, *Psychological Review*, 57, 145–58

Corsini, R. J. and A. J. Auerbach, 1996, *Concise Encyclopedia of Psychology*, New York: Wiley

Craik, K. J. W., 1940a, On the sone scale, *Advancement of Science*, 1, 335–340

    1940b, In defence of the measurability of sensation intensity, *Advancement of Science*, 1, 343

Crombie, A. C., 1952a, *Augustine to Galileo: Vol. 1, Science in the Middle Ages 5th to 13th Centuries*, London: Heinemann

    1952b, *Augustine to Galileo: Vol. 2, Science in the Later Middle Ages and Early Modern Times 13th to 17th Centuries*, London: Heinemann

    1994, *Styles of Scientific Thinking in the European Tradition*, London: Duckworth

Cronbach, L. J. and G. C. Gleser, 1957, *Psychological Tests and Personnel Decisions*, Urbana: University of Illinois Press

Crosby, A. W., 1997, *The Measure of Reality: Quantification and Western Society, 1250–1600*, Cambridge University Press

Danto, A. and S. Morgenbesser, 1960, *Philosophy of Science*, New York: World Publishing Co

Danziger, K., 1990, *Constructing the Subject: Historical Origins of Psychological Research*, Cambridge University Press

Dawes Hicks, G., 1913, Are the intensity differences of sensation quantitative? II, *British Journal of Psychology*, 6, 155–74

Debreu, G., 1960, Topological methods in cardinal utility theory, in K. J. Arrow, S. Karlin, and P. Suppes, (eds.), *Mathematical Methods in the Social Sciences*, Stanford University Press, pp. 16–26

228 *References*

Dedekind, R., [1872] 1901, Continuity and irrational numbers, in *Essays on the Theory of Numbers*, trans. by W. W. Beman, Chicago: Open Court, pp. 1–27

De Morgan, A., 1836, *The Connexion of Number and Magnitude*, London: Taylor and Walton

Denzin, N. K. and Y. S. Lincoln, 1994, *Handbook of Qualitative Research*, Thousand Oaks, CA: Sage

Descartes, R., [1637] 1954, *The Geometry*, trans. by D. E. Smith and M. L. Latham, New York: Dover

  [1641] 1934, Objections and Replies, in E. S. Haldane and G. R. T. Ross, (eds.), *The Philosophical Works of Descartes*, Vol. 2, Cambridge University Press

  [1644] 1985, Principles of Philosophy, in J. Cottingham, R. Stoothoff and D. Murdoch, (eds.), *The Philosophical Works of Descartes*, Vol. 1, Cambridge University Press

Díez, J. A., 1997a, A hundred years of numbers, an historical introduction to measurement theory 1887–1990, Part I, *Studies in History and Philosophy of Science*, 28, 167–185

  1997b, A hundred years of numbers, an historical introduction to measurement theory 1887–1990, Part II, *Studies in History and Philosophy of Science*, 28, 237–65

Domotor, Z., 1992, Measurement from empiricist and realist points of view, in C. W. Savage and P. Ehrlich, (eds.), *Philosophical and Foundational Issues in Measurement Theory*, Hillsdale, NJ: Erlbaum, pp. 195–221

Drake, S., 1957, *Discoveries and Opinions of Galileo*, New York: Doubleday

  1978, *Galileo at Work: His Scientific Biography*, University of Chicago Press

Drever, J., 1938, The quantitative relation between physical stimulus and sensory event, *British Association for the Advancement of Science*, 108, 331–4

Dummett, M., 1991, *Frege: Philosophy of Mathematics*, London: Duckworth

Ebbinghaus, H., 1908, *Psychology: An Elementary Textbook*, trans. by M. Meyer, Boston: Heath

Ellis, B., 1966, *Basic Concepts of Measurement*, Cambridge University Press

Fagot, R. F., 1961, A model for equisection scaling, *Behavioral Science*, 6, 127–33

Falmagne, J-C. and G. Iverson, 1979, Conjoint Weber laws and additivity, *Journal of Mathematical Psychology*, 86, 25–43

Fechner, G. T., [1851] 1987, Outline of a new principle of mathematical psychology, *Psychological Research*, 49, 203–7

  1860, *Elemente der Psychophysik*, Leipzig: Breitkopf and Hartel; Eng. trans. by H. E. Adler, 1966, *Elements of Psychophysics*, Vol. 1, D. H. Howes and E. G. Boring, (eds.), New York: Rinehart and Winston

  [1887] 1987, My own viewpoint on mental measurement, *Psychological Research*, 49, 213–19

References 229

Fehér, M., 1995, *Changing Tools: Case Studies in the History of Scientific Methodology*, Budapest: Akadémiai Kiadó

Ferguson, A., C.S. Myers, R. J. Bartlett, H. Banister, F. C. Bartlett, W. Brown, N. R. Campbell, J. Drever, J. Guild, R. A. Houstoun, J. C. Irwin, G. W. C. Kaye, S. J. F. Philpott, L. F. Richardson, J. H. Shaxby, T. Smith, R. H. Thouless and W. S. Tucker, 1938, Quantitative estimates of sensory events: interim report of the committee appointed to consider and report upon the possibility of quantitative estimates of sensory events, *British Association for the Advancement of Science*, 108, 277–334

Ferguson, A., C. S. Myers, R. J. Bartlett, H. Banister, F. C. Bartlett, W. Brown, N. R. Campbell, K. J. W. Craik, J. Drever, J. Guild, R. A. Houstoun, J. O. Irwin, G. W. C. Kaye, S. J. F. Philpott, L. F. Richardson, J. H. Shaxby, T. Smith, R. H. Thouless, and W. S. Tucker, 1940, Quantitative estimates of sensory events: final report of the committee appointed to consider and report upon the possibility of quantitative estimates of sensory events, *Advancement of Science*, 1, 331–49

Field, H., 1980, *Science Without Numbers*, Princeton University Press

Field, J. V., 1997, *The Invention of Infinity: Mathematics and Art in the Renaissance*, Oxford University Press

Fishburn, P. and B. Monjardet, 1992, Norbet Wiener on the theory of measurement, 1914, 1915, 1921, *Journal of Mathematical Psychology*, 36, 165–84

Forrest, P. and D. M. Armstrong, 1987, The nature of number, *Philosophical Papers*, 16, 165–86

Fowler, D. H., 1987, *The Mathematics of Plato's Academy*, Oxford: Clarendon Press

Freeman, F. N., 1929, The individual in school: II, special abilities and their measurement, in C. Murchison, (ed.), *Foundations of Experimental Psychology*, Worcester, MA: Clark University Press, pp. 705–737

Frege, G., 1884, *Die Grundlagen der Arithmetik*, Wilhelm Koebner, Breslau, trans. by J. L. Austin, 1950, *The Foundations of Arithmetic*, Oxford: Blackwell and Mott

1903, *Grundgesetze der Arithmetik*, Vol. 2, Hildesheim: Georg Olms

Freud, S., 1895, A project for a scientific psychology, *Standard Edition of the Complete Psychological Works of Sigmund Freud*, Vol. 1, London: Hogarth Press, pp. 335–69

1915, Instincts and their vicissitudes, *Standard Edition of the Complete Psychological Works of Sigmund Freud*, Vol. 14, London: Hogarth Press, pp. 109–40

Friedenberg, L., 1995, *Psychological Testing: Design, Analysis and Use*, Boston: Allyn and Bacon

Gage, F.H., 1934a, An experimental investigation of the measurability of auditory sensation, *Proceedings of the Royal Society, Series B, Biological Sciences*, 116, 103–22

230   *References*

1934b, An experimental investigation of the measurability of visual sensation, *Proceedings of the Royal Society, Series B, Biological Sciences*, 116, 123–38

Galileo Galilei, 1623, *Il saggiatore*, trans. in E. A. Burtt, 1932, *The Metaphysical Foundations of Modern Physical Science*, New York: Humanities

Galton, F., 1869, *Hereditary Genius*, London: Macmillan

1879, Psychometric experiments, *Brain*, 2, 147–62

Gaukroger, S., 1995, *Descartes: An Intellectual Biography*, Oxford: Clarendon Press

Gigerenzer, G., 1993, The superego, the ego, and the id in statistical reasoning, in G. Keren and C. Lewis, (eds.), *A Handbook for Data Analysis in the Behavioral Sciences: Methodological Issues*, Hillsdale, N.J: Erlbaum, pp. 311–39

Gigerenzer, G., Z. Swijtink, T. Porter, L. Daston, J. Beatty, and L. Krüger, 1989, *The Empire of Chance: How Probability Changed Science and Everyday Life*, Cambridge University Press

Gödel, K., 1931, Über formal unentscheidbare Sätze der *Principia Mathematica* und verwandter Systeme I, *Monatshefte für Mathematik and Physik*, vol. 38., trans. B. Meltzer, 1962, *On Formally Undecidable Propositions of Principia Mathematica and Related Systems*, Edinburgh: Oliver and Boyd

Goldstein, H. and R. Wood, 1989, Five decades of item response modelling, *British Journal of Mathematical and Statistical Psychology*, 42, 139–67

Gould, S. J., 1981, *The Mismeasure of Man*, New York: W. W. Norton and Co

Grant, D. A., 1952, Measurement in psychology: review of 'mathematics, measurement, and psychophysics': S. S. Stevens. Ch 1, Handbook of Experimental Psychology, *Psychological Bulletin*, 49, 158–9

Grant, E., 1971, *Physical Science in the Middle Ages*, New York: Wiley

1974, *A Source Book in Medieval Science*, Cambridge, MA: Harvard University Press

1996, *The Foundations of Modern Science in the Middle Ages*, Cambridge University Press

Grattan-Guinness, I., 1997, *The Fontana History of the Mathematical Sciences*, London: Fontana

Grayson, D. A., 1988, Two–group classification and latent trait theory: scores with monotone likelihood ratio, *Psychometrika*, 53, 383–92

Griffin, N., 1991, *Russell's Idealist Apprenticeship*, Oxford: Clarendon Press

Griffin, N. and A. C. Lewis, 1990, *The Collected Papers of Bertrand Russell*, Vol. 2, *Philosophical Papers 1896–99*, London: Hyman Unwin

Grosholz, E. R., 1987, Some uses of proportion in Newton's Principia, Book I: a case study in applied mathematics, *Studies in History and Philosophy of Science*, 18, 209–20

1991, *Cartesian Method and the Problem of Reduction*, Oxford: Clarendon Press

References 231

Guild, J., 1933, Discussion, *Proceedings of the Physical Society*, 45, 573–576
  1938, Are sensation intensities measurable? *British Association for the Advancement of Science*, 108, 296–328
  1940, In denial of the measurability of sensation intensity, *Advancement of Science*, 1, 344–7
Guilford, J. P., 1954, *Psychometric Methods*, New York: McGraw–Hill
Guilford, J. P. and A. L. Comrey, 1951, Measurement in psychology, in H. Helson, (ed.), *Theoretical Foundations of Psychology*, New York: Van Nostrand, pp. 506–56
Haack, S., 1993, *Evidence and Inquiry. Towards Reconstruction in Epistemology*, Oxford: Blackwell
Hacking, I., 1983, *Representing and Intervening*, Cambridge University Press
Hambleton, R. K. and H. Swaminathan, 1985, *Item Response Theory: Principles and Applications*, Dordrecht: Kluwer
Hardcastle, G. L., 1995, S. S. Stevens and the origins of operationism, *Philosophy of Science*, 62, 404–24
Harriman, P. L., 1947, *The New Dictionary of Psychology*, New York: Philosophical Library
Hearnshaw, L. S., 1962, Sixty years of psychology, *Bulletin of the British Psychological Society*, 15, 2–10
  1964, *A Short History of British Psychology, 1840–1940*, Westport, CT: Greenwood
Heath, T. L., 1908, *The Thirteen Books of Euclid's Elements*, Vol. 2, Cambridge University Press
Heidelberger, M., 1993, Fechner's impact for measurement theory, *Behavioral and Brain Sciences*, 16, 146–8
  1994, The unity of nature and mind: Gustav Theodor Fechner's non–reductive materialism, in S. Poggi and M. Bossi, (eds.), *Romanticism in Science*, Dordrecht: Kluwer, pp. 215–36
Heiman, G. A., 1995, *Research Methods in Psychology*, Boston: Houghton Mifflin
Helmholtz, von H., 1887, Zählen und Messen erkenntnistheortisch betrachtet, *Philosophische Aufsätze Eduard Zeller zu seinum fünfzigjährigen Doktorjubiläum gewindmet*, Leipzig: Fues' Verlag, pp. 17–52, trans. R. Kahl, 1971, An Epistemological Analysis of Counting and Measurement, in R. Kahl, (ed.), *Selected Writings of Hermann von Helmholtz*, Connecticut: Wesleyan University Press, pp. 437–65, trans. M. F. Lowe, 1977, Numbering and measuring from an epistemological viewpoint, in P. Hertz and M. Schlick, (eds.), *Hermann von Helmholtz: Epistemological Writings. Boston Studies in the Philosophy of Science*, Vol. 37, Dordrecht: Reidel, pp. 72–114
Herrnstein, R. J. and E. G. Boring, 1965, *A Source Book in the History of Psychology*, Cambridge, MA: Harvard University Press
Hill, M. J. M., 1914, *The Theory of Proportion*, London: Constable

232   *References*

Hirsch, M. W., 1995, Review of 'realism in mathematics', P. Maddy. Oxford University Press: London, 1993, *Bulletin of the American Mathematical Society*, 32, 137–47

Hölder, O., 1901, Die Axiome der Quantität und die Lehre vom Mass, *Berichte über die Verhandlungen der Königlich Sächsischen Gesellschaft der Wissenschaften zu Leipzig, Mathematisch–Physische Klasse*, 53, 1–46; trans. in Michell and Ernst, 1996, 1997

Holt, E. B., 1904, The classification of psycho–physic methods, *Psychological Review*, 11, 343–69

  1915, *The Freudian Wish and its Place in Ethics*, London: T. Fisher Unwin Ltd

Hornstein, G. A., 1988, Quantifying psychological phenomena: debates, dilemmas, and implications, in J. G. Morawski, (ed.), *The Rise of Experimentation in American Psychology*, New Haven: Yale University Press

Huntington, E. V., 1902, A complete set of postulates for the theory of absolute continuous magnitude, *Transactions of the American Mathematical Society*, 3, 264–84

Hutcheson, F., 1725, *An Inquiry into the Original of our Ideas of Beauty and Virtue*, London: Darby

James, W., 1890, *Principles of Psychology*, New York: Holt, Rinehart and Winston

Jastrow, J., 1887, A critique of psycho-physic methods, *American Journal of Psychology*, 1, 271–309

Jerrard, H. G. and D. B. McNeill, 1992, *Dictionary of Scientific Units*, London: Chapman and Hall

Jevons, W. S., [1873] 1958, *The Principles of Science*, New York: Dover

Johnson, H. M., 1936, Pseudo-mathematics in the social sciences, *American Journal of Psychology*, 48, 342–51

Kant, I., [1764] 1970, Inquiry concerning the distinctness of the principles of natural theology and morality, in D. Walford, (ed.), *The Cambridge Edition of the Works of Immanuel Kant: Theoretical Philosophy, 1755–1770*, Cambridge University Press, pp. 243–86

  [1781] 1978, *Critique of Pure Reason*, trans. by Norman Kemp Smith, London: Macmillan

  [1786] 1970, *Metaphysical Foundations of Natural Science*, trans. J. Ellington, Indianapolis: Bobbs–Merrill

Kaplan, R. M. and D. P. Saccuzzo, 1993, *Psychological Testing: Principles, Applications, and Issues*, Pacific Grove, CA: Brooks/Cole

Keats, J. A., 1967, Test theory, in P. R. Farnsworth, O. McNemar and Q. McNemar, (eds.), *Annual Review of Psychology*, Vol. 18, Palo Alto, CA: Annual Reviews Inc, pp. 217–38

Kelley, T. L., 1923, The principles and technique of mental measurement, *American Journal of Psychology*, 34, 408–32

  1929, *Scientific Method*, Ohio State University Press

References 233

Kelley, T. L. and E. Shen, 1929, The statistical treatment of certain typical problems, in C. Murchison, (ed.), *The Foundations of Experimental Psychology*, Worcester, MA: Clark University Press, pp. 855–83

Kerlinger, F. N., 1979, *Behavioural Research: A Conceptual Approach*, New York: Holt, Rinehart and Winston

Klein, J., 1968, *Greek Mathematical Thought and the Origins of Algebra*, Cambridge, MA: MIT Press

Kneale, W. and M. Kneale, 1962, *The Development of Logic*, Oxford: Clarendon Press

Koyré, A., 1968, *Metaphysics and Measurement*, London: Chapman and Hall

Krantz, D. H., 1964, Conjoint measurement: the Luce-Tukey axiomatization and some extensions, *Journal of Mathematical Psychology*, 1, 82–100

1972, A theory of magnitude estimation and cross modality matching, *Journal of Mathematical Psychology*, 9, 168–99

Krantz, D. H., R. D. Luce, P. Suppes, and A. Tversky, 1971, *Foundations of Measurement*, Vol. 1, New York: Academic Press

Von Kries, J., 1882, Über die Messung intensiver Grössen und über das sogenannte psychophysische Gesetz, *Vierteljahrsschrift für wissenschaftliche Philosophie*, 6, 257–94

Kuhn, T., 1961, The function of measurement in modern physical science, *Isis*, 52, 161–93

1970, *The Structure of Scientific Revolutions*, University of Chicago Press

Laming, J. and D. Laming, 1996, J. Plateau: On the measurement of physical sensations and on the law which links the intensity of these sensations to the intensity of the source. J. Plateau: report on 'Psychophysical study: theoretical and experimental research on the measurement of sensations, particularly sensations of light and of fatigue' by Mr Delbœuf, *Psychological Research*, 59, 134–44

Leary, D. E., 1980, The historical foundation of Herbart's mathematization of psychology, *Journal of the History of the Behavioral Sciences*, 16, 150–63

Levy, P., 1973, On the relation between test theory and psychology, in P. Kline, (ed.), *New Approaches in Psychological Measurement*, London: Wiley

Lindberg, D. C., 1982, On the applicability of mathematics to nature: Roger Bacon and his predecessors, *British Journal for the History of Science*, 15, 3–25

Van der Linden, W. J. and R. K. Hambleton, 1997, *Handbook of Modern Item Response Theory*, New York: Springer-Verlag

Lindzey, G., 1954, *Handbook of Social Psychology*, Vol. 1, Reading, MA: Addison–Wesley

Link, S. W., 1994, Rediscovering the past: Gustav Fechner and signal detection theory, *Psychological Science*, 5, 335–40

Locke, J., [1690] 1894, *An Essay Concerning Human Understanding*, Oxford University Press

234 *References*

Lord, F. M. and M. R. Novick, 1968, *Statistical Theories of Mental Test Scores*, Reading, MA: Addison-Wesley

Lorge, I., 1951, The fundamental nature of measurement, in F. Lindquist, (ed.), *Educational Measurement*, Washington: American Council of Education, pp. 533–59,

Lovie, A. D., 1997, Commentary on Michell, quantitative science and the definition of measurement in psychology, *British Journal of Psychology*, 88, 393–4

Lucas, J. R., 1984, *Space, Time and Causality*, Oxford: Clarendon Press

Luce, R. D., 1956, Semiorders and a theory of utility discrimination, *Econometrica*, 24, 178–91

1972, What sort of measurement is psychophysical measurement? *American Psychologist*, 27, 96–106

1977, Thurstone's discriminal processes fifty years later, *Psychometrika*, 42, 461–89

1979, Suppes' contributions to the theory of measurement, in R. J. Bogdan, (ed.), *Patrick Suppes*, Dordrecht: Reidel, pp. 93–110

1987, Measurement structures with Archimedean ordered translation groups, *Order*, 4, 165–89

1988, Goals, achievements, and limitations of modern fundamental measurement theory, in H. H. Bock, (ed.), *Classification and Related Methods of Data Analysis*, North-Holland: Elsevier, pp. 15–22

1989, R. Duncan Luce, in G. Lindzey, (ed.), *A History of Psychology in Autobiography*, Vol. VIII, Stanford University Press, pp. 245–89

1990, 'On the possible psychophysical laws' revisited: remarks on cross modality matching, *Psychological Review*, 97, 66–77

1993, Let's not promulgate either Fechner's erroneous algorithm or his unidimensional approach, *Behavioral and Brain Sciences*, 16, 155–6

1994, Thurstone and sensory scaling: then and now, *Psychological Review*, 101, 271–7

1996a, The ongoing dialog between empirical science and measurement theory, *Journal of Mathematical Psychology*, 40, 78–98

1996b, When four distinct ways to measure utility are the same, *Journal of Mathematical Psychology*, 40, 297–317

1997, Quantification and symmetry: commentary on Michell, 'Quantitative science and the definition of *measurement* in psychology', *British Journal of Psychology*, 88, 395–8

Luce, R. D. and W. Edwards, 1958, The derivation of subjective scales from just noticeable differences, *Psychological Review*, 65, 222–37

Luce, R. D. and L. Narens, 1994, Fifteen problems concerning the representational theory of measurement, in P. Humphries, (ed.), *Patrick Suppes: Scientific Philosopher*, Vol. 2, Dordrecht: Kluwer, pp. 219–49

Luce, R. D. and J. W. Tukey, 1964, Similtaneous conjoint measurement: a new type of fundamental measurement, *Journal of Mathematical Psychology*, 1, 1–27

References   235

Luce, R. D., D. H. Krantz, P. Suppes, and A. Tversky, 1990, *Foundations of Measurement*, Vol. 3: *Representation, Axiomatization, and Invariance*, San Diego: Academic Press

Lumsden, J., 1976, Test theory, in M. R. Rosenzweig and L. W. Porter, (eds.), *Annual Review of Psychology*, Vol. 27, Palo Alto, CA: Annual Reviews Inc, pp. 251–80

McCormack, T. J., 1922, A critique of mental measurements, *School and Society*, 15, 686–92

McDonald, R. P., 1985, *Factor Analysis and Related Methods*, Hillsdale, NJ: Erlbaum

McEvoy, J., 1982, *The Philosophy of Robert Grosseteste*, Oxford: Clarendon Press

McGregor, D., 1935, Scientific measurement and psychology, *Psychological Review*, 42, 246–66

McKeon, R., 1941, *The Basic Works of Aristotle*, New York: Random House

Mackie, J.L., 1962, The philosophy of John Anderson, *Australasian Journal of Philosophy*, 40, pp. 265–82
    1973, *Truth, Probablility and Paradox: Studies in Philosophical Logic*, Oxford: Clarendon Press

Mancosu, P., 1992, Descartes's Géométrie and revolutions in mathematics, in D. Gillies (ed.), *Revolutions in Mathematics*, Oxford: Clarendon, pp. 83–116

Massey, B. S., 1986, *Measures in Science and Engineering: Their Expression, Relation and Interpretation*, Chichester: Ellis Horwood

Maxwell, J. C., 1891, *A Treatise on Electricity and Magnetism*, London: Constable and Co

Meehl, P. E., 1991, Why summaries of research on psychological theories are often uninterpretable, in R. E. Snow and D. E. Wiley, (eds.), *Improving Inquiry in Social Science: A Volume in Honor of Lee J. Cronbach*, Hillsdale, N.J: Erlbaum, pp. 13–59

Meier, S. T., 1993, Revitalizing the measurement curriculum: four approaches for emphasis in graduate education, *American Psychologist*, 48, 886–91

Merton, R. K., D. L. Sills and S. M. Stigler, 1984, The Kelvin dictum and social science: an excursion into the history of an idea, *Journal of the History of the Behavioral Sciences*, 20, 319–31

Mertz, D. W., 1980, On Galileo's method of causal proportionality, *Studies in the History and Philosophy of Science*, 11, 229–42

Michell, J., 1986, Measurement scales and statistics: A clash of paradigms, *Psychological Bulletin*, 100, 398–407
    1988, Maze's direct realism and the character of cognition, *Australian Journal of Psychology*, 40, 227–49
    1990, *An Introduction to the Logic of Psychological Measurement*, Hillsdale, N.J.: Erlbaum
    1993, The origins of the representational theory of measurement:

Helmholtz, Hölder, and Russell, *Studies in History and Philosophy of Science*, 24, 183–206

1994a, Numbers as quantitative relations and the traditional theory of measurement, *British Journal for Philosophy of Science*, 45, 389–406

1994b, Measuring dimensions of belief by unidimensional unfolding, *Journal of Mathematical Psychology*, 38, 244–73

1997a, Bertrand Russell's 1897 critique of the traditional theory of measurement, *Synthese*, 110, 257–76

1997b, Quantitative science and the definition of *measurement* in psychology, *British Journal of Psychology*, 88, 355–83

Michell, J. and C. Ernst, 1996, The axioms of quantity and the theory of measurement, Part I, An English translation of Hölder (1901), Part I, *Journal of Mathematical Psychology*, 40, 235–52

1997, The axioms of quantity and the theory of measurement, Part II, An English translation of Hölder (1901), Part II, *Journal of Mathematical Psychology*, 41, 345–56

Mill, J. S., 1843, *A System of Logic*, London: Parker

Mill, J. S., [1865] 1965, An examination of Sir William Hamilton's philosophy, in J. M. Robson, (ed.), *Collected Works of J. S. Mill*, Vol. 9, London: Routledge

Moyer, A. E., 1991a, P. W. Bridgman's operational perspective on physics. Part I: Origins and development, *Studies in History and Philosophy of Science*, 22, 237–58

1991b, P. W. Bridgman's operational perspective on physics. Part II: Refinements, publication and reception, *Studies in History and Philosophy of Science*, 22, 373–97

Mundy, B., 1987, The metaphysics of quantity, *Philosphical Studies*, 51, 29–54

1994, Quantity, representation and geometry, in P. Humphreys, (ed.), *Patrick Suppes: Scientific Philosopher*, Vol. 2, Netherlands: Kluwer, pp. 59–102

Myers, C. S., 1913, Are the intensity differences of sensation quantitative? I, *British Journal of Psychology*, 6, 137–54

Nagel, E., 1931, Measurement, *Erkenntnis*, 2, 313–33

Narens, L., 1985, *Abstract Measurement Theory*, Cambridge, MA: MIT Press

1996, A theory of ratio magnitude estimation, *Journal of Mathematical Psychology*, 40, 109–29

Narens, L. and R. D. Luce, 1986, Measurement: the theory of numerical assignments, *Psychological Bulletin*, 99, 166–80

1990, Three aspects of the effectiveness of mathematics in science, in R. E. Mirkin, (ed.), *Mathematics and Science*, Singapore: World Scientific Press, pp. 122–35

1993, Further comments on the 'nonrevolution' arising from axiomatic measurement theory, *Psychological Science*, 4, 127–30

Newman, E. B., 1974, On the origin of 'scales of measurement', in H. R,

References

Moskowitz, B. Scharf, and J. C. Stevens, (eds.), *Sensation and Measurement: Papers in Honor of S. S. Stevens,* Dordrecht: Reidel, pp. 137–45

Newton, I., [1728] 1967, Universal arithmetic: or, a treatise of arithmetical composition and resolution, in D. T. Whiteside, (ed.), *The Mathematical Works of Isaac Newton,* Vol. 2, New York: Johnson Reprint Corp., pp. 3–134

Niederée, R., 1992, What do numbers measure? A new approach to fundamental measurement, *Mathematical Social Sciences,* 24, 237–76

1994, There is more to measurement than just measurement: measurement theory, symmetry, and substantive theorizing. A discussion of basic issues in the theory of measurement, *Journal of Mathematical Psychology,* 38, 527–94

O'Neil, W. M., 1944, Factors and faculties, *Australasian Journal of Psychology and Philosophy,* 22, 55–69

Pandora, K., 1997, *Rebels within the Ranks: Psychologists' Critique of Scientific Authority and Democratic Realities in New Deal America,* Cambridge University Press

Parsons, C., 1990, The structuralist view of mathematical objects, *Synthese,* 84, 303–46

Passmore, J., 1935, The nature of intelligence, *Australasian Journal of Psychology and Philosophy,* 13, 279–89

1952, *Hume's Intentions,* Cambridge University Press

Perline, R., B. D. Wright and H. Wainer, 1979, The Rasch model as additive conjoint measurement, *Applied Psychological Measurement,* 3, 237–55

Pieters, J. M., 1979, A conjoint measurement approach to color harmony, *Perception and Psychophysics,* 26, 281–6

Pintner, R., 1929, The individual in school: I. General ability, in C. Murchison, (ed.) *Foundations of Experimental Psychology,* Worcester, MA: Clark University Press, pp. 661–704

Porter, T. M., 1995, *Trust in Numbers: The Pursuit of Objectivity in Science and Public Life,* Princeton University Press

Quine, W.V., 1941, Whitehead and modern logic, in P. A. Schilpp, (ed.), *The Philosophy of Alfred North Whitehead,* Chicago: Northwestern University Press, pp. 125–63

1953, *From a Logical Point of View: Nine Logico–Philosophical Essays,* Cambridge, MA: Harvard University Press

1963, *Set Theory and its Logic,* Cambridge, MA: Harvard University Press

Ramsay, J. O., 1975, Review of 'Foundations of measurement, Volume I.' *Psychometrika,* 40, 257–62

1991, Review of 'Foundations of measurement, Volumes II and III.' *Psychometrika,* 56, 355–8

Ramul, K., 1960, The problem of measurement in the psychology of the eighteenth century, *American Psychologist,* 15, 256–65

238 *References*

Rasch, G., 1960, *Probabilistic Models for Some Intelligence and Attainment Tests*, Copenhagen: Danish Institute for Educational Research

Reese, T. W., 1943, The application of the theory of physical measurement to the measurement of psychological magnitudes, with three experimental examples, *Psychological Monographs*, 55, 1–89

Reid, T., [1748] 1849, An essay on quantity, in W. Hamilton, (ed.), *The Works of Thomas Reid*, Edinburgh: Maclachlan, Stewart and Co., pp. 715–19

Resnick, D. P., 1982, History of educational testing, in A. K. Wigdor and W. R. Garner, (eds.), *Ability Testing: Uses, Consequences and Controversies*, Washington, D. C.: National Research Council, pp. 173–94

Resnick, M., 1981, Mathematics as a science of patterns: ontology and reference, *Noûs*, 15, 529–50

Rich, G. J., 1925, Psychophysical measurement methods, *Psychological Bulletin*, 22, 613–48

Richardson, L. F., 1933, Reply, *Proceedings of the Physical Society*, 45, 585–8

Rieber, R. W., 1980, *Wilhelm Wundt and the Making of a Scientific Psychology*, New York: Plenum Press

Rodewald, H. K., 1974, A conjoint–measurement analysis of control by dimensions of compound stimuli, *Perceptual and Motor Skills*, 38, 551–6

Ross, S., 1964, *Logical Foundations of Psychological Measurement*, Copenhagen: Scandinavian University Books

Rozeboom, W. W., 1966, Scaling Theory and the Nature of Measurement, *Synthese*, 16, 170–233

Ruml, B., 1920, The need for an examination of certain hypotheses in mental tests, *The Journal of Philosophy Psychology and Scientific Methods*, 17, 57–61

Rusnock, P. and P. Thagard, 1995, Strategies for conceptual change: ratio and proportion in classical Greek mathematics, *Studies in History and Philosophy of Science*, 26, 107–31

Russell, B., [1896] 1983, The a priori in geometry, in K. Blackwell *et al.*, (ed.), *The Collected Papers of Bertrand Russell: Vol. 1, Cambridge Essays, 1896–99*, London: Allen and Unwin, pp. 291–304

  1897, On the relations of number and quantity, *Mind*, 6, 326–41

  1903, *Principles of Mathematics*, Cambridge University Press

  1919, *Introduction to Mathematical Philosophy*, London: Routledge

  1959, *My Philosophical Development*, London: George Allen and Unwin

Salkind, N. J., 1994, *Exploring Research*, New York: Macmillan

Scheerer, E., 1987, The unknown Fechner, *Psychological Research*, 49, 197–202

Scheerer, E. and H. Hildebrandt, 1988, Was Fechner an eminent psychologist? in J. Brozek and H. Gundlach, (eds.), *G. T. Fechner and Psychology*, Passavia Universitätsverlag, pp. 269–82

Scott, D., 1964, Measurement models and linear inequalities, *Journal of Mathematical Psychology*, 1, 233–47

References

Scott, D. and P. Suppes, 1958, Foundational aspects of theories of measurement, *Journal of Symbolic Logic*, 23, 113–28

Smith, T., J. Drever, J. H. Shaxby, W. Brown, R. A. Houstoun, R. J. Bartlett, S. G. Barker and C. G. Winson, 1932, The quantitative relation of physical stimuli and sensory events, *British Association for the Advancement of Science*, 102, 300

South, E. B., 1937, *An Index of Periodical Literature on Testing, 1921–1936*, New York: The Psychological Corporation

Soyfer, V. N., 1994, *Lysenko and the Tragedy of Soviet Science*, Newark, NJ: Rutgers University Press

Spearman, C., 1904, General intelligence, objectively determined and measured, *American Journal of Psychology*, 15, 201–93

1908, The method of 'right and wrong cases', ('constant stimuli') without Gauss's formulae, *British Journal of Psychology*, 2, 227–42

1923, *The Nature of 'Intelligence' and the Principles of Cognition*, London: Macmillan

1927, *The Abilities of Man*, New York: Macmillan

1930, C. Spearman, in C. Murchison, (ed.), *History of Psychology in Autobiography*, Vol 1, New York: Clark University Press, pp. 299–333

1937, *Psychology Down the Ages*, Vol. 1, London: Macmillan

Stankov, L. and A. Cregan, 1993, Quantitative and qualitative properties of an intelligence test: series completion, *Learning and Individual Differences*, 5, 137–69

Stein, H., 1990, Eudoxos and Dedekind: on the ancient Greek theory of ratios and its relation to modern mathematics, *Synthese*, 84, 163–211

Stevens, S. S., 1935a, The operational definition of psychological terms, *Psychological Review*, 42, 517–27

1935b, The operational basis of Psychology, *American Journal of Psychology*, 47, 323–30

1936a, Psychology: the propaedeutic science, *Philosophy of Science*, 3, 90–103

1936b, A scale for the measurement of a psychological magnitude: loudness, *Psychological Review*, 43, 405–16

1939, Psychology and the science of science, *Psychological Bulletin*, 36, 221–63

1942, Operationism, in D. D. Runes, (ed.), *The Dictionary of Philosophy*, New York: Philosophical Library, pp. 219–20

1946, On the theory of scales of measurement, *Science*, 103, 667–80

1951, Mathematics, measurement and psychophysics, in S. S. Stevens, (ed.), *Handbook of Experimental Psychology*, New York: Wiley, pp. 1–49

1956, The direct estimation of sensory magnitudes – loudness, *American Journal of Psychology*, 69, 1–25

1958, Measurement and man, *Science*, 127, 383–9

240 *References*

1959, Measurement, psychophysics and utility, in C. W. Churchman and P. Ratoosh, (eds.), *Measurement: Definitions and Theories*, New York: Wiley, pp. 18–63

1961, To honour Fechner and repeal his law, *Science*, 133, 80–6

1966a, On the operation known as judgement, *American Scientist*, 54, 385–401

1966b, Operations or words? *Psychological Monographs*, 80, 627, 33–8

1967, Measurement, in J. R. Newman, (ed.), *The Harper Encyclopedia of Science*, New York: Harper and Row, pp. 733–4

1968, Measurement, statistics, and the schemapiric view, *Science*, 161, 849–56

1974, S. S. Stevens, in G. Lindzey, (ed.), *A History of Psychology in Autobiography, Vol VI*, Englewood Cliffs, NJ: Prentice Hall, pp. 393–420

1975, *Psychophysics: Introduction to its Perceptual, Neural, and Social Prospects*, New York: Wiley

Stevens, S. S. and H. Davis, 1938, *Hearing: Its Psychology and Physiology*, New York: Wiley

Still, A., 1997, Stevens, Stanley Smith, in N. Sheehy, A. J. Chapman and W. A. Conroy, (eds.), *Biographical Dictionary of Psychology*, London: Routledge, pp. 540–3

Strieder, P., 1982, *Albrecht Dürer*, trans. by N. M. Gordon and W. L. Strauss, New York: Abaris Books

Suen, H. K., 1990, *Principles of Test Theories*, Hillsdale, NJ: Erlbaum

Suppes, P., 1951, A set of independent axioms for extensive quantities, *Portuguliae Mathematica*, 10, 163–72

1954, Some remarks on problems and methods in the philosophy of science, *Philosophy of Science*, 21, 242–8

1960, *Axiomatic Set Theory*, New York: Van Nostrand

1979, A self-profile, in R. J. Bogdan, (ed.), *Patrick Suppes*, Dordrecht: Reidel, pp. 3–56

Suppes, P. and M. Winet, 1955, An axiomatization of utility based on the notion of utility difference, *Journal of Management Science*, 1, 259–70

Suppes, P. and J. Zinnes, 1963, Basic measurement theory, in R. D. Luce, R. R. Bush and E. Galanter, (eds.), *Handbook of Mathematical Psychology, Vol. 1*, New York: Wiley, pp. 1–76

Suppes, P., D. H. Krantz, R. D. Luce and A. Tversky, 1989, *Foundations of Measurement, Vol. 2*, New York: Academic Press

Swoyer, C., 1987, The metaphysics of measurement, in J. Forge, (ed.), *Measurement, Realism, and Objectivity*, Dortrecht: Reidel, pp. 235–90

1991, Structural representation and surrogative reasoning, *Synthese*, 87, 449–508

Sylla, E., 1972, Medieval quantifications of qualities: the 'Merton School', *Archive for History of Exact Sciences*, 8, 9–39

Terrien, J., 1980, The practical importance of systems of units; their trend parallels progress in physics, in A. F. Milone and P. Giacomo, (eds.), *Proceedings of the International School of Physics 'Enrico Fermi' Course LXVIII, Metrology and Fundamental Constants*, Amsterdam: North-Holland, pp. 765–9

Thom, P., 1981, *The Syllogism*, Munich: Philosophia Verlag

Thomson, W., 1891, *Popular Lectures and Addresses, Vol. 1*, London: Macmillan

Thorndike, E. L., 1904, *Theory of Mental and Social Measurements*, New York: Science Press

    1918, The nature, purposes, and general methods of measurements of educational products, in G. M. Whipple, (ed.), *Seventeenth Yearbook of the National Society for the Study of Education, Vol. 2*, Bloomington, Illinois: Public School Publishing, pp. 16–24

    1923, Measurement in education, in G. M. Whipple, (ed.), *Twenty First Yearbook of the National Society for the Study of Education, Vol. 1*, Bloomington, IL: Public School Publishing, pp. 1–9

Thouless, R. H., 1938, Notes on Mr Guild's statement, *British Association for the Advancement of Science*, 108, 328–9

Thurstone, L. L., 1927a, A law of comparative judgment, *Psychological Review*, 34, 278–86

    1927b, Three psychophysical laws, *Psychological Review*, 34, 424–32

    1931, The measurement of social attitudes, *Journal of Abnormal and Social Psychology*, 26, 249–69

    1937, Psychology as a quantitative rational science, *Science*, 85, 228–32

    1947, *Multiple Factor Analysis*, University of Chicago Press

Titchener, E. B., 1905, *Experimental Psychology: A Manual of Laboratory Practice*, London: Macmillan

Tversky, A., 1967, Additivity, utility and subjective probability, *Journal of Mathematical Psychology*, 4, 1–20

Venn, J., 1889, *The Principles of Empirical or Inductive Logic*, London: Macmillan

Warren, H. C., 1934, *Dictionary of Psychology*, Cambridge, MA: Houghton Mifflin

Watt, H. J., 1913, Are the intensity differences of sensation quantitative? III, *British Journal of Psychology*, 6, 175–83

Weber, E. H., 1834, *De pulsu, resorptione, auditu et tactu: annotationes anatomicae et physiologicae*, Leipzig: Koeher

    [1846] 1978, Der Tastsinn und das Gemeingefühl, in H. E. Ross and D. J. Murray, (eds.), *E. H. Weber: The Sense Of Touch*, trans. D. J. Murray, New York: Academic Press

Weyl, H., 1949, *Philosophy of Mathematics and Natural Science*, Cambridge, MA: Princeton University Press

    1970, David Hilbert and his mathematical work, in C. Reid, *Hilbert*, Berlin: Springer-Verlag, pp. 245–83

Whitehead, A. N. and B. Russell, 1913, *Principia Mathematica, Vol. 3*, Cambridge University Press

242 *References*

Whitley, B. E., 1996, *Principles of Research in Behavioral Science*, Mountain View, CA: Mayfield

Wiener, N., 1919, A new theory of measurement: A study in the logic of mathematics, *Proceedings of the London Mathematical Society*, 19, 181–205

Wigner, E. P., 1960, The unreasonable effectiveness of mathematics in the natural sciences, *Communications on Pure and Applied Mathematics*, 13, 1–14

Winter, H. J. J., 1948, The work of G. T. Fechner on the galvanic circuit, *Annals of Science*, 6, 197–205

Wise, M. N., 1995, *The Values of Precision*, Cambridge, MA: Princeton University Press

Woodbridge, F., 1930, *Hobbes Selections*, New York: Scribners

Wooldridge, A., 1994, *Measuring the Mind: Education and Psychology in England, c. 1860–c. 1990*, Cambridge University Press

Wundt, W., [1896] 1907, *Outlines of Psychology*, trans. by C. H. Judd, Leipzig: Engelmann

Zupan, M. L., 1976, The conceptual development of quantification in experimental psychology, *Journal for the History of the Behavioral Sciences*, 12, 145–58

Index

abilities, 4, 5, 9–12, 19, 93–94, 97–98, 103, 106, 159, 164, 201–204, 206–207
Adams, E. W., 200, 84n.14
Anderson, J., 47, 61n.21
Aristotelianism, 30, 36, 40, 68
Aristotle, 22, 27, 29n.7, 35n.11, 36, 68
Armstrong, D. M., 16n.15, 47, 61, 66, 80n.7, 114, 124
attribute,
  non-quantitative, 33, 34, 41, 48, 103, 156
  ordinal, 128, 131, 142, 157, 189
  quantitative, *see* quantity
automorphism, 209–211
axiomatisation, 194

Bartlett, F. C., 144, 146
Bartlett, R. J., 144, 145, 149, 153, 155
Bergson, H., 44, 89–90
Berkeley, G., 170
Bigelow, J., 47, 63n.23, 64n.24
Binet, A., 9, 94, 95
Boring, E. G., 83n.12, 99, 103–104, 141, 142
Bostock, D., 28n.6, 47, 62
Brentano, F., 34, 83n.12, 142
Bridgman, P., 163, 169–170, 171n.12, 184n.21
Brown, W., 91–92, 94, 144n.9, 152, 185
Burt, C., 96, 143

Campbell, N. R., 121, 140, 142, 157–158, 160–161, 164, 165
  concept of number, 122–125, 178–179
  critique of psychophysical measurement, 44, 145–147, 151–152, 156
  theory of measurement of, 121–131, 136–139, 145, 151, 167, 168, 204–205

Carnap, R., 163
categories of being (or existence), 3, 125
Cattell, J. McK., 34, 38, 97–101, 102n.26
causality, 3, 56, 74, 94–95, 114, 115, 214, 218
Cliff, N., 211–216, 217
Comrey, A., 156, 157–160, 162
concatenation, 48, 54, 56, 73, 114, 129, 196–197
Coombs, C., 91n.19, 198
correlation, 93–94
Craik, K. J. W., 144, 153–154, 205
critical inquiry, 2, 107, 143, 144, 154, 191, 219
Cronbach, L. J., 159

Dedekind, R., 29, 58–59, 62
De Morgan, A., 30, 33, 64
Descartes, R., 32, 36, 40–41, 44, 68, 80n.6
Drever, J., 144, 153

Ebbinghaus, H., 34
Ellis, B., 65–66, 110, 131
Euclid, 27, 28, 31, 59, 85, 114, 202
  The Elements, 25–33, 58, 62–63, 109, 112, 193
Eudoxos, 26n.1

factor analysis, 94–96, 206–207, 215
Fagot, R. F., 174n.15, 200
Fechner, G. T.,
  psychophysics, 3, 6, 79–90, 148, 173, 177
  reaction to quantity objection, 69, 80, 87–90
  understanding of measurement, 85–87, 185
Feigl, H., 163, 170

Index

Ferguson Committee, 78, 143–144, 154, 155, 160–161, 172
Frege, G., 47, 61, 63, 124, 178–179, 193
Freud, S., 37

Galileo, 31–32, 36, 40, 63, 200n.10
Galton, F., 38, 93, 96, 99, 143
Gauss, K. F., 7n.5
Gödel, K., 179
Guild, J., 145, 147–153
Guilford, J. P., 15, 157

Hearnshaw, L. S., 146, 156
Helmholtz, H. von, 47, 68–74, 131, 219
Herbart, J. F., 79
Hilbert, D., 179, 182–183
Hobbes, T., 40
Hölder, O., 29, 47, 60, 85, 130, 138, 168, 193, 199
    conditions (axioms): for intervals, 74–75, 91–92, 120, 149, 152
    of quantity, 29, 51–54, 56–57, 84, 115, 129, 134–135
    theorem, 198, 200, 211
homomorphism, 197
Hume, D., 42

isomorphism, 118, 164, 168

James, W., 80, 90–91, 93n.20
Johnson, H. M., 138, 142

Kant, I., 37, 42, 69, 124
Kelley, T. L., 99, 104–107
Kerlinger, F. N., 187–189
Krantz, D. H., 128, 129, 152, 174n.16, 200, 202, 208, 212
Kries, J. von, 44, 88–89, 95, 219
Kuhn, T., 24, 36n.13, 108, 140, 142

Locke, J., 40
Lord, F. M., 20–21, 189, 213
Luce, R. D., 30, 82n.10, 128, 174n.16, 198, 213, 219
    conjoint measurement theory, 199–200, 204–205, 212
    representational measurement theory, 195
    theory of automorphisms, 208–211

Mackie, J. L., 47n.2, 61n.21, 132n.13
Maxwell, J. C., 14, 33
magnitudes,
    concept of, 31n.10, 85, 109, 118n.7, 131–133, 136, 164, 198n.7
    fundamental/derived, 121, 123, 126, 128, 145n.16, 147–148
    indivisibility of, 111, 114–116
    of quantities, theory of, 52–59, 69–74, 116–120
    ratios of, 13–14, 16, 18, 25–33, 58–67, 75, 105, 116, 137, 211
McGregor, D., 141–142
measurability thesis, 25, 33–39, 44–45, 143, 157, 162, 188, 189, 191, 192, 207
measurement,
    Campbell's theory of, see Campbell, N.R., theory of
    classical concept of, 14, 16–19, 25–33, 44–45, 78, 85, 109–110, 118–119, 137–139, 185–186
    conjoint, 199–207, 211–215
    definition of, 5, 145–146, 154, 156, 185; in psychology, 15–23, 186–190; Stevens' see Stevens. S. S., definition of measurement of
    derived, 121, 126, 128–130, 136, 145n.16, 147–148, 198, 204–205
    extensive, 196–197, 208
    fundamental, 121–122, 125–126, 129, 134, 145n.16, 147–148, 157, 198
    Nagel's theory of, see Nagel. E., theory of measurement of
    precision of, 34, 98
    representational theory of, 118–121, 123, 127–128, 131, 136–138, 142, 160–161, 164–169, 176–177, 195–199
    rhetoric of, 99n.24, 160, 192
    Russell's theory of, see Russell, B., theory of measurement of
    scales of, interval 20; 142, 161, 176; nominal, 142, 172, 174, 176, 185; ordered metric, 91n.19; ordinal, 142, 157, 174, 176, 185; ratio, 20, 142, 172, 176, 197, 208
    traditional concept of, see classical concept
    unit of, 12–14, 50, 90, 103–106, 153
Meehl, P. E., 217
mental tests, see psychological tests
Mertonians, 31, 68
Mill, J. S., 56, 80, 123n.10, 124
mind-body relation, 43, 80, 87

Index

245

Mundy, B., 36, 47, 198n.7
Myers, C. S., 144

Nagel, E., 110, 156, 164, 193, 198
  theory of measurement, 131–137, 140–141
Narens, L., 195, 208, 211, 213
Newton, I., 32, 36, 42, 56, 169, 200n.10
Niederée, R., 47, 199n.9
non-quantitative,
  attributes, *see* attributes,
    non-quantitative
  causes, 94–95, 218–219
  structures, *see* structures,
    non-quantitative
normal science, 108, 140, 142, 191, 217, 219
Novick, M. R., 20–21, 189, 213
number, 26, 35n.11, 117–119, 123–125, 177–185
  cardinal, *see* natural
  concept of, 29, 59–67, 123–124, 179;
    formalist, 178–183;
    intuitionist, 117, 130;
    logicist, 117, 130, 179;
    operationist, 184;
    physicalist, 123–124;
    set theoretical, 117, 119, 194
  integer, 61, 117
  natural, 49, 60–61, 115, 117, 123–124
  rational, 28, 58, 62, 63, 64
  real, 29–30, 58–66, 117, 127, 137, 210
numerals,
  measurement and, 76, 156, 160–161, 164, 165, 172
  numbers and, 16n.14, 122, 178–179, 184
numerical coding, 185

operationism, 71–72, 110, 114, 131, 141, 158, 162, 169–177, 184, 187–189, 199
Oresme, N., 29n.7, 31, 33, 55, 73, 75

Pearson, K., 93, 96, 143
phenomenological movement, 42
Plateau, J., 83, 90, 91
Plato, 35–36
positivism, 71, 110, 114, 134, 136, 169, 170n.9, 178
practicalism, 96–97, 100–101, 106
psychological tests, 9–10, 93, 94, 95, 97–99, 102, 106–107, 142, 159–160, 166–167, 188–189, 206–207
psychometrics, 102, 105–107, 186–187, 189
  item response theories, 10–12, 212
  test theory, 107, 212n.21, 213
psychophysics, 5, 6–9, 79–93, 141–142, 148–154, 172–175, 186, 189, 211
psychophysical methods,
  average error, 82
  bisection, 83–84, 91, 150
  cross-modality matching, 173
  just noticeable differences, 82–84
  magnitude estimation, 173
  pair comparisons, 6–7
  right and wrong cases, 82
Pythagoras, 35
Pythagoreanism, 19, 35, 67–68, 88, 98, 101, 125, 139

qualitative methods, 42n.18
qualities, 54n.14, 68, 89
  primary, 40
  secondary, 40–41
quantification, 42, 67, 73–77, 104, 218
  instrumental task of, 75–77, 79, 86
  scientific task of, 75–77, 79, 86, 92, 94, 97, 106, 151, 189
quantitative imperative, 38–39, 96, 99, 101
quantity, 19, 33, 37, 71–76, 85, 114, 218–219
  as category of being, 3, 87, 125, 140
  concept of, 25, 43, 47–49, 52–55, 56n.16, 63, 89, 111, 117, 120, 125, 198, 208
  continuous, 47–59, 66, 110, 111, 127, 137, 204
  discrete, 112–113, 115–116, 181
  extensive, 54–56, 67
  intensive, 29, 34, 54–56, 88
  objection, 25, 39–44, 78, 88–93, 106–108, 139, 155, 177, 186, 189–90, 215
  view of mathematics, 37

Rasch, G., 11–12, 166n.6, 212
ratios, 25–29, 55, 109, 120, 181, 204
  of magnitudes, *see* magnitudes, ratios of
Reese, T., 156–157, 162
Reid, T., 43–44, 68, 102n.27
relations, 60–62, 111–114, 132–133, 195–196

246 Index

asymmetric, 165, 168, 176
difference, 90, 120, 201–202
interval, 74–75, 90–92, 120, 198, 200
ordinal, 89
reflexive, 138, 168, 174
symmetric, 69, 138, 126, 150, 168, 174
transitive, 69, 103, 138, 126, 150, 165, 168, 174, 176, 197
Richardson, L. F., 144, 145, 153
Rozeboom, W. W., 166
Russell, B., 47, 64, 110, 174, 198n.7
concept of number, 117, 123, 178–179
relation of number to quantity, 111–116, 117n.6
theory of measurement, 91, 116–121, 131, 164, 165, 167

Schlick, M., 170
scientism, 39, 98, 192
Scott, D., 196, 203
sensations,
differences between, 7, 82–84, 89, 92, 150–152
intensities of, 4, 6–9, 19, 81–84, 148–155, 172–173
Spearman, C., 9, 38, 93–97, 143, 159, 206–207
Stein, H., 47, 62
Stevens, S. S., 104, 127, 131, 137, 194
concept of number, 16n.14, 177–184
definition of measurement, 15–23, 45, 46, 76–77, 78, 108, 109, 138, 160,

163–165, 177, 186–189, 191, 192, 216
operationism, 169–177, 184n.21, 199
representation, 164–169
theory of scales of measurement, 20, 136, 138n.15, 161, 175–177
structures,
additive, 48–49, 52–56, 64–67, 72–74, 105, 115, 121–122, 125–126, 199
non-quantitative, 103, 164, 219
ordinal, 116–117, 127, 131, 164, 166, 168
Suppes, P., 19n.19, 128, 168, 175, 193–199, 208, 219
Swoyer, C., 47, 198n.7

Tarski, A., 194
Thomson, G. H., 91, 94, 152, 185
Thorndike, E. L., 97, 98, 101–104
Thurstone, L. L., 7, 94, 139
law of comparative judgment, 7–9
Titchener, E. B., 91, 143
Tukey, J. W., 30, 75, 199–200, 204, 212

Wallis, J., 29, 63
Weber, E. H., 81
Weber's law, 81–82
Weyl, H., 179, 183
Whitehead, A. N., 47, 64, 110, 163
Wundt, W., 34, 79, 80, 90, 96, 99, 109

Zinnes, J., 76, 168, 175, 196, 198–199

IDEAS IN CONTEXT

Edited by QUENTIN SKINNER (*General Editor*)
LORRAINE DASTON, WOLF LEPENIES, J. B. SCHNEEWIND
and JAMES TULLY

1 RICHARD RORTY, J.B. SCHNEEWIND and QUENTIN SKINNER (eds.)
Philosophy in History
Essays in the historiography of philosophy*

2 J.G.A. POCOCK
Virtue, Commerce and History
Essays on political thought and history, chiefly in the eighteenth century*

3 M.M. GOLDSMITH
Private Vices, Public Benefits
Bernard Mandeville's social and political thought

4 ANTHONY PAGDEN (ed.)
The Languages of Political Theory in Early Modern Europe*

5 DAVID SUMMERS
The Judgment of Sense
Renaissance nationalism and the rise of aesthetics*

6 LAURENCE DICKEY
Hegel: Religion, Economics and the Politics of Spirit, 1770–1807*

7 MARGO TODD
Christian Humanism and the Puritan Social Order

8 LYNN SUMIDA JOY
Gassendi the Atomist
Advocate of history in an age of science

9 EDMUND LEITES (ed.)
Conscience and Casuistry in Early Modern Europe

10 WOLF LEPENIES
Between Literature and Science: The Rise of Sociology*

11 TERENCE BALL, JAMES FARR and RUSSEL L. HANSON (eds.)
Political Innovation and Conceptual Change*

12 GERD GIGERENZER *et al.*
The Empire of Chance
How probability changed science and everyday life*

13 PETER NOVICK
That Noble Dream
The 'objectivity question' and the American historical profession*

14 DAVID LIEBERMAN
The Province of Legislation Determined
Legal theory in eighteenth-century Britain

15 DANIEL PICK
Faces of Degeneration
A European disorder, c. 1848–c. 1918*

16 KEITH BAKER
Approaching the French Revolution
Essays on French political culture in the eighteenth century*

17 IAN HACKING
The Taming of Chance*

18 GISELA BOCK, QUENTIN SKINNER and MAURIZIO VIROLI (eds.)
Machiavelli and Republicanism*

19 DOROTHY ROSS
The Origins of American Social Science*

20 KLAUS CHRISTIAN KOHNKE
The Rise of Neo-Kantianism
German Academic Philosophy between Idealism and Positivism

21 IAN MACLEAN
Interpretation and Meaning in the Renaissance
The Case of Law

22 MAURIZIO VIROLI
From Politics to Reason of State
*The Acquisition and Transformation of the Language of Politics
1250–1600*

23 MARTIN VAN GELDEREN
The Political Thought of the Dutch Revolt 1555–1590

24 NICHOLAS PHILLIPSON and QUENTIN SKINNER (eds.)
Political Discourse in Early Modern Britain

25 JAMES TULLY
An Approach to Political Philosophy: Locke in Contexts*

26 RICHARD TUCK
Philosophy and Government 1572–1651*

27 ROBERT R. YEO
Defining Science
*William Whewell, Natural Knowledge and Public Debate
in Early Victorian Britain*

28 MARTIN WARNKE
The Court Artist
The Ancestry of the Modern Artist

29 PETER N. MILLER
Defining the Common Good
Empire, Religion and Philosophy in Eighteenth-Century Britain

30 CHRISTOPHER J. BERRY
The Idea of Luxury
A Conceptual and Historical Investigation*

31 E. J. HUNDERT
The Enlightenment's 'Fable'
Bernard Mandeville and the Discovery of Society

32 JULIA STAPLETON
Englishness and the Study of Politics
The Social and Political Thought of Ernest Barker

33 KEITH TRIBE
Strategies of Economic Order
German Economic Discourse, 1750–1950

34 SACHIKO KUSUKAWA
The Transformation of Natural Philosophy
The Case of Philip Melancthon

35 DAVID ARMITAGE, ARMAND HIMY and QUENTIN SKINNER (eds.)
Milton and Republicanism

36 MARKKU PELTONEN
Classical Humanism and Republicanism in English Political
Thought 1570–1640

37 PHILIP IRONSIDE
The Social and Political Thought of Bertrand Russell
The Development of an Aristocratic Liberalism

38 NANCY CARTWRIGHT, JORDI CAT, LOLA FLECK and
THOMAS E. UEBEL
Otto Neurath: Philosophy between Science and Politics

39 DONALD WINCH
Riches and Poverty
An Intellectual History of Political Economy in Britain, 1750–1834*

40 JENNIFER PLATT
A History of Sociological Research Methods in America

41 KNUD HAAKONSSEN (ed.)
Enlightenment and Religion
Rational Dissent in Eighteenth-Century Britain

42 G. E. R. LLOYD
Adversaries and Authorities
Investigations into Ancient Greek and Chinese Science*

43 ROLD LINDNER
The Reportage of Urban Culture
Robert Park and the Chicago School

44 ANNABEL BRETT
Liberty, Right and Nature
Individual Rights in Later Scholastic Thought

45 STEWART J. BROWN (ed.)
William Robertson and the Expansion of Empire

46 HELENA ROSENBLATT
Rousseau and Geneva
From the *First Discourse* to the *Social Contract*, 1749–1762

47 DAVID RUNCIMAN
Pluralism and the Personality of the State

48 ANNABEL PATTERSON
Early Modern Liberalism

49 DAVID WEINSTEIN
Equal Freedom and Utility
Herbert Spencer's Liberal Utilitarianism

50 YUN LEE TOO and NIALL LIVINSTONE (eds.)
Pedagogy and Power
Rhetorics of Classical Learning

51 REVIEL NETZ
The Shaping of Deduction in Greek Mathematics
A Study in Cognitive History

52 MARY MORGAN and MARGARET MORRISON (eds.)
Models as Mediators

53 JOEL MICHELL
Measurement in Psychology
A Critical History of a Methodological Concept

Titles marked with an asterisk are also available in paperback

For EU product safety concerns, contact us at Calle de José Abascal, 56–1°,
28003 Madrid, Spain or eugpsr@cambridge.org.

www.ingramcontent.com/pod-product-compliance
Ingram Content Group UK Ltd.
Pitfield, Milton Keynes, MK11 3LW, UK
UKHW010900060825
461487UK00012B/1253